BEDLAM ON THE STREETS

Caroline Knowles

with photography by Ludovic Dabert

London and New York

First published 2000
by Routledge
11 New Fetter Lane, London EC4P 4EE

Simultaneously published in the USA and Canada
by Routledge
29 West 35th Street, New York, NY 10001

Routledge is an imprint of the Taylor & Francis Group

Typeset in Garamond by Taylor & Francis Books Ltd
Printed and bound in Great Britain by
TJ International Ltd, Padstow, Cornwall

British Library Cataloguing in Publication Data
A catalogue record for this book is available from the British Library

Library of Congress Cataloging in Publication Data
Knowles, Caroline
Bedlam on the streets / Caroline Knowles; photographs by Ludovic Dabert.
p. cm.
Includes bibliographical references and index.
1. Mentally ill–Care–Québéc (Province)–Montréal. 2. Mentally ill–Québéc
(Province)–Montréal–Social conditions. 3. Community mental health services–Québéc
(Province)–Montréal. 4. Mentally ill–Deinstitutionalization–Québéc (Province)–Montréal.
5. Mentally ill–Services for–Québéc (Province)–Montréal. 6. Montréal (Québéc :
Province)–Social conditions. I. Title.
RC480.53 .K56 2000
362.2'042'0971428–dc21
00-38253

ISBN 0–415–23298–8 (hbk)
ISBN 0–415–23299–6 (pbk)

CONTENTS

LIST OF PLATES

Plate 1

PREFACE

This is not the book I intended to write. It grew, monstrously and insistently from research material collected by myself and a multi-disciplinary team of research assistants based at Concordia University in Montréal between 1992 and 1998. It began as another contribution to a growing collection of instalments produced by the author in the social analysis of ethnicity's multiple associations with marginality, organized, on this occasion, by what I expected to discover about the regimes of psychiatry operating in the 'community'. My starting point was deeply flawed by the assumptions transferred from similar research I had done in the UK, and sustained by the liberal and well-intentioned rhetoric of Canadian and Québec mental health care policy documents. I had assumed there was, as the rhetoric insisted, a community system of mental health provision in which the outreach of psychiatry could be described, documented and taken to task for its forms of racial marginalization. There wasn't. At least there was not one that I recognized. What there was wasn't obvious. It had to be excavated from the fabric of the city and its suburbs: its clients disentangled from the city's poor and multiply disenfranchised. As the research re-focused on the task of excavating the system's social and spatial relationships, so its forms of racialization and ethnicization took a back seat because they were not what was most striking about it. To have persisted with the original plan and foregrounded race and ethnicity, rather than the system in which they are articulated and given meaning, would not have done justice to the research findings and the voices we heard, which quite clearly told us that race was a second-order issue when compared to the operation of the system itself. Consequently, this is not primarily a book about race, at least it is only about race in the sense that everything is, as Winant insists, about race (and we should add, gender). Race and ethnicity (and gender) were present in what people said and did: they were present in who people are and the ways in which they moved about the streets of the city, and to have edited them out would have distorted the narratives in which these things were embedded and would have misrepresented the lives they organized. Therefore, this is a book in which ethnicity and race (and to a lesser extent gender) hover menacingly beneath the surface of the text, erupting in the appropriate places into narrative and analysis. It is always present and a part of the broader social landscape. Race, ethnicity and madness are ways of describing social processes and social relationships that, throughout the investigation and the resulting text, form complex matrices in the geographies of the city.

Bedlam tells a story of urban space and its social geographies of madness: a local story set within the broader parameters of systems of social welfare and globalization.

Unable to trace the contours of a non-existent system, we pieced together this story by tracing its clients' trajectories from the revolving doors of the local psychiatric wards and hospitals. They led us to the local foster homes, homeless shelters, rooming houses and streets where they lived; and to the day centres, soup kitchens, food banks and streets where they spent their days. This, we were to discover, was the operational meaning of 'community mental health care': that which goes on outside of the hospital and which is stitched together by those (clients) who use it. It was here, on these sites, that we interviewed clients and those who cared for or watched over them in an effort to establish a sense of how their lives were lived. The fragmented matrices of social relationships we describe are the 'post-asylum geographies of madness' in Montréal, and, we suspect in many cities beyond. They invoke hybrid and highly mediated forms of psychiatric knowledge and practice that are quite remote from the operation of psychiatry in clinical settings. In these newly opened hybrid spaces of community and psychiatric neglect the mad themselves are able to direct their lives and theorize their madness in ways that were not previously possible in the time of the great incarcerations of the asylum. It is this, and the urban and administrative contexts in which it is set, that *Bedlam* tries to capture.

This task of capturing some of the vitality, dynamic and meaning of this system and the lives it organized quickly revealed the inadequacy of my existing research tools and theoretical repertoire. I approached the task tentatively with a residual commitment to Foucauldian notions of forms of 'governmentality' overlain by Ricoeurian hermeneutics that demanded the inclusion of 'people narratives' and not just the 'grand narratives' I had once presumed to govern people. The system I wanted to describe demanded more. It demanded the analysis of 'space' in the sense in which Lefebvre captures it. It demanded a grasp of 'performance' in the sense of De Sade's productions in the eighteenth-century lunatic asylums in which he was himself an inmate. And it demanded a visual dimension in order to enliven the representation of the cast of characters and spatial contexts on which the text was to be based. I was stretched and challenged conceptually and methodologically by the lives I attempted to describe: the lives that had re-routed my intention to write about race. While I am responsible for having produced the account of the lives described in this book, this was an interactive process in which the lives under consideration shaped, through their stories and challenges, the resulting analysis. My attempts to capture the 'lived-ness' of their lives has meant relegating theoretical and methodological debates and justification of the framework to passing references and footnotes. I hope the reader will see this as it was intended: not as sloppy scholarship but as an attempt to tell a story in an accessible way.

Because this book is the result of a collaborative, interdisciplinary university research project based at Concordia University in Montréal where I worked for over six years, I owe many debts of gratitude to the students of sociology, anthropology, medical anthropology, art therapy, fine arts and geography at Concordia and McGill universities who worked on it with me as interviewers. In particular I thank Pascale Annoual, Leanne Joanisse, Francine Robillard, Mary Ellen Macdonald, Catherine Degnen, Marc Paulse, Norva St Bryce, James Roach, Richard Element, Clara Khuderverdian, Kim Matthews, Margaret Bartha, Stephanie Premji and Noemi Toussignant for their help with interviews and observations. I would like to thank the many transcribers who have turned tapes into text; my colleagues in the Culture and

Mental Health Unit at McGill University and the Jewish General Hospital, especially Allan Young and Laurence Kirmayer, who provided me with an intellectual context in which to work. I gratefully acknowledge the financial support of the conseil Québécois de la recherche sociale, which provided the majority of the funding for this project as well as other contributors – the Department of Sociology and Anthropology at Concordia, Erica Besso at the Office of Research Services and Robert Roy in the Faculty of Arts and Sciences – who bailed me out when I ran out of money. I also gratefully acknowledge the intellectual support of colleagues at Concordia and my new colleagues at the University of Southampton as well as Prue Chamberlayne and Michael Rustin at the Centre for Biography in Social Policy at the University of East London. I would also like to thank Patrick Knowles for his practical and policy insights, David Mofford for his editorial suggestions and Jessica, William and Sophia Knowles-Mofford for their customary good-humoured tolerance of my preoccupation with writing. The patient support of June and Eric Litton is also gratefully acknowledged. Mari Shullaw at Routledge guided this through to completion with her customary wisdom and enthusiasm. Routledge's anonymous reader provided insightful comments and an important guide to the text's major flaws. But most of all I should like to acknowledge a tremendous debt of gratitude to those who provided the material for this book by sharing their often very painful stories with us. It would be impossible to work with this particular group of informants without developing a deep respect for the ways in which they garner the courage to rise each morning and get through the day. Their struggles are highly deserving of respect and contain many lessons from which we can learn not just about them but about ourselves, the lives we live and the things we take for granted.

The acknowledgement of funding agencies and academic institutions customarily obscures and forgives the difficulties and frustrations incurred in doing funded research. Because of this we lack honest accounts of the conditions of intellectual production that persists in universities. With this in mind I would like to underscore the ambivalence of my grateful acknowledgement of Concordia University as a place that simultaneously sustained and discouraged me: conditions that, I suspect, are replicated throughout North American, and maybe other, universities too.

Caroline Knowles,
University of Southampton, January 2000

INTRODUCTION

> It was an age of great fortunes and great private generosity, but it was
> also an age of hunger and deprivation for large segments of the popula-
> tion.
>
> ('History of The Mission', describing the nineteenth-century
> conditions in which it came to be founded)

The history of the 'Mission' – a homeless shelter based on principles of nineteenth-
century Christian philanthropy and undergoing something of a renaissance – contrasts
in this quote the social polarities of railway and insurance barons, produced by the
boom of the 1890s, with the declining fortunes of the poor in Montréal. Its narrative
imitates Dickens' *Tale of Two Cities*: 'It was the best of times and the worst of times.'
This is the story of modernity – and its sequels. *Bedlam on the Streets* is a tale of one city
– Montréal – and it is the tale of many cities. It is a tale of global economic realignment and its shifting fault lines of privilege and entitlement. It details the local
consequences of global restructuring. It is a tale of the collapse of social welfare and its
attendant conceptions of inclusion and social citizenship,[1] and the renewed importance of the religious and philanthropic organizations that preceded it. It is a tale of
the downloading of the responsibility for welfare from public to private institutions
and from the state to the municipality. It is a tale of the realignment of the psychiatric
gaze onto a domain of less serious, more treatable, conditions covered by insurance
policies and away from the antics of the chronically and incurably mad.[2] It is a tale of
personal crises, of terrifying descent into madness, homelessness, joblessness, loneliness, and dependence on cocktails of legal/illegal drugs. It is a tale about the
production and management of contemporary madness. It is a tale about what
happened on the streets when the local asylums and psychiatric wards closed and there
was nowhere else for the mad to go. In using the term 'mad' to tie into popular narratives and avoid inappropriate psychiatric categorization, it is necessary to insist that
the use of a single term to invoke multiply varied lives is in no sense intended to
confer a unitary status or situation upon them. Using one term to collectivize subjectivities as a group of course carries this implication. On the contrary, the pages that
follow show the mad to occupy different parts of the city's geography, and speak with
many different voices about madness, their situation and what it means to be them.
The mad, even in a single city, are a diverse group of people with individual biographies, pathways into madness and ways of coping. The lives described in this book are
'manufactured' by the global and local, macro and micro social processes that interface

1

with the individual trajectories that make up the living of a life. These lives are in no sense accidental or the product of individual misfortune. They are about paths taken and decisions made in the context of forms of provision underwritten by a broader and deliberate political agenda and set of social priorities with which we march determinedly into the twenty-first century.

The local situation in Montréal and elsewhere is the result of global restructuring and its social consequences. The strategic economies of the G7 countries and beyond were substantially restructured by the de-industrialization of the 1980s. The shift from (production line) Fordism to flexible, disorganized capital ushered in an era of fragmentation in production processes, of contracting out, an explosion of consultants and an overall shift from production to service-led economies (Wolch and Dear 1993: 4–5; Sassen 1994: 43). In North America and beyond the growth of flexible part-time working practices produced a polarization of personal wealth and assets. The 1980s in the United States produced a concentration of personal wealth, an explosion of the number of millionaires and billionaires and broke new records for the number of Americans cast into poverty and homelessness (Wolch and Dear 1993: xvii). Sassen's (1991) *The Global City* insightfully documents the impact of the strategic cities of London, New York and Tokyo on their national and urban hinterlands in terms of the social polarities that are generated to service the global flows and lifestyles of the few. Globalization and its spatial and economic re-alignments is a 'narrative of eviction' (Sassen 1994: 56) etched in its own peculiarities upon local urban landscapes. This volume illuminates some of the local manifestations of these processes.

As the new economic and spatial orders of globalization consolidated themselves transnationally so the social polarities created manifested themselves locally. The intensification of poverty noted by Wolch and Dear (1993) and Sassen (1994) in the context of the US placed new demands on the welfare state at a time when it, too, was undergoing strategic realignment. If the general trend of money, industry and services was global: welfare (in North America and in Britain) was moving in the opposite direction. It was becoming more local. The 'deinstitutionalization' that restructured American welfare in the 1980s retrenchments were spearheaded by mental health reforms that began in the sixties (Wolch and Dear 1993: 9). Mental health provided a model that was to be repeated for other problematic populations – the disabled, the elderly, probationers and parolees – whose care could be 'downloaded' from the nation state to municipal or local government levels around a rhetoric that posited the 'community' as a better environment for care and one that respected the civil rights of those previously incarcerated. The state simultaneously divested itself of its strategic place in welfare and the organization of the economy by transferring these things in opposite directions. At the same time as economies became more globally configured, so its social consequences and the means by which they were to be addressed – welfare – became even more local.

Localization and deinstitutionalization are not inherently problematic developments in the welfare systems of the global order. Much depends on the deals cut between the national and the local municipal state and whether this is seen as an opportunity to roll back welfare spending in favour of other priorities. Montréal is caught in a three-way struggle between levels of government – municipal, provincial and federal – about levels of contribution to social programmes. Like other jurisdictions its concerns have shifted from broad commitments to redistributive social justice to the politics of balanced budgets and deficit reduction. In this context, as in the US, deinstitutionalization and localization parallel the growth of a shadow welfare system: 'a proliferation of private, quasi public, voluntary and commercial agencies (like the mission) providing services hitherto supplied by government' (Wolch and Dear 1993: 14). In the US, this sector created 3.1 million new jobs during the Reagan years in health, education and social services (Wolch and Dear 1993: 14). Shadow states have their own forms of fragmentation, geographies, and configuration of social relations, services and practices that merit investigation. Twenty years of financial retrenchment, shifts in political priorities away from the disadvantaged, deinstitutionalization, local-ization and reliance on shadow services has had much the same impact on Montréal as Wolch and Dear describe for the US: 'the safety nets of the U.S. welfare state is thread-bare; its ability to protect the security of imperilled lives has been significantly compromised' (Wolch and Dear 1993: 15–16).

Why Montréal? Montréal is not one of Sassen's (1991) global cities. But the global/local configurations outlined above describe exactly the situation and recent history of Montréal. Its economic base has shifted from manufacture and mineral resources to service industries. Its welfare state, a part of the jurisdiction of the province of Québec, was consolidated and secularized in the 'Quiet Revolution' of the 1960s,[3] when the politics of modernity and attendant conceptions of citizenship and entitlement challenged the existing theocratic order, already being dismantled by the 1980s and returned on new terms to the very hands – in private and religious philan-thropy – from which it had been wrested only twenty years previously. Montréal is a culturally and historically distinct space on the periphery of the North American continent where French is the language of public culture, and the majority of people operate in either or both of Canada's two official languages. For this same reason Montréal also occupies a peripheral position within the nation state. Local politics are configured between two sides in a political debate about whether Québec is a nation-in-waiting or a constituent part of the confederated state of Canada that urgently needs to revisit the original terms of confederation in the light of modern political circumstances that seem to favour another global trend: the devolution of nation states. The political debate about the future of the nation has produced its rival white (French and English) civil and uncivil (ethnic) nationalisms that contextualize the local politics of race. This is a place where whiteness and its attendant forms of belonging mediate the politics of multi-racism. Politically and demographically Montréal also occupies a distinctive position within the province of Québec. It is far more equally divided than other parts of the province on the issue of Québec sovereignty, something that shows its political diversity. And it houses most of the province's Anglophone and immigrant populations (12 per cent of the city's popula-tion are 'visible minorities'), factors that make it more cosmopolitan and multi-lingual than other parts of the province.

Montréal is also an important site in the French Canadian Diaspora, although Québec City is nationalism's political power base and Lac St Jean to the north its former industrial heartland. Welfare budgets and the deals cut between the federal and provincial governments is one of the strategic sites on which the nation debate is conducted. Montréal is indisputably part of the global social order, its trend in the reconfiguration of nation states and the welfare regimes they are willing and able to sustain. It is a local city with extra local significance. It is emblematic of broader

Plate 2 Montréal street scene

trends affecting the US (and Britain) and hence a good place from which to take a closer look at how some things actually work in the local regimes of community mental health. Successive United Nations quality of life indexes have rated Canada number two in the world as a country in which to live. That this is achieved at the price of some highly selective forms of social marginalization – of the poor, mad and homeless – is not readily apparent because it is obscured beneath a liberal rhetoric of inclusivity and compassion.[4]

Montréal, with an urban population of around 2 million of Québec's 6 million citizens, has an estimated homeless population of 20,000, half of which are juveniles,[5] and a long winter in which temperatures fall well below zero to beyond the point at which human flesh freezes. Its homeless population may be small by US standards, and there is a greater supply of affordable housing than in global cities like New York, London and Tokyo, where housing costs far out-strip local average wages, but like US cities it has seen a 'democratization of homelessness' (Wolch and Dear 1993: xxii) to include the young, the old, women and children, the unemployed, the working poor, those discharged from psychiatric treatment, drug addicts and alcoholics: the product of globalization, localization and the privatization of welfare. Enhancement in the quality of life for some has come at a cost to others. This can be justified only in a moral and political order in which some lives are more worthy and socially valuable than others: a point that places the operation of liberal democratic orders, including those that are highly skilled in impression management, in question. The rhetoric of Canadian and Québec nationhood cannot admit these political priorities but subscribes to them in practice.

The chapters that follow document the operation of some aspects of what Wolch and Dear loosely refer to as 'the shadow state': those aspects that organize the lives of the mentally distressed in the absence of more formal systems of community psychiatric care. This system is referred to as 'psychiatric care in the community' but it has little to do with psychiatry and its conception of community is rather particular and restricted. *Bedlam on the Streets* maps the transactions between a specific group of welfare clients and the various, multi-purpose, regimes through which they are dealt with. It examines some of the spatial practices and the social relationships that make up this system and the life-story narratives of the mentally distressed. Unconcerned with the veracity of psychiatric diagnoses, it looks at the meaning which diagnoses have for those to whom they are applied.[6] It looks at what occupies the space in the social management of madness once occupied by the asylums, psychiatric wards and clinics, but abandoned in accumulated deinstitutionalization, downloading and the emergence of informal networks in which the mad are able to make decisions about their lives in the context of what are, effectively, newly configured geographies of neglect.

Bedlam on the Streets is written in order to disturb the cosy picture of civility and its wholesome certainties about the nature of the 'community' imagined as 'community mental health' that allows the Québec Minister of Health and Social Services to announce that: 'It is with a certain amount of pride that I present this mental health policy' (Therese Lavoie-Roux 1990). Her version of 'community' as a collection of 'family and friends' providing the best environment for 'care' (Lavoie-Roux 1990: 14, 17) is highly selective in its attention to a less serious and chronic range of psychiatric difficulties, and hopelessly optimistic in its expectations of friends and family when those with serious and persistent psychiatric difficulties have placed considerable stress on the very relationships which are supposed to sustain them. The minister's version of community as 'natural surroundings' (Lavoie-Roux 1990) is premised on a particular version of the lives of the mentally distressed in which they are reincorporated into the existing social relationships without disturbing or challenging them, or the socially worked conceptions of 'personhood', which, as you will see, have difficulty in incorporating madness as a legitimate way of being in the world. The 'natural surroundings' of community described in the pages that follow are not at all what the minister had in mind. Montréal does not have a community mental health care system that reaches those with serious and persistent mental health difficulties. What it does have are the chaotic geographies of psychiatric retreat and social neglect described in the pages that follow. In this it is not unique but a consistent part of a North American trend.[7] Like other places it saw the closure of hospital psychiatry as an opportunity to balance budgets and cut back expenditure on a seemingly intractable social problem. Like other places, its policy rhetoric contains lofty intentions that make it possible for the minister to speak with pride and researchers to claim that: 'Québec is the only Canadian province to have organized its health and social services into a co-ordinated network, integrating hospitals, rehabilitation and convalescence centres, and social services agencies' (Mercier and White 1994: 41). We will see that lofty intentions are not matched in the provision of resources to all, but only some, citizens so that community care for the mad is a comforting myth, a delicate veneer that cannot sustain the demands made upon it.

The significance of psychiatry in community settings has been overestimated from a number of directions and this has contributed to sustaining the myth of the orga-nizing power of psychiatry over the lives of the mad. Desjarlias' (1997) poignant, Goffmanesque, anthropological account of a community unit in Boston does not consider the broader context of local and state provision of the jurisdiction in which it is set. Are all Boston facilities this good? Is it a flagship? Who gets to use it? And what happens to those who don't? Desjarlais' text creates the impression that Massachusetts has extensive and rather excellent community provision. But does it? Goodwin (1997: 12), who documents the rapid decarceration of American mental health care into the private sector combined with poor coverage through Medicare for those with mental health problems in Massachusetts and elsewhere, however, sets Desjarlais' text in its political context. There has been a shift away from the jurisdic-tion of psychiatry and formal provision that parallels our findings in Montréal. Wolch et al. (1988: 266–70) show that Californian decarceration in the years of the Reagan governorship did not occur around a transfer of resources to facilitate the outreach of psychiatry into the community, but in the context of a political strategy favouring cut backs in social spending, gentrification and urban renewal that left the mentally ill ghettoized and ignored in deteriorating parts of the inner city. The evidence suggests that the facility of which Desjarlias writes is far from typical. Survivor stories of mental distress told as powerful tales of individual suffering (Church 1995; Spaniol and Koehler 1994; Burstow and Weitz 1988) that hit out at the awful managing power of psychiatry over that of suffering leave the impression that it is psychiatry and not its absence or the systems that replace it that are problematic. Psychiatry's most eloquent critics, many of them trained as psychiatrists and anthropologists (Littlewood 1998; Fernando 1991; Littlewood and Lipsedge 1989) similarly give the impression that psychiatry is the problem and, in the manner of survivor tales, extend psychiatry's apparent domain of influence by not placing it in its broader political context as a service selectively aimed at a range of lives with less serious and attractively treatable conditions. Similarly Parker et al. (1995) claim that psychiatric knowledge is so ubiq-uitous that the mad cannot avoid constituting their own subjectivity in these terms – a claim that should be treated with a certain amount of scepticism given the arrange-ment of contemporary community mental health care characterized by psychiatric neglect.

Bedlam is an attempt to set the practice of psychiatry and its outreach into the community into some kind of broader context. It shows that psychiatry itself has only a residual influence in the contemporary management of madness when it comes to those with chronic and persistent difficulties. Although versions of psychiatric knowl-edge are in play, they are articulated by the plethora of multi-purpose voluntary associations and private arrangements as well as popular cultural assumptions in oper-ation around the management of madness in the context of urban life. Above all it shows that these are anyway powerfully mediated by the life trajectories and accounts of madness of those whom it supposedly manages. The interface between welfare regimes and their subjects is a two-way process in which crucial decisions are made about the deployment of available resources in the alleviation of individual tragedy: decisions that reflect individual life paths, interpretations of madness and the narrative structures in which they are rendered. Bedlam is not intended as another attack on psychiatry for its managing power over human affairs. Rather, it is an attempt to provide some sort of commentary on the absence of psychiatry. It is an account of the mechanisms and processes that make up the new forms of community where there is little or no provision of formal services. It is an attempt to document and comment on the broader social relationships between the mad and the not so mad in the sharing of urban space. And it suggests that the problem is not the failure of psychiatry or the inadequacy of community care, although it certainly is inadequate, but a broader social problem concerning the terms on which the mad and the rest of society might coexist. It is about what happens when the aliens are let out of the asylum and there is nowhere special for them to go.[8]

What follows is a journey traversing some of the post-asylum geographies of madness that inflect the cityscape through which they are constructed. This is not a departure but a part of an intellectual tradition that dates back at least to the Chicago school and its concern with the social geographies of the city. Faris and Dunham's (1965 [1939]) *Mental Disorders In Urban Areas* is an ecology of mental disorder that plots the distribution of mental disorder onto the urban landscape connecting personal disorganization with the social disorganization and anomie of city life. In Burgess's classic model of concentric city zones, Faris and Dunham insert another map linking human mobility as migration and drift through the city with rates of breakdown and mental pathology. Transience, now an accepted condition of the global order, was seen as inherently problematic in the forging of the social bonds anchoring the individual to the community as a geographical space: and so rates of schizophrenia were mapped onto indices of mobility (Faris and Dunham 1965: 177). Just as the asylum once received the disordered products of city life as human crises implied in Faris's and Dunham's urban geographies, it has now sent them back on terms requiring examination and discussion. The Los Angeles social geographers Wolch and Dear have documented some of these *Landscapes of Despair* (1987) in which the mentally distressed are more recently ghettoized by zoning laws that protect wealthier neighbourhoods from itinerants. Chris Philo (1989: 260) has challenged Wolch and Dear's accounts of the geographies of social exclusion and provided insights into the social geographies of madness in Britain (Parr and Philo 1995). Taylor and Dear (1982) have examined neighbourhood tensions over the siting of community facilities in Toronto. It is these discussions of madness and urban space that provided the impetus for *Bedlam*, along with Peter Barham's (1992: 101) provocative account of the mad as hovering between other and self, stripped of their human subjectivity in the asylums, returned to make their own way in the urban landscape. *Bedlam* is an attempt to understand the social and spatial relationships of which these geographies of madness are composed, through the voices and movements of those whose lives they organize. It mines the interface between the manner in which people are administered and the actions and decisions they make around these contexts. Agency and structure are different ends of the same set of processes that are negotiated within a set of finite possibilities with outcomes that are not especially predictable but form the substance of local micro-studies of welfare cultures. In these concerns the broad intellectual parameters of the book owe debts to Bourdieu's notion of habitus; Foucauldian accounts of the networks of power through which lives are sustained; de Certeau's concept of practical action and the quotidian as a focus for social analysis; Nietzsche's notion of true existence; and Lefebvre's concept of space as a domain of social relationships and political priorities. These intellectual tools are put to work in a series of journeys that take us from the revolving doors of Montréal's psychiatric wards to some of the recesses of the city and through the trajectories of the lives lived in these settings – assembling a collage of voices, visual images and text in an attempt to understand the life world of the mad.

1

VOICE, IMAGE AND TEXT

Don't let them put you under a microscope.
(Overheard reference to the research
in a centre where we were interviewing)

The reflexive turn in the social sciences, its contingent knowledge claims, its imaginative recreation of life worlds and micro-social processes, and its use of free-association interpretation carries a responsibility to expose its principles of textual production to critical scrutiny and counter-argument. In the absence of truth and validity, there is reasonable interpretation – what Freeman (1993) calls veracity – and the philosophical, theoretical and political positions on which it is premised. The collage of voices (authorial and informant), images (visual and textual), urban spaces and practical lives featured in this volume are the product of theoretically and politically driven decisions. These decisions are complicated by the multiple layers of intertextuality that drive multi-disciplinary research teams in which individual student-researchers operate their own understanding of the research in the field in ways which articulate *their* experiences, personal/professional conceptions of themselves as interviewers/observers, and ways of managing interaction with informants.[1] Research fields are textured by a collage of practical and intellectual activity as well as the social relationships between researcher and researched: activities in which researchers' biographies are neither central nor incidental and mostly opaque.[2] In involving ourselves in the lives of others in the course of research, we change them and we change ourselves: we help them write *their* story in specific terms and we rewrite our own in the process. If research is a highly edited activity, then so are its products which are subjected to further processes of scrutiny and selection in the production of a final text. The ensuing chapter represents an attempt to discuss some of the principles of *Bedlam*'s production.

This is evidently a text that is politically framed in the sense that it is responding to an implicit political agenda that has produced the situation under investigation. It is responding to it by exposing it, making it visible, so that those who wish to defend it must do so openly and in a critical dialogue that places madness in a broader social framework governed by principles of fairness and social justice. This text is politically framed in that it exposes a situation in order to raise the question of change and to suggest some of the directions in which this might occur. The critique lies in the framing of the exposure to foreground forms of social exclusion: versions of subjectivity and lifestyle; forms of provision and their appropriateness; versions of

9

citizenship loosely concerned with the nature of the social bonds connecting the individual to the collectivity of individuals composing the social world; and the connections between a particular group of welfare subjects and the regimes through which their lives are organized. It is intended to show some of the lines of fragmentation in liberal democratic states and to expose some of those features that are commonly thought of as attending less liberal, affluent and highly developed political regimes. Its political framing justifies what is otherwise a perverse voyeurism in placing under the microscope – as the whispered comment referred to above so aptly puts it – lives which are already highly scrutinized at the same time as they are unseen. They are scrutinized, as will become apparent, by the myriad apparatuses, bureaucratic systems and personnel that manage them. And yet they remain hidden from the popular gaze by the absence of political debate about their situation, and by the ways in which they are inserted (and insert themselves) into the grammar of the city where they are not ghettoized, in the way Wolch and Dear (1987) describe, but centrally placed in ways that make them both marginal and invisible.

Bedlam's political framing is theoretically managed. Marleau Ponty's 'situated human subjectivity' (Crossley 1994) provides a mode of grasping the ways in which social and spatial contexts generate specific forms of personhood and ways of being in the world. Lefebvre's (1996) conception of space as product and producer of social activity and relationships also provides a means of thinking about the relationships between people and the spaces in which their lives are produced and given meaning.[3] In this dialogical formulation, spaces, and the activities performed around them, produce a range of possible ways of being that contribute to the production of space on certain terms.[4] People produce the spaces that *produce them* as human subjects. Just as important as space in the production of people and lives are the stories people tell about themselves and their lives.[5] The telling of everyday life contains vital clues about social morphology (de Certeau 1988) and the lives lived through it (Ricoeur 1991). The living and telling of life as stories highlights the individual choices unique to each biography, in which individual life trajectories are as significant as the broader (social) spatial and policy contexts in which they are cast. In this schema the individual and its social context form and transform each other in a dialogically constituted tension.[6]

Bedlam's theoretical framing, expanded in the appropriate places throughout the text, serves the political objectives of critical exposure and provides the basis for the textual production of the group of lives that follow. Within these general political/theoretical acts of framing are more practical decisions that make up research activity and produce the material from which textual selections are made. Threading together voices, space and images involves deciding which voices, which spaces, and which images to present from the available casts of characters and the scenes on which they operate: issues which require more detailed examination.

Voices

The concept of 'voice' invokes a politics of recognition and places the theorization and experience of the unheard at the centre of research activity. The voices at the centre of our investigation in *Bedlam* are those of the mentally distressed users of the community system. But significant information about the operation of services and the relations between them was provided by those who worked as volunteers and as paid employees in foster homes, in day centres, in soup kitchens, food banks and homeless shelters.[7] The most insightful accounts came not from those – community and social workers – who were more centrally placed in informal services, but from those strategically placed intermediaries who ran the showers, sorted laundry and served soup. These, along with the researchers' impressions, provide the subsidiary voices arranged around the accounts solicited from our mentally distressed informants and massaged into an overarching narrative by the author. The centrality of mad voices in our analysis differentiates *Bedlam* from texts concerned with the operation of psychiatry and the standpoint of services: and attention to the social circumstances in which those voices are set differentiates *Bedlam* from 'survivor accounts' that foreground the terror of the psychiatrically managed experience of madness without placing it in its broader administrative and social contexts.

The use of *voice* in the task of social analysis positions lives as a key source of social knowing. The voice narrating the story of its life in a particular set of circumstances opens a window onto that life, other lives and the broader social circumstances in which they are cast.[8] The voices of those who worked in and around informal community facilities were produced with the invitation to 'tell us what it is you do here' and were intended to provide an alternate commentary to the impression management of brochures and publicity documents and to provide detail of work practices and commentaries on what it meant, from their perspective, to be a client. Our invitation to mentally distressed informants to 'tell us about *your life* and how you came to be *here*' in which the *here* referred to the soup kitchen, foster home, shelter or day centre in which the interview took place, produced narratives in which they drew the connections between themselves and their present circumstances, rearranging the scenes of their past which formed this particular trajectory.[9] This was an invitation to speak on certain terms and it produced particular kinds of stories and consequently forms of social knowing. Lives were told as the product of individual struggles and decisions in specific social and administrative circumstances because interviews were specifically framed in this way.

Although we avoided the lexicon of mental health in order to allow informants to speak about their circumstances in their own terms, the purpose of our conversations had somehow to be simply described and most often this got reduced to their 'experiences with the health care system'. Hence *Bedlam*'s voices narrate stories of individual suffering and triumph *and* collective stories about a particular group of welfare subjects and the social and political regimes through which their lives are managed.[10] The collection of voices is a highly manipulated source of social knowing. There is yet a further level to its forms of manipulation and that concerns the invitation to 'speak' itself. This draws the speaker into the conventions of storytelling – beginning, middle and end – which work against episodic and non-sequential remembering. One person pointed the difficulties of this out to us:

> And you want, and you want to straighten out [the story he was telling us]. If you want a cohesion of this tape, you should accept that it is episodic. I'm not lecturing I'm just saying that you should accept that it's episodic and to try to piece it together like a jigsaw puzzle ... that's fine by me, it doesn't have to be linear.
>
> (A warning delivered by Evan)

Plate 3   Derrik being interviewed at Burger King

It also demands the narrative ordering of non-narrative forms of remembering associated with trauma and the disordering experience of psychotic and schizophrenic episodes. These may be experienced as sounds, smells or feelings, which cannot easily be translated into words. The demand that delusional experiences be rendered in narrative form therefore involves extensive work of translation by storytellers.

As well as being an invitation to speak on certain terms, interviews are invited 'performances of the self' in which the self is substantially recreated (Freeman 1993) in telling the story of a life.[11] In these dramas informants' agendas interface with those of researchers and can take off in directions which are difficult to predict. In Pras's first interview, he picked up on one of our sub-themes concerned with trying to understand peoples' sense of belonging. He arrives at the second wearing padlocks and chains on his neck and hands, which, he explains, he had just purchased from Canadian Tire. Speaking from the apparently white skin of his Canadian–Haitian ancestors, he deploys his newly acquired props in a narrative of racial enslavement in which Jamaica and Africa substitute for Haiti in symbolizing black enslavement and a sense of homeland.

> In America when the English and the other Europeans went to Africa, they brought with them ... the black people ... the Africans to America as slaves in chains on ships and eventually what happened is slaves rebel against their masters ... they killed them ... they broke their chains. FREEDOM ... in Jamaica ... Black freedom.
>
> (Pras)

His performance leaves us in no doubt about how he sees himself and what his apparent whiteness obscures. It shows us how close narratives of race and ethnicity are to the surface of people's lives. And it shows the entwining of forms of racial and mental suffering. It also leaves us with the sense that we have helped to generate this particular narrative in providing the scene, the audience and the questions which unleashed its performance.

Anne *performed* the story she does not tell by other means. Refusing to be interviewed, she detaches an interviewer and photographer from the day centre where they are interviewing. She enlists them to carry her bags and hold an arm each as she picks her way through the snow in a peculiar knee-high lifted gait back to her apartment. She performs for them on the bongos, prepares a meal from the things she has available and then she directs the camera onto herself, posing in different wigs and hats, and onto selected items in her apartment: a performed visual account of herself and her life accomplished without words and reproduced in Chapter 5, in an exploration of the meaning of madness.

As well as being displays (accounts) of the self that enliven certain themes and ignore others in their acts of selective disclosure, and as well as switching proceedings to other genres of narrative (visual ones in the case of Anne), interview performances are ways of dealing with interviewers who are placed in the position of audience in what are essentially two-way transactions. In various interviews we have been placed in the position of substitute psychiatrists, substitute social workers, confessors, advisors, sounding-board for various theories especially the theory that someone is 'better'

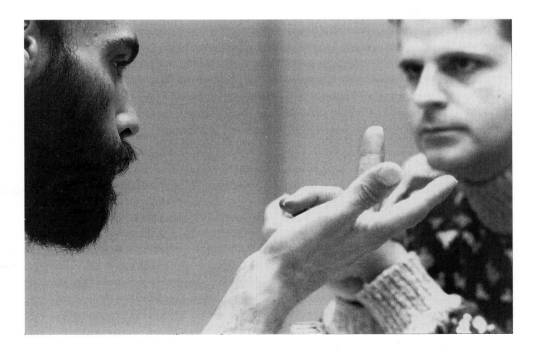

Plate 4   Getting the interviewer's attention

or 'normal', and kindly visitors or potential friends. We were also occasionally reminded of our position as a part of the problem we were embarked upon investigating.

> I want it understood on the tape that I repeat it and repeat it and repeat it, that I don't care about what people feel about what I should do or did or didn't do, I'm in a revenge vendetta mode against society. ... You're, you're a threat to me, who reads that [his story] is a threat to me I want to make it clear that I don't really much care how anybody feels about the economy or welfare or mental illness or anything. ... I'm not exactly angry but I want to get it across that you can't get away with the shit that you do to people like me. ... I feel that the tape will be read and it will be misused.
>
> (Evan)

Researchers' insecurities, conceptions of themselves and comfort levels in dealing with madness were often astutely observed and blatantly exploited by informants who drew them into their performances, also on certain terms. These dialogues of performance significantly shape the production of voices in the processes of investigation.

The deployment of *mad* voices in the task of social analysis poses particular problems. Does their madness detract from the value of these voices as social testimony? Are theirs *not* the voices that provide a window onto a particular constellation of social circumstances but the voices of delusion or the medication used to treat delusion? And if so, must they therefore be discounted? Or should they be accepted as a legitimate account of the social (and pharmacological) conditions in which the seriously mentally distressed live? Many of our stories were told through the fog of medication: but these *are* the conditions in which these lives are lived and negotiated and for this reason alone must be seen as legitimate social testimony. Stories collected under the influence of heavy medication – particularly evident in those living in foster care arrangements – were of limited use and form only a small portion of the voices in this volume. Medication has a bearing on the issue of delusion as it acts to produce a moderating effect. Freeman's (1993: 163) 'narrative order of experience', which asks whether stories make sense of the available information in a coherent and plausible way, helps cut a path through the issues raised by delusion. Barham's (1984) interviews with the schizophrenics with whom he worked as a psychiatrist show how apparently delusional reasoning makes sense in the contexts in which it is set. He shows how delusional reasoning works as a reasonable interpretation of how the world of the schizophrenic and the psychiatric hospital operates once we understand the assumptions with which the schizophrenic is operating. Even delusional reasoning is socially located. Schizophrenics, too, are social beings, productive and useful agents of history, who make sense of their own lives (Barham 1984: 6). None of our informants, with the exception of Walter, made us work this hard to interpret their testimony. Badges occupied Walter's world (including his Nelson Mandela T-shirt): symbols and markers of identity and allegiance that differentiate 'our people' from enemy 'aliens' and their space-ship invasions and conspiracies. The Queen – of Canada, England and Jamaica – as well as the great kings of Africa occupied his personal landscape. What appears as a delusional rant in which he is involved in an inter-galactic war with the bureaucracies of the Canadian Federal Government in fact contains moments in which it is possible to understand his position as a Jamaican immigrant, processed by immigration and other procedures, and recruited by the Nation of Islam to serve in the world-wide struggle against black oppression.[12] The other voices in *Bedlam* are not delusional. They are surprisingly ordinary, banal even. The many stories we collected support the view that the mad are eminently capable of examining, theorizing and rendering their own lives in narrative terms. Ultimately all voices, even delusional ones, are a product of the social and administrative conditions in which they operate, as well as the research conditions in which they are offered and collected. One or two further comments on the research process and the selection of voices serves to clarify some further aspects of *Bedlam*'s production as a text.

In the absence of obvious community mental health care facilities in which to interview, *Bedlam*'s voices were tracked from the hospital gates to the informal facilities and sites with which they came into contact. This brought us into contact with people with serious and persistent difficulties – primarily schizophrenics,[13] who had not been reabsorbed invisibly into the landscape of the city. We collected stories from each of the different kinds of living arrangements that constituted the community. Foster homes and shelters were approached directly; and through day centres, soup kitchens and food banks we found those who lived in private rooming houses and on the streets. Intending to collect as many different kinds of story as possible, our interviews were spread over all of the different kinds of sites we found and were as demographically spread as possible.

Of the sixty schizophrenics we interviewed, two-thirds were men, reflecting a difficulty in finding women and getting into what were specifically women's shelters. Two-thirds are classified by the Canadian Federal Government as 'visible minorities' (their term for non-whites) mostly Caribbeans, with smaller numbers of Africans and South Americans. The non-visible (white) group was dominated by those who identified themselves as 'Canadian' or 'Québécois' and contained more Anglophones than Francophones, with the remainder identifying themselves as 'Irish', 'Jewish', 'Italian' or 'Greek'. Gender, origin and ethnicity are not the sole architects of experience, and a great deal of attention was paid to collecting different kinds of narratives and hence versions of experience. Sixty people were interviewed on tape between one and six times each – a process that generated over a hundred user interviews. The number of times we interviewed someone depended on the usefulness of what they had to say and their facility for telling stories. Storytellers – those who seemed most easily able and willing to reflect on their own lives – got the most tape time.

Forty-three workers were interviewed, not all of them on tape and once each only. Because we worked from sites and not by personal contact, all of our mad informants were a part of some centre or facility's turf and access had to be negotiated with workers. Interviewing workers (and volunteers) was hence a part of our entry routine. It was *their* conceptions of their clients and the purpose of our research that determined who we were able to interview. We were steered away from the volatile, the dangerous, the unsuitable and hence the voices we were able to collect owed much to their selections on our behalf. When two interviewers turned up to interview Vincent at one of the drop-in centres as arranged, the centre co-ordinator called Vincent over and briefed him:

Co-ordinator:	These students from the university would like to talk to you Vincent, is that okay? But I'm warning you, none of that bullshit. None of that God stuff either.
Vincent:	I don't lie.
Co-ordinator:	Bull shit and lying are not the same thing. I'm just warning you Vincent, none of that bull shit. None of the God stuff either. These are serious students.

Their selections were also sometimes visibly organized by the broader nature of relationships between workers and their client/users. In some homeless shelters and foster homes it seemed that certain people were *instructed* to give interviews as part of a set of obligations we were not a party to, but which had to do with the ways in which systems of obligation and expectation were internally arranged between workers and their clients. This, of course, laid waste to our careful preparation and vetting of ethics protocols involving written 'informed' consent being given by the informant: a requirement in North American universities. In other kinds of sites it was clearer when people *wanted* to speak to us and when they didn't, and sometimes we were hijacked by those who had special reasons for wanting to tell their stories. Some of these interloper voices are included in the final text because generally they express more politically worked narratives that speak for others as well as the storyteller, something that, of course, provided the impetus for wanting to be heard. A striking example of someone who wanted to speak to us was Craig, who sees himself as a historian of the forgotten memories of the asylum. He speaks about his asylum experiences – although we were initially reluctant to collect them – on behalf of those who are unable to speak and remember, something he sees as a political duty. We will meet him later. Jonathan, a street musician, who we will also meet later, offered to speak to us as someone who lives among the mad and has observed them, and the others who occupy the streets, at close quarters. He is the self-appointed spokesman of life on the streets: an expert in the grammar of the city.

The final text itself of course contains further selection by the author, of a tiny proportion of the many voices heard and collected. The most powerful voices – those, which give a vivid sense of the life, lived in a particular set of circumstances – were included. Priority was ceded to voices articulating common views and themes and these are often set beside the alternate voices challenging them. Sometimes narratives are detached from the lives in which they were produced in order to give more thorough treatment to a particular theme. On other occasions the coherence of themes is sacrificed in order to respect the integrity of the narrated life from which it was drawn because in detaching voices from their biographies important details of individual lives and tales of suffering are lost. The resulting text juggles these two priorities. Whether it does so successfully is for the reader to decide.

Space

Bedlam was intellectually conceptualized as a people narrative enterprise and it was the limitations of this type of narrative that led to it being reconceptualized in spatial terms. People narratives – the windows onto lives – articulate the spatial contexts in which they are set. As de Certeau (1988: 115) reminds us: 'every story is a travel story', a narration of spatial practice, movement from here to there. So the problem with narrative is not that it is without space: on the contrary it is full of space. My dissatisfaction with verbal narrative was about its failure to give an adequate sense of some of the spectacular spatial contexts in which daily lives were set. It matters where the mundane practices of daily life occur: there is a world of difference between getting up and having breakfast in a private home and getting up in a shelter and panhandling for the money to buy breakfast in a public place. These are quite different activities in spatial terms and, if spaces produce people and their forms of subjectivity or inner being (Lefebvre 1996; Pile and Thrift 1995), then who and what we are and how we operate in the world are space-related. Some, but not all, space is revealed in talk. Space can unseat or reinforce narrative: it works in no particular configuration. An example is found in the narratives of popular culture that Phil Cohen (1996) writes about as 'racialized territory' in London's Docklands. In these stories narrative and place (as spaces with identities) underscore each other: the symbolism of race and its narratives of collective suffering and exclusion/belonging, entitlement and inclusion mark territory. In Montréal narratives of racial suffering remain *private* matters and hence are not mapped onto the city landscape symbolically and territorially in the same way as Cohen's examples in East London. This is because of the different ways in which racial politics are configured in the two cities. Consequently, an interview with a black man in Montréal about the extent to which 'ethnicity matters' will typically be met with indifference and bland statements about the 'family of man', which repeats the party line of three layers of governance in which Canadian society is a mosaic of difference without inequality. The man telling you this will typically be wearing a Nelson Mandella T-shirt like the one worn by Pras, and will have been recruited, like others living in Little Burgundy – a 'black area' next to the railway station traditionally occupied by railway porters whose employment was once restricted to this occupation – by the Nation of Islam and their narratives of black nationalism. This is not misrepresentation, but a mode of operating through the dominant myths and stories of the locale. In this case the reading of space and its symbolism counters the narrative: providing a parallel narrative to those articulated as the voices of people. In this example of popular narrative people are not the sum of what they *say*, and talk and space are brought to bear upon each other in contradictory (or mutually sustaining) ways. Space can, in certain circumstances, fill the silences in talk by adding another dimension to the analysis, and this highlights the importance of old-fashioned ethnography and the skills of observation, sometimes eclipsed by the collection of stories as the basis of contemporary social analysis.

Ethnographic observation revealed the gap between practice and talk; between living and telling stories about life. While much of the mundane or quotidian is revealed in talk, there are things that remain unsaid, not because they cannot be said, but because they are not said. Instead they are embedded in the habitual, the taken-for-granted background assumptions of living, which are beyond narrative. Living is essentially a practical activity: it is 'done' rather than reflected upon and hence not necessarily told as narrative. This unformulated 'practical grasp of the world' (Taylor 1999: 34) is best captured in Bourdieu's 'habitus', the social rules and background understanding that is animated in *practical action*. This is embodied. It is about the ways in which we move about the world. And it is about a contemporary 'sense of self' (Taylor 1999: 33). Descriptions of practical action are hence a point of access to this intangible but essential part of the social fabric. Practical action is essentially (although not exclusively) a set of spatial practices: the imposition of human agency upon the social, built environment in which human existence is cast. Space can be seen as a repository of action shaped by practice and social relationships.[14] Everyday actions and movements are embedded in the unreflected-upon use of space. Hence analytically, space operates as a text that can be read for the silent narratives that are not told by other means and are certainly not told by people. But it none-the-less operates as a domain of definite lived experiences and social relationships (Keith and Pile 1993; Cohen 1996; Massey 1993: 156). Space is a 'field of action' transformed by the lives of its social subjects (Lefebvre 1996: 190–1) that it, in turn transforms. The spaces in which madness operates produce, and are produced by, certain kinds of lives. They can be read for their particular social relationships and the kinds of practical activity they sustain.

Space has many analytical advantages as a setting for life-story narrative. It takes up where narrative leaves off and fills the gaps in narrated accounts of lives structured by public, personal and popular stories. It places lives in a broader context of social relationships; of built environments; of practices and actions that are habitual and not just consciously reflected-upon and narrated; and of the moral and political priorities embedded in the grammar of the city. Space is also a domain of aesthetics that is particularly amenable to visual representation (Parr and Philo 1995). Space then can be read for its practical activities, its implied social relationships, the subjectivities it produces, and for important clues about the political and moral order of which it forms a part. Although lives remained at the centre of our analytic framework these became 'narrated lives in their spatial contexts'. In understanding spatial context, we better understand lives and the subtle differences between them.

Visual images

The spectacular spaces we encountered in tracking the community system in Montréal demanded visual representation. Photographs (like space, the people we didn't want to interview and the overall direction of the research itself) grew from the field and the material we were collecting. At one level photographs, like writing, are simply texts raising the same issues of representation and political/theoretical framing. But on another level they have some special properties. Two are particularly significant. Photographs expose people and places that would otherwise remain anonymous. Real names of people and places are substituted for others, but the photographs are the real thing and not mock-ups. Second, photographs are much more open to interpretation and alternate reading than the text, which is rather precisely pinned-down by its political and theoretical orientation. It is precisely around the visual images (as well as the voices heard in the direct quotes) that the text opens up and lets the reader in. The risks are exposure (of those who might prefer anonymity),[15] and loss of control (of the text to the reader). Apart from these differences, photographs raise the same issues of textual construction as writing: issues of representation, meaning, ethics, politics and theory. A discussion of visual images is a good place to consider some of these issues – already raised in a broader form in relation to voice and space – in greater detail.

Photographing the mad raises important questions about representation, the meaning of madness and its legitimate forms of management, all of which hinge on interpretations of how the mad look. There are many images to choose from. How should they look? Normal or deranged? We have examples of both. Should they look like victims of political neglect? Or like the survivors of multiple forms of private suffering? Or like the combatants of internal demons? They are all of these things. Picturing madness, like other acts of textual representation raises the age-old theoretical question in sociology – are they really mad or simply being administered by the state and its technologies of surveillance because their forms of eccentricity violate the boundaries of social interaction and are too much to absorb? Is theirs a private or a political suffering? Or are these two things connected in some way? This is a fundamental question not centrally addressed in our investigations because they were structured by other concerns, but we take the position that madness is a fundamental crisis of the nature of human existence that is produced and managed by broader social and political forces. Having spent a number of years with some of our interviewees and having listened to their stories, it would be dishonest to air-brush out their private suffering and the torturing persistence of the voices that speak to them in their episodes of delusion. But while their suffering is real and experienced as individual pain, there can be no doubt that it is socially produced and managed, and that these things, too, are part of the problem. Failed relationships and difficult economic circumstances prominently feature in the stories we collected: things that are socially framed. It soon became apparent that we were speaking to the graduate class of the child welfare system: that their madness was the outcome of previous life stress and the failure of other, earlier forms of social management. Evidently this was a case of vulnerability compounded by earlier vulnerability, and administrative failure compounded by earlier administrative failure.

Plate 5   Wycliff attending to his 3-year-old daughter

Photography is not extensively deployed as a tool in social analysis and for this reason there is not much to draw on by way of previous discussion. Anthropology, cultural studies and oral history have made more extensive use of photography than sociology. Although anthropology has embraced the visual, visual anthropology relies primarily on film seeing photography as a tool in ethnographic fieldwork promoting 'holistic and accurate observation' (Collier and Collier 1986: 5).[16] Photography is deployed in anthropology as a method in the effective documentation of artefacts of material culture (inventory); a way of preserving the initial vivid impressions formed in the field; a means of orientation in the field; a way of establishing a rapport with locals; a record of which cannot be easily turned into text descriptions; a tool for detailing uses of space; and an index of social relationships: 'precise records of material reality' (Collier and Collier 1986: 10). In these contexts photography is seen as a means of documenting the real in which the construction of that reality is not placed in question. Oral historians such as Alicia Rouverol (1999) in her study of the closure of an American poultry factory ' was Content and Not Content'. The Story of Linda Lord and the Closing of Penobscot Poultry and Michael Frisch and Milton Rogovan's (1993) Portraits in Steel have used photography most effectively to convey the spaces in which working lives are lived but with only scant consideration of their textual practices that implicitly rely on having captured a layer of social realism. In sociology photography has remained a marginal concern despite the pioneering work of the American Journal of Sociology discussed by Henny (1986); and Bourdieu's (1990: 1–8) attempts to constitute the practices and images of photography as an object of sociological investigation. Despite current attention to space and spatial metaphors (Fyfe and Law 1988: 1–2) sociology has remained firmly focused on text and on narrative: on the written and the spoken word. Sociologists listen and map and turn what they see into text. And yet, photographs and other means of depicting visual images are a part of everyday life – the object of social analysis (Denzin 1989; Lefebvre 1994; de Certeau 1988). We live in a visual culture in which photography is a part of the 'furniture of the environment' (Sontag 1990: 21). Visual images and their social messages of which we are all skilled interpreters surround us. Despite this sociology is effectively visually illiterate: picturing features neither as a technique for recording nor as a tool in social analysis.

Photographs offer a way of entering the world of others, of visualizing what we are not: a means of 'class tourism' which places before our gaze unfamiliar social realities (Sontag 1990: 57) drawn from either end of the social scale. Photographs are the tool of the Baudelaireian flaneur – able to confront us with celebrity lives captured by the paparazzi and with the city's 'dark seamy corners' and 'neglected populations' (Sontag 1990: 55–6). Bedlam's photographs bring the mad into public focus with an invitation to imagine their lives. But the invitation to imagine also intrudes (Sontag 1990: 13). There is a voyeurism in photographing unguarded moments, apartments, meager possessions and rows of beds ranged in dormitories. These are the trappings of what are anyway highly scrutinized lives in which distinctions between what is public and what is private differ markedly from what holds for the rest of the population. This kind of intrusion requires a clear political rationale (Hevey 1992: 60) that questions, repositions and reinterprets madness and the lives it touches. The invitation to imagine turns lives into spectacle at the same time as it brings the invisible into public view. The New York photographer Diane Arbus is criticised for her photographic freak shows of giants and dwarfs on the grounds that she manipulates their images into projections of her own preoccupation (Hevey 1992: 64). Photographs displaying the human body *are* spectacles (Bordieu 1990: 83). This cannot be avoided. They are also the projections of authorial intention. This, too, is unavoidable. The only honest course is to discuss the photographer's relationship to his work and, because his work is rendered in an analysis of madness, the relationship between the photographer, the author and the text. More of this later.

Although all of the people photographed signed consent forms they will have imagined the use of their photograph in many ways. They cannot have imagined its precise deployment in this text as we ourselves were uncertain about this when the photographs were taken: and to see people as they cannot see themselves, if not a form of violation (Sontag 1990: 15), exercises certain power relationships over representation and hence carries a moral debt to those whose images are used not to cause them further harm, and if possible to do a bit of good. The general aim in using photographs in this text is to help create a space in which both the social position and social world of the mad can be re-imagined in more positive, inclusive, and less defensive terms.

There are many other things which can be said about the meaning of photographs and have a bearing on their use in this text. Photographs are a commentary on the social systems in which they are produced and which can only produce certain images. In this sense they operate as an archive of the possible depictions of the social world. As well as being individually authored acts of representation, they form a part of the 'scopic regime' (Jenks 1995: 15) or collective ways of seeing and understanding in which we are all implicated. In this they are an archive of the popular imaginary. Photography, like vision itself, is a 'skilled social practice' (Jenks 1995: 10): What we see and the manner in which we see it, is bound up with the social arrangement of knowledge, strategies of power and systems of desire (Jenks 1995: 1). Photographs are eminently significant social texts. They depict elements of the social fabric for skilled interpretation and are hence to be seen as a resource in the task of social analysis.

As well as being an expression of a given scopic regime and its social order, photographs acquire meaning – and must hence be read – in the context of the political regimes in which they are deployed. Photographs have been of service as a tool of governance in which they are deployed as a means of surveillance to record and identify as in police photographic records (Tagg 1988: 10). But they have also been deployed in more progressive campaigns as in the liberal documentary welfare traditions of the nineteenth century, where they were used as evidence of social conditions, for example, to display the living conditions of the poor as part of a demand for slum clearance (Tagg 1988: 119–20).[17] Photographs have no necessary political agenda but can be deployed in the techniques of either governance or critique. Not a straightforward record of social conditions, they can be made to show any set of social circumstances in any mode of political framing, as 'good' or 'bad'. Not just the product of the social conditions they represent, they are a 'politically mobilized rhetoric of truth' (Tagg 1988: 13) which is given meaning by the frameworks in which they are deployed (Law and Whittaker 1988: 161). Photographs are hence a tool, a resource, to be deployed in all manner of campaigns and projects. They are no more a resource of oppressive regimes – although they display aspects of these regimes – than they are a resource in the task of social criticism. They serve well the task of critical exposure by opening up certain arenas and strategies for social action: valorizing as

Plate 6

well as objectifying and subjugating (Tagg 1998: 91–3). It is of course with this intention – valorization and critical exposure of the system – that photographs are deployed in *Bedlam*.

In historical terms photography has a special relationship to madness that is concerned with its deployment as a strategy of social management, its part in therapeutic regimes and the broader social and political contexts in which both of these things were set. Sander Gilman's (1982) brilliant visual grammar of madness *Seeing the Insane* explores the aesthetic and therapeutic strategies in eighteenth-century portraiture, early psychiatry and popular culture through which madness was *seen*.[18] Gilman's work is a history of psychiatry through the iconography of madness.[19] By the end of the seventeenth century he shows how the therapeutic regimes of psychiatry had transformed the sketches of wild men belonging to the middle ages (Gilman 1982: 21). Conceptions of madness through species occupied eighteenth-century craniometry and its concern with facial angles,[20] concomitantly a feature of early anthropology.[21] Later drawings of the melancholic depict passions as the site of dysfunction which could be *read* in the face (Gilman 1982: 102) by a skilled therapist.[22] Gilman is arguing that madness was navigated visually in the popular imagination and therapeutic strategies until the nineteenth century, when the idea that the mad could be restored to the community through the disciplines of work, normality of daily routines and psychiatric treatment narrowed the gap between sanity and insanity and the mad were 'normalized' at the same time as they were whisked away from public view (Gilman 1982: 161). This normalization process may be seen as having continued with the discoveries of chemical management and decarceration. In the regimes of community psychiatry the mad – and this has a direct bearing on *Bedlam* – had become indistinguishable from others and hence the most insidious of public threats: they *look* like everyone else but they are not. In this respect the mad are incorporated into the scopic regimes of the inner city where we both see them and don't see them. They are invisible except when they draw attention to themselves in their erratic performances of 'crazy' behaviour.

It should be clear from this brief attempt to position photography in this text that visual narratives are as highly manipulated as written texts. With no meaning of their own they display the regimes in which they are set and take on the intellectual and political frameworks of the texts in which they are deployed. They are not an index of the 'real' as Bordieu (1990: 74) claims and, in being open to manipulation, they inflect meaning rather than reflect it – producing new social realities (rather than reflecting old ones) and transforming daily life rather than reproducing it (Tagg 1988: 3, 63–4, 119). *Bedlam*'s photographs are intended, not as illustration of the 'really real', but as a parallel narrative to the written narrative and its voices. They are often images that cannot be reduced to words, and so are accompanied by captions only. Eyes and facial expressions convey the horrors of untellable stories. To describe these images in words would undermine them and their purpose in the text as they are intended to expand the range of intertextualities between reader and text: opening the text to the visual faculties of the reader for further interpretation that goes beyond that text. They are, however, strategically placed in the text in order to add, strategically, things which cannot be *said* but which must be *seen*.

Plate 7   Dominique sitting in Dunkin Donuts

Strategies of representation

Tagg's (1988) 'strategies of representation' provides a way of discussing the more detailed selection of the images placed within *Bedlam*'s pages. Although the ensuing discussion focuses on visual images, it equally applies to the selection of voices and *their* arrangement in the text. The strategy of representation obviously services the political/theoretical framing raised earlier: the discussion of diversity; the suggestion that the mad exercise high levels of social agency; an exploration of the life worlds of the mad and the meaning of madness; and the critical exposure of the regimes through which madness is organized and managed.

The images recorded photographically and chosen for inclusion in the text were intended to give a sense of active relationships between people, and between people and the environments in which they live, without lapsing into the nostalgia of 'ethnographic theatre' (Tagg 1988: 12) or tagging the mad as an object of pity. Images (and voices) were chosen to show people negotiating and manipulating, as well as sometimes being temporarily defeated by, the spatial and administrative contexts in which their lives are cast: choosing paths from those available and making contextually rational decisions about their lives. In this way we hoped to expose some of the existential threads in lives and use them to question the sociological categories – madness, homelessness, dangerousness, welfare, clients and so on – through which lives are grouped and understood administratively and sociologically. Existential is used in this volume in two senses. It is used in the sense in which Sartre and Camus used it to refer to the processes of individual decision making in which one rather than another of the available paths – trajectories – is chosen in the living of a life. And it is used to refer to some of the inner processes which guide these choices of trajectory: an inner sense of selfhood as a bundle of gut reactions and emotions that people *feel* to be unique to them and form a part of western conceptions of personhood. The existential in this sense is a core of unique and personal being. The self may be written by the available cultural script but not – as Freeman (1993) suggests – without 'remainder'. It is this individual bit of creativity – the remainder – that approximates to the existential, that inner gut reaction with which people negotiate their cultural scripting and adminis-trative processing. Without it we would have to admit to being cultural automatons. The existential is a small but significant part of that which is played out in active biography. Active biography, delivered through voice and pictures, muddies and frag-ments social positioning and its categorical imperatives. Although we wanted to expose and challenge the therapeutic/welfare arrangements through which madness is dealt with, we didn't want to provide images of passive recipients of the neglectful regimes of psychiatry in the community. Neither did we want to suggest unrealistic levels of individual 'choice' and action, individualizing (and blaming on a lack of self-determination) what are also social and political problems. In addition to active social agency, our representational strategy attempted to convey the diversity and contradic-tory nature of madness and its impact on lives by placing together discordant images that disturb popular assumptions – such as the picture of a single (schizophrenic) father gently tending his 3-year-old daughter.

Our (and here the collective intention refers not to the research team but decisions made between the author and the photographer) representational strategy demanded a balancing of people and places. Existential 'choices' as paths taken are cast in the administrative frameworks of welfare and its political systems, and our intention was to show how these looked and worked and to document their shaping of the lives lived through them. We wanted to document the aesthetics of the social geographies of madness composing the community system – to show what it looked like because it was so strikingly different from other parts of the urban landscape and the social scenes on which other people lived. Photographs of shelter dormitories and so on invite the reader to imagine the lives that can be led in those circumstances. In other words, lives are visually *placed* in their spatial, administrative and political contexts without simply reducing them to that context. In maintaining a tension between the existential threads of lives and their contexts we circumvent images of 'victimhood' and total individual responsibility by stressing the political and collective aspects of responsibility for the modern disposal of madness. In the 'rejection of tragedy in favour of mobilization' (Hevey 1992: 104–5), it is important to pursue a representa-tional strategy which opens up a critical dialogue with systems of governance by drawing attention to their effects.

Two forms of authorship mediated the representational strategies of this text: one textual and one visual. Authorship weaves together the threads of who we are and what we do. In autobiographical terms the photographer, Dabert, and I, as the author of the text, are both recent immigrants to Québéc and the research which produced *Bedlam* was one of the mechanisms by which we each got to know parts of Montréal we might not otherwise have discovered. Being an immigrant conveys its own forms of marginality and opportunities for self-reinvention as well as extensive possibilities to live as an interested 'tourist' at least in the short-term. We each originate from opposite sides of Québec history and the current configuration of local politics, as well as from quite distinctive intellectual environments. My (British) training in French Philosophy and Sociology – Marx, Foucault, Lefebvre – is deeply ingrained in my social analysis. Dabert's masters' degree in photography from a French university had caused him to spend many years photographing objects – sculptures, icons – (rather than people) in which he experimented with meaning in the composition of the photograph. He says that his work – photographing mice and other small animals with little dresses, accessories and wigs against landscapes of plastic toys – was about himself and his 'disguises'. He became involved in the project when it was well under way: entering through an established role – as one of a team of research assistants and through the stories we had already collected which he spent days pouring over.[23] His mandate was to extend the narrative with visual images which could take us beyond the limitations of text and represent somehow the aesthetic dimensions of space and people. In order to do this he asked some challenging questions in which he was forced to deal with my visual illiteracy. While we had a representation strategy, the difficulty was in deciding what the strategy meant in terms of images as it was worked out in textual terms. The difficulty was that I worked textually, analytically and politically; and he worked in images in ways that were about the perfection of the image and its ability to communicate aesthetically and not (understandably) in a way that was textured by social analysis and politics. In order for us to have a dialogue about image and analysis, we each had to upgrade the understanding of the other and many of our meandering meetings and conversations were concerned with precisely this business.

Authorship is about intellectual and personal identities, but it is also a product of the ways in which we work. Dabert would let his camera wander (with permission) during selected interviews that centred on the work of interviewing rather than picturing. Although he spent a long time getting to know people, he was unnerved by their lack of concern about intrusion once photographing started. This was the first time he had pictured people who had not asked to be photographed. We had agreed that he would photograph people in ways that showed other dimensions of their identity – things about them – that had not been revealed in their stories; relationships between people; the spaces on which they operated; and relationships between people and spaces. This was adjusted in some of the institutional spaces where we and the staff became uneasy about our 'captive audience' who were forced by necessity to use certain spaces to alleviate their hunger or because they had nowhere else to sleep, and so we shot these scenes during the day when they were closed to those who normally used them. Some of these photographs have a rather eerie 'unpeopled' feel to them that, perhaps, appropriately reveals a sense that these are depersonalized spaces of human warehousing.

Dabert's photographs are about the people and places they feature – but they also display his own thoughts, feelings and reactions to these people and to their lives. Some of the apartments he photographed challenged his (and my) sense of hygiene and interior aesthetics. Faced with one particular 'grey and greasy' interior, he demands to use colour (we had agreed on black and white) and moves between colour and black and white as the situation demands. He was asked to work with people he had difficulty understanding and whom we knew we could not help. Reflecting my own and the interviewers' feelings he says he 'didn't know how to live with these stories' at first. In settling on an explanation for the distance between his own life and theirs he decides that this must be a life they have chosen at some unconscious level, and this thought served to 'protect myself from a reality I wasn't ready to see'. My own theory is more fettered by the organization of administrative apparatuses and space that constrain individual choice. He eventually decides that he doesn't need to understand but simply accept. For my own part, I have tried as far as possible to stand in the position of those whose lives we seek to understand. As my job was to co-ordinate the research rather than do it all myself – although I couldn't write this without doing some of it – my own horror, incomprehension and sympathy is sometimes vicarious and sometimes visceral. My office was the place where the interviewers deposited their feelings and stories along with the tapes and transcripts. I spent hours listening to their stories of the stories, as well as to the stories themselves. It was here that I felt I sat among stories of human struggle in the most difficult of circumstances: stories that expose the outer limits of human existence and stand as a testament to human survival. These were stories I felt both troubled and privileged to hear, and which I have struggled to understand and retell with integrity while weaving them into a text. Contrary to fashionable claims, it is possible to operate reflexively in understanding others in situations that do not mobilize the researcher's experience as central to the research frame. As I have no experiential relationship to madness – although like everyone else I am positioned by my ethnicity, which, as a British immigrant in my research field, I did not share with any of my informants – my motivation for doing this research is political. I, temporarily or so it turned out, shared this city. The photographs of it included in this text express my own ambivalence and sometimes nostalgia for another version of my own life. My children, who grew up there, think of it as 'home'. The existence of the system I describe is offensive. It dehumanizes us all and deserves to be exposed.

The final product – the image – is also a technical accomplishment: definition and detail background, framing and cutting of the image are all-important concerns. In consulting me over these decisions Dabert had to 'read' the visual text for me and advise on the techniques that would provide the desired result. In deciding which images to include in the text, I set out some broad themes and he selected the images that achieved the most powerful effects. *Bedlam*'s visual images are hence the result of multiple negotiations with the text, with their subjects, with those who guarded their spaces, with our own sense of ethics, with the limits of current theory and social understanding, with the limits of technical accomplishment and with the range of things it was possible to picture.

Relations between visual image, text and voice

The analysis pursued in *Bedlam* is thus composed of three narratives: stories told by people about their personal or professional (in the case of workers) lives and experiences; the (silent) narratives of space and their political and moral context; and a visual narrative. Each of these, to some extent, compensates for the deficiencies of the others and the result – I hope – is an account with more depth and substance – texture – than it would otherwise have had. To some extent these are discrete narratives: neither can be reduced to the others because they perform different functions in the overall production of the text. The dialogue of voices contains different kinds of detail from the visual dialogue of the photographs: to render the photographs in a written narrative would negate their purpose, which is to offer possibilities of interpretation not offered in the text. The photographs are therefore strategically placed but not translated into text. Each kind of narrative – space, voice and image – has meaning in the context of the others and to this extent they are interdependent. Pictures can counter, support or explore the tensions in the written narrative. They are positioned intentionally to offer another layer of narrative and as an invitation to further interpretation by the reader which the text does not attempt to control, save by the authorial acts of selection and positioning. An 'inexhaustible invitations to deduction, speculation, and fantasy' (Sontag 1990: 23); visual images can also be more powerful when they are unspoken in the text. Our images were not easily collected. They were a source of tension between research team members and much criticised for their exposure of people, for what were assumed to be their objectifying properties, and for providing a source of distraction from the proper work of interviewing and collecting voices to turn into text. Ultimately their cost bankrupted the project bringing it to an abrupt end with many questions unanswered. I think it was worth it. But the reader will judge for her/himself.

2

MADNESS AND THE GRAMMAR OF URBAN SPACE

And they put me on the streets. With a prescription and then no money.
No place to live. So what I did was, I walked back into the hospital.

(Rick)

As discharged patients are released through the revolving doors of the local psychiatric
wards they are 'reinserted' into the texture of the city: into what Wolch and Dear
describe as 'landscapes of despair', and as 'asylums without walls' (Wolch and Dear
1987). This chapter is concerned with the terms and conditions of their reinsertion:
with the ways in which the text of human life writes the text of the urban landscape
upon which it is itself written. It is concerned with how the social morphology of
urban space is etched between the distributive practices of those who man the
revolving door, and the movements and decisions made by the mad themselves. It is
an attempt to map some of the 'local geographies of madness' (Parr and Philo 1995) as
the outcome of administrative distributive mechanisms and existential choices. Not
working on a blank canvas, the discharged patient will interface with the
fiscal/aesthetic priorities of local business, urban planning and local government.
Cities are textured by their multiplicity as domains of occupation, activity and lives.
They are sites of multiple meaning and memory (Donald 1995: 78) sculpted by
competing forms of coexistence and uses of space: not one place but many places, as it
is meaning and memory that, among other things, turn space into place. This chapter
describes a 'slice of life' in Montréal, but it could be any North American city. This is
significant in its ability to unsettle the other slices living around it, and, ambiguously,
for its invisibility as an object of local political consideration. The significance of the
mad in the city lies in their social insignificance. An analysis of their insignificance
exposes the moral and political strategies (de Certeau 1988: 95) of city governance and
welfare regimes, and raises important questions concerning levels of social tolerance.

Ultimately this chapter is an attempt to tap into the grammar of the city from the
window opened onto it by discharged psychiatric patients; and to be able to say something about the places occupied by madness on the urban landscape. The aim is not to
discover the underlying principles (as grammar) by which the city works, but to
understand the forms of social practice to which it gives rise: a grammar which is
talked and walked by human bodies operating in space and time. The significance of
time in the etching of space is evident in the architecture of any city. Space and place
have temporal depth: cities are textured by 'accumulated times' (de Certeau 1988:
108), the monuments and markings of past *and* present activity (Lefebvre 1996: 78–9,

84). What is of rather more immediate interest, given the project upon which we are
in this volume embarked, are the ways in which Montréal's monuments of the past are
re-deployed in the service of current social relationships and practices. Its religious and
industrial past has been co-opted to service the new welfare regimes of the twenty-first
century – widely utilized as *ad hoc* services by the mad. Constructed to service a particular political order, and its social relations and practices, buildings and cities are
plastic – constantly recycled to the service of new purposes and new clients. Hence,
any discussion of Montréal's new geographies of madness must consider the intricate
interconnections of time and space in the production of urban/social morphology.
Places and sometimes people are recycled in a system that rotates its mad around the
city and in and out of the asylum doors. Because of the significance of time in the
manufacture of place, and because the social practices and social relationships of the
present are only intelligible in the context of their micro-histories, this chapter begins
with an account of the revolving door's genealogy in the 'making of the city' and in
the 'making of the apparatus for the social management of madness'. The local manufacture of these two things – the city itself and its means of managing madness – are
the outcome of global shifts and the attendant retrenchment of welfare. The precise
forms taken by these twin processes are locally varied despite being the product of the
same processes and similar political frameworks at a macro-level. Place and space are
the outcome of purposive human activity, past and present. And the administrative
structures in which they are set gives a sense of the mechanisms through which lives
are managed.

The revolving door's geneology: religion, industry and asylums

The revolving door's genealogy and political context lies in the making of Montréal's
industrial and transportation fortunes and in the deals cut between state and church
over the management of social welfare in the nineteenth century. By the nineteenth
century, the island of Montréal, strategically positioned in the St Lawrence Seaway, had
seen the first waves of sixteenth-century French settlers, traders, trappers and mission-
aries displacing the indigenous population, and had become an industrial and
transport centre dominated by English–Canadian interests. The corridor of land
surrounding the railway and connecting it to the port and the old (sixteenth-century)
city – now a significant tourist attraction – on the one side, and the post-modern city
of bank and insurance towers and underground shopping malls on the other, is marked
by the monuments of its industrial (nineteenth-century) past in the form of factory and
warehouse buildings now being recycled as homeless shelters, as artists' studios and as
desirable urban lofts. This nineteenth-century corridor of partially re-deployed land
with derelict spaces is a significant site in Montréal's version of *Bedlam* as the place
where many of the homeless live in shelters and occupy empty spaces and buildings.

As trading gave way to settlement, the theocratic order of the Catholic world established its hold on the lives of the citizens of New France. The Catholic Church's power
and wealth shaped the development of the city: the parcelling-up and distribution of
the land on which the city is built was under the jurisdiction of religious orders to the
extent that even today there are places in the west end where the meandering street
pattern respects monastic orchard pathways in contrast to the grid pattern of streets
that otherwise dominates the city. The contemporary built-landscape is still marked

by large convents and magnificent, ornate, gothic revival churches built in the second half of the nineteenth century: a testament to the church's power and wealth, now the scene of dwindling religious orders and congregations. No longer needed for the purposes for which they were built, churches and convents have found new uses as colleges, theatres, comedy clubs, entrances to shopping malls and, most importantly for our purposes, soup kitchens and day centres. The Gray Nuns are now the owners of some impressive pieces of city heritage conceptualized, at least by them and the property developers, as real estate. Seeing buildings and land in these terms is highly significant in understanding the political agendas of this and other cities. Like the factories and warehouses, churches and convents have new custodians, new memories and new purposes. They form a part of the new moral and political order servicing the swelling ranks of the city's poor and the demands made by the lifestyles of the affluent. The province of Québéc today is a highly modern, secular and urban society. Eighty per cent of its population is urban-based and one-third of this is concentrated in Montréal itself (Health Services and Promotion Branch of Health and Welfare Canada 1990: 113). New social forces and patterns occupy the spaces once built for the monuments of religion and industry. Quite different, new, lives are lived and turned into stories in the spaces once occupied by old ones: but, as we shall see, 'what came earlier continues to underpin what follows' (Lefebvre 1996: 229) in terms of architectural legacies *and* the restructuring of welfare so that the needs of certain sectors of the population call less upon state provision and the interface between church and state shifts once more.

The uniqueness of the local situation in the disposal of lunacy lies in the interface between state and church in the organization of incarceration. The first provision for 'fols et infirmes' in 1720 in the Québéc General Hospital occurred under the management of the Catholic Church but was funded by the government in what was then British colonial territory (Keating 1993: 32).[1] The church under government contract and in receipt of government fees was to 'garde des alienes' (Keating 1993: 32), first in the general hospital and then later in the two psychiatric hospitals: the St-Jean de Dieu – the Catholic-run 'holding tank' in the east French-Canadian end of the city and the Verdun Protestant Hospital, now re-named the Douglas, its Protestant counterpart in the west English-Canadian, end of the city (Gillmor 1987: 29). In this peculiar arrangement of language and confessional separation, the government discharged its responsibility for the mad, a pattern repeated for education and other forms of welfare provision. Until the 1960s the Catholic Church ran most of the hospitals, orphanages, asylums and welfare agencies in the province (Gillmor 1987: 29): responsibilities ceded to the state twenty years later than in the rest of North America and marking the rapid secularization and modernization of the *Révolution Tranquille*. Other North American cities cut other deals between church and state, the mad and the not so mad, producing locally variant histories of psychiatry and its hold over the lives of mad citizens and their relatives.

In other respects, in terms of type of regime and therapeutic strategies, there were many similarities between Québéc, Canadian, British and American treatment of lunatics. The principle of physical separation of the mad from the rest of the population was the same in the state jurisdictions of the United States, the provincial jurisdictions of Canada and in Britain. By 1850 most states in the United States had an asylum (Rothman 1990: 142–3), as did most parts of Britain and Canada, as part of a general strategy of incarceration (applied also to other populations such as orphans). The well-documented trends in therapeutic strategies – the mid-nineteenth-century belief in cure, which was abandoned by the 1870s, the use of moral treatments and discipline, the expansion of asylums as custodial institutions, the ideas of Tuke and Pinel – circulated between Britain, France, Canada, Québec and the United States (Rothman 1990: 265; Scull 1981: 145). In common with these trends in treatment by the second half of the ninteenth century, the church in Québec ran the asylums as custodial, rather than treatment-based, operations in which psychiatrists sought access to their patients through the nuns. By the 1950s psychiatrists would be responsible for up to 3,000 'suicides, schizophrenics and criminals' (Gillmor 1987: 12) crammed into wards in one of Montréal's two asylums. St-Jean alone had more than 6,000 'psychotics, neurotics, alcoholics, mad aunts and disturbed sinners' (Gillmor 1987: 29) – so many that they were shunted from building to building on the asylum's own railway system. Gillmor (1987: 29) suggests that it was easy to get *in* to St-Jean and hard to get out, as in order to be released patients had to prove they were sane and had somewhere to go as, unlike today, no-one was released onto the streets (Gillmor 1987: 114).[2]

There are, of course, people who remember the later years of this period of the great incarceration in which the mad occupied a specific and *enclosed* space in the grammar of the city. Although Alfred, in speaking about asylums, told us 'They are all forgot', Craig (referred to in Chapter 1), who contacted us out of his sense of obligation to 'remember' on behalf of those who cannot, gives striking testimony of the period just before decarceration. Much of his account is precise and factual. He tells us that he was in hospital from 1953 to 1967 and that he was given fifty shock treatments in that time.

> and those days, oh it was terrible, the smell, everybody, all the place seemed to smell. They hadn't washed for months the patients … most of the people lie on the floor in the hallway, there are no seats [he uses the present tense]. If there were chairs they probably would have sit in the chairs but there were no chairs, so along the hallway they would sit and do their business along the hallways. There was a small room where me and four other patients sat, we sat in our small room, so I became very withdrawn and was within myself, and I became very sick [the hospital, he claims, contributes to his sickness] … we waited in vain for a visitor, but there were none in sight. Those that came were refused admittance. I broke a window, we had no air, we had no air conditioning. There were 300, 300 of us in a small room with no air.
>
> (Craig)

The imagery of Craig's story sets the asylum in its classic nineteenth-century context as a den of squalor and neglect, although the period he is describing is, of course, much later. His account of its airlessness is corroborated by Gillmor (1987), who says that in summer, the heat and humidity were so oppressive that patients would smash the windows, which were kept shut for security and other reasons. But the meaning of the asylum, as opposed to a version of its social conditions, is only revealed when the extract from Craig's story quoted above is placed in its overall narrative context. His account of the asylum, from which the extract above is taken, is a catalogue of abuses perpetrated on patients by staff; and it is this, of course, that he wants us to note. Nurses administer lethal injections in the middle of the night to patients who are found dead in the morning. Craig escapes death by changing beds with another patient. Patients are tied to beds and drugged after they have broken windows. They are used as human guinea pigs for experimental surgery and to test medication. Although informed consent didn't penetrate North American psychiatry until the 1970s and prior to that individual psychiatrists had a fairly free hand – as medical mavericks – to experiment with treatment (Gillmor 1987), Craig's story begins to sound like fantasy, or at the very least exaggeration, when he 'slips' into another, parallel, narrative and refers to the psychiatrists as 'the Nazis'. This places a new complexion on his account of the asylum as a place of death and displays (once more) a link between narratives of racial and mental suffering. Race and the political strategies established to administer it – in this case genocide – is never far below the surface as we saw with Pras.

> I've seen a patient die, and, they just left him in his bed for four or five days tied up, and there was a terrible smell and the body turned blue, so right away we know he is dead. But they didn't care, nobody seemed to care, the conditions were very bad, people were dying, almost every minute that goes by people were dying, till there was nobody left in the ward. There's a ward next to me, it is called medical, surgical ward, no doctors there had ever gone in that ward, and there were about 10–12 patients that were all blind. But they didn't feed 'em, they didn't wash 'em, I went in to give them a shave, and they smelt so bad it was terrible. But they, most of them were crying when I went in there, they were hungry and thirsty … it wouldn't happen today, 'cos people would complain, but 1953 till 1967 just nobody complained, nobody, nobody went in these wards.
>
> (Craig)

As this part of Craig's testimony reveals, the meaning of the asylum, at least in his life, draws upon a version of Jewish wartime suffering in the death camps with its own catalogue of medical experiments, brutality and mutilation of body and spirit. These stories of racialized ancestral suffering – for Craig is too young to have been in a concentration camp himself – clearly inflect Jewish childhood in different ways. Craig is both saved and cured in his story when he is moved to the safety of the Psychiatry Department of the Jewish General Hospital in Montréal: his own version of wartime liberation. This story is instructive on the level of meaning, memory and narrative. There are common characteristics in general terms between the experience of the death camps and the asylum; at least there are enough to fix the meaning of the asylum in these terms as a type of human experience and allow Craig to 'remember and speak'. His ancestors' wartime experiences provided Craig with a mechanism for remembering and a narrative model – suffering, survival, escape and bearing witness – on which to hang his experiences in the asylum. His story is also a striking example of the ways in which ethnic and Diaspora memories and experiences inflect remembering and telling. There are many more of these examples in the pages that follow bringing other versions of racialized and ethnicized experience to bear on the meaning of madness, the administrative mechanisms managing it and its place in the grammar of the city. Race and ethnicity are, of course, extremely difficult to excavate from the broader social texts in which they are embedded. In many ways they are best left there and reviewed in context.

The revolving door's genealogy: decarceration

Craig's story also captures some of the local social significance of decarceration as a form of liberation: something that is rather dismissed in subsequent critiques of community care in Canada, the US and elsewhere. Québéc's asylum period in line with others ended abruptly in 1961 with the Report of the Beddard Commission when a number of processes came to a head. Ex-patient Jean-Charles Page in his best seller *Les Fous Crient au Secours* detailed 36-day sleep treatments, excessive use of electro-convulsive therapy and insulin shock treatments spearheading an assault on the asylums by exposing their conditions and treatment of patients to public view. At the same time as these revelations, the sisters declared a one million dollar profit at St-Jean de Dieu from *per diem* per head payments made by the provincial government (Gillmor 1987: 89) – accusations of cruelty and corruption had found their time. A general disenchantment with forms of religious governance had found its time by a number of routes. Concomitant with the deplorable state of its asylums, Montréal was also a centre of world expertise in psychiatry, something that clearly remained separate from the manner in which psychiatry was practised in public institutions at that time. Indeed, it remains a centre of expertise – now in trans-cultural psychiatry – while local psychiatric services struggle with the significance of ethnicity and culture in their routine practice. A curious disjunction! By 1943 Montréal was something of a medical Mecca. The McGill medical school had a worldwide reputation along with the local work of Wilder Penfield. Cameron, worked as a psychiatrist at the Allen Memorial Hospital and his work attracted a great deal of international attention not least because he was later exposed for running clinical tests for the CIA on de-patterning (Gillmor 1987: 5).[3] And at the Verdun Protestant Hospital, also in the 1950s, Lehman was pioneering the use of Largactil (Gillmor 1987: 147), which changed forever the regimes of chemical management of madness. It was in this uneven intellectual, research and professional practice context that local decarceration occurred. When Beddard's findings abruptly signalled the end of the asylum era, Québéc had seventeen asylums containing 22,000 long-term patients, 40 per cent of which were abruptly released into the 'community' (Health Services and Promotion Branch of Health and Welfare Canada 1990: 114–15). This was, as is easily imagined, a very makeshift arrangement which set the tone for later decarcerations. One of the patients released at this time was Evan, who now lives in a homeless shelter, and who showed-up in our group of informants. He had this to say about it:

> Nowadays they're spending more money for staff and they've hidden all the patients out at the barns. In the country, farmers winterize the barns, old churches and everything and it's full of psychiatric patients, and the medication is distributed ... they're out in farms and Eastern Townships and Laurentians with nowhere to go. They take their heavy medication and sleep all day, and if they, their foster mother or foster father has time he'll change their sheets or he won't change their sheets ... they tie them to the chairs and

they don't wash them and they get gangrene and they die. … I saw all this, the world, it's just a matter of ignorance on the streets.

(Evan)

The waves of decarceration, that occurred in the United States, were similarly abrupt and makeshift. Was this a temporary stopgap or did it establish the terms and conditions of the new services of human storage? The evidence suggests the latter. And yet – at least in Québec – it was billed as a gradual shift to community-based models of treatment and support (Goodwin 1997: 11–12, 86) that define the 'character' of contemporary community services.

Decarceration – in Québec and throughout North America – brought some important changes in the practice of psychiatry: significant because they contributed to manufacturing the situation we are describing – the place of madness in the grammar of the city. With decarceration, psychiatry relinquished its former custodial role in the social management of madness in favour of the new therapeutic order of the 'brief encounter'. In this model patients were treated in outpatient departments. Only acute episodes required brief hospitalization followed by stabilization and release. Developments in neuroleptic medication made the long-distance chemical management of madness possible. This restructuring of psychiatric services so that treatment and psychiatric expertise remained *inside* the hospital with care, management and storage being down-loaded onto the *outside* of the hospital is a process that is still gaining momentum in Québec as elsewhere. Further downsizing of former asylums and psychiatry's clinical bed base is currently in process. Local reports contend that the Québec government plans to close 50 per cent of its remaining 6,000 beds by the year 2002 (*Montréal Gazette* 16 April 1997) and to reduce hospital stays in line with the neighbouring province of Ontario.[4] In future even fewer people will be hospitalized and for shorter periods of time and more treatment will be offered on an outpatient basis. More than 90 per cent of Montréal's estimated 10,000 schizophrenics now live outside of hospital and more than half the remaining beds in any one day are occupied by 'revolving door' patients (Farquhar 1997: 1–2). It is these people who showed up in our group of informants.

The restructuring of psychiatry as an outpatient service with brief hospital stays coincided with its expansion. In 1950 there were fifteen psychiatrists in the province of Québec. In 1962, at the start of decarceration, there were 170 and by 1990 there were 815 (Mercier and White 1994: 42–3). This is clearly a response to a growth in the demand for psychiatric services. Versions of psychiatric knowledge are now a significant part of popular culture deployed to discuss relationships, circumstances and life in general (Rose 1989). It is not surprising that there would be an increased demand for psychiatric services in this kind of social context. Many countries make expansive claims about the proportion of its population using psychiatric services. Canada claims that 8 per cent of its population, and in the US, 20 per cent of its population, will use psychiatric services in any 6-month period (Goodwin 1997). Psychiatry has redirected its professional gaze onto the mental health status of the population and in the process averts its gaze from madness. It is concerned with a range of more treatable and less serious psychiatric difficulties of the sort that can be successfully resolved in the therapeutic contexts of the brief encounter. As others have claimed, psychiatric outpatient departments deal with 'neuroses or situational problems, and this created a class of psychiatric patients not previously seen in mental hospitals' (Freeman 1994: 19): the 'worried well' (Barham 1992: 107). This new client group displaced those with serious and persistent difficulties – such as schizophrenics – who did not fit well in the new therapeutic context. Locally, the gradually down-sizing asylums continued to deal with these patients whose condition was less amenable to treatment as a two-tier system developed in which psychiatric services in general hospitals catered for the needs of the less seriously and persistently distressed. In the realignment of the inter-face between psychiatry, health seeking populations and their governments, the seriously mentally distressed were sidelined. It is this group that needs and doesn't get community services that were overwhelmingly represented in our group of informants.

At the time of writing, Québec still had nineteen gradually closing asylums 'our heritage from the past' (Health Services Promotion Branch of Health & Welfare Canada 1990: 117). Accounts of conditions within them are remarkably similar to those relating to the period before the decarceration of the sixties in their reference to dirt, body odour and overcrowding, although their therapeutic strategies have moved on. In terms of therapeutic scenes the seriously mentally distressed are stuck in a time warp. But in other respects they have been abruptly moved on – many of them on to the streets and other storage facilities. Evan captures this rather well:

> The nurse ... very experienced RN ... after breakfast she asked us to gather in the day room, the TV room there and she had herself and her staff in a little semicircle, we were all around like that. And she said would any one like to say anything about the ward, any complaints? And I said the patients stink, I said they don't wash and their bodies are stinking. When we're in the cafe-teria lined up to get our food, it smells and it turns my stomach. So **** [name of the nurse] turns around on me. 'How do you feel about Evan saying you stink?' ... so I said they asked me ... back and forth and there was not much progress, the other patients didn't want to talk, I did all the talking ... ridden with unions. ... In the **** [name of the hospital] the last person to be accounted for, the last person to care about, is the patient, as the last person. ... [And has it changed?] Yeah they put people in foster homes ... and now **** [name of hospital] is getting empty. The rooms used to hold patients, small rooms and small dormitories are now full of computers and *people that do research*.
>
> (Evan)

Asylums belong to a previous era – a legacy of time passed. Evan is one of those with serious and persistent difficulties (schizophrenia) stranded by the reorganization of psychiatric care. His hospitalization spanned the shift of the sixties and, although he was always admitted on a voluntary basis, he clearly felt he was a prisoner in the hospital, the object (he was told) of an '18 foot high stack of charts' making up his medical records, which was, 'not surprising considering every time a nurse has to do something or a doctor, they write it down'. The operation of psychiatry through outpatient services and short hospital stays means that Evan and the others have become 'revolving door' patients who move back and forth in and out of hospitals for brief stays. The mad are 'system nomads' (Knowles 1997) consigned to a life of constant mobility by the ways in which services are structured and operated. Some of

Plate 8   A suburban foster home

our informants had been through the revolving door routine on a yearly or twice-yearly basis reporting fifteen or more 'tours' through the hospital, while for others admission was so common it was impossible to distinguish one from another. In the shift in psychiatry from treatment and storage to treatment only, Evan is of marginal interest because his condition cannot be treated but only managed. He presents a problem of storage, and he revolves in and out of hospital on a yearly or more frequent basis. Evan and the others rely on what has been put in place to substitute for the shrinkage of psychiatric beds – the community. Storage rather than treatment is not necessarily a problem, although its implied batch-life passivity clearly is. What matters are the types of storage on offer and whether they are appropriate for those who have no other option but to use them. The rest of this chapter is devoted to describing these storage options, the conditions of their creation and use, and their overall place in the grammar of the city.

Distributive practices of the revolving door

The post-hospital distribution of those with serious psychiatric difficulties such as schizophrenia – those with less serious diagnoses are left to fend for themselves – is orchestrated by Community Liaison Services. There are three of these services operating in different geographical areas of the city and they form the key administrative mechanisms matching ex-patients with trajectories and places in the city. One of these operates out of a former asylum, which gives a distinct impression of being abandoned. Its imposing nineteenth-century façade is eerily empty. Beneath the desk in the entrance, labelled as 'reception', is another notice that says 'there is no reception' and visitors can – in contrast to the high security of earlier times when people were kept in and the flow of visitors controlled – just wander into the hospital and take a look around. Our investigations revealed that effectively there are four categories of discharged patient: those who leave under their own steam; those who are directed to homeless shelters; those who enter some kind of supported accommodation system; and those who are boarded-out, technically under the administrative/clinical jurisdiction of the asylum in a re-invention of the nineteenth-century practice of 'boarding out lunatics' (Busfield 1986: 277). These four categories become five when living arrangements break down and people end up living on the streets. These are not anyway discrete categories, as people move between them, and because those who live in their own apartments, on the street, in shelters and in supported housing arrangements meet in the city's soup kitchens, food banks and day centres and hence share a set of social conditions beyond housing arrangements. There are more than 200 food banks throughout the city distributing food donated by individuals, schools and corporations to those who need it. The diverse congregations of the food banks and soup kitchen are the result of the structure of welfare payments. Welfare cheques are inadequate to cover both rent *and* food, and the city contains a substantial number of people whose employment, nutritional and housing status is precarious. Among them are discharged psychiatric patients.

Community mental health facilities

We commence our tour of the city with the elite of the community system: those who are released into some kind of supported accommodation and its system of other supports. There are three things to note about this sector: it is tiny; it is highly selective in terms of the type of client it will take; and it occupies a highly significant place in policy and government rhetoric.

Supported accommodation and its related services form a tiny network of formal community services. Formal means set up specifically to deal with people with mental health difficulties, staffed by some trained professionals with mental health or social/community work backgrounds, and funded out of the provincial health and social services budget. In all of these respects these services form a contrast with other parts of the community system, which form an *ad hoc* patchwork sewn together by those who use them. The formal sector consists of a small number of sheltered residential situations, day centres, support groups, advocacy pressure groups, respite-care and family-support services set up in the late 1980s and early 1990s to deal with (selected) aspects of decarceration. It has remained tiny and token: a respite-care facility that can serve only ten families at a time; a community follow-up service that can track only 120 people; and a transitional housing facility with only seven apartments housing three people each. Many of these services have a two-year waiting list and very little turnover. One of the workers in this system – Donald – expresses this rather well:

> We're sort of like a sore thumb sticking out. ... If you took us and put us in a mid-western state ... if you put us in Chicago, or you put us in Miami or you put us in New York, or you put us in Vancouver, we are pretty much gonna

look like everybody else. You put us ... [in Montréal] and we just don't fit.

(Donald)

Donald indicates the anomalous situation of formal community mental health facilities in Montréal, although he may overestimate levels of services in the other areas he lists. Visibly higher levels of resources than are available in the other sectors mark it: it has smart interiors, excellent staffing ratios and professionally trained and qualified staff. Workers in this sector are visibly less stressed and do not speak of users as dangerous, aggressive or unmanageable. They have open and people-centred versions of their client group. They operate with concepts like 'individual situations': they speak about 'lives' and not 'cases' or diagnostic categories. They are rarely required to sort out fights, call the police or lend people money to buy their medication. The reason for this is that they carefully select their clients.

It is clear from the contracts clients sign in order to enter this sector and use facilities like transitional housing that 'suitable clients' are: compliant with medication regimes; able to live collectively in a responsible manner in a rule-bound environment; and are without a history of violence or drug/alcohol abuse. The basis for client selection is incorporated and justified by the community care catchword 'reintegration', which appears in all of the provincial policy statements. One transitional housing facility stipulated that its residents should have 'better functioning than normal for those needing institutional care' and be 'ready to integrate into the community'. Barham (1992: 12–13) points out that community care in most places is premised on the assumption that mental patients can be transformed into useful citizens; and that it was only ever considered to be a stepping stone from hospital to an independent life. Consequently, there is a ready-made rationale for denying facilities to anyone unlikely, unwilling or unable to measure up to this standard of self-determination. The patient incapable of citizenship is not, by implication, worthy of public expenditure on community facilities: an easily defensible position in a political climate in which all claims on the public purse are judged for worthiness on the basis of their willingness to 'contribute' in employment terms. The ability to contribute in employment terms has become the dominant qualification for citizenship in the welfare rhetoric of the United States, Canada and Britain.

The other central point in community care policy statements, and in this Québéc is also unexceptional, concerns family support networks. These underwrite reintegration and also form the basis for selecting clients for this sector. The Québéc Government's (1990) assessment that the 'community' is the 'natural' locus of care implicates the family as the 'main living environment for many people with mental health problems' (Governement du Québéc 1990: 42). Follow-up and respite care facilities are clearly aimed at supporting families to provide care as opposed to substituting for family care. In fact, much of the apparatus of community care in general assumes the active participation of family. The *'virage ambulatoire'*, for example, only works on those who can go home from hospital early because there are people apart from nurses who can care for them. But this approach invokes a version of family that is roundly contradicted in the stories we were told in which family is a focus for a great deal of ambivalence and often as not cited as a contributory factor in mental breakdown. The emergence of the asylum is a monument to the family's unwillingness or inability to cope with the mad in the first place: and most of our informants were connected with psychiatric services by their nearest and dearest out of fear, concern and lack of alternate solutions and resources. The existence of family is symbolic of a general willingness to wield a semblance of support in the task of achieving self-determination. Those who show they are willing and able to support themselves will be supported. Class also, covertly, textures selection. The newsletter of one of the main family support and advocacy organizations connected with the formal sector is concerned with 'education' of families and 'information meetings' with professionals in psychiatry and community services – activities it combines with support for local museums. Those who are successful in becoming the clients of formal community services have active families who form support groups and go in for fund raising and show the required amount of self-determination to become once again useful citizens. They are educated, articulate and disadvantaged only by (less serious forms of) mental illness and not by poverty and related forms of social marginality and compound social/psychological difficulties.[5] The formal community system occupies a strategic position in implementing and validating a moral agenda ironically developed by liberal and social democratic regimes and concerned with differentiating the deserving (of resources) from the undeserving.

It also occupies a strategic position in the rhetoric of policy makers and governments – a system in microcosm that obscures the absence of a general system of public provision by creating the impression that there *is* a system. It is this micro-system that allows the Minister for Health and Social Services referred to in the introduction to boast about community facilities. The ideal – re-integrateable – client serves as the model for all clients and the object of the much vaunted 'multi-disciplinary teams', 'diversified integrated services': the people who are followed with 'individualized service plans' (Mercier and White 1994: 44–5) around which health and social services ostensibly cohere. This micro-system successfully creates the impression that it is the starting point in a much bigger project. Fed by successive government reports extolling the virtues of community care, those who operate Community Liaison Services and who are hence responsible for positioning ex-patients in the community believe that the integrated community mental health services envisioned by government and policy moguls *will* eventually appear. Indeed, they are enormously enthusiastic about it. But this is a service still waiting to be born. Donald, who works in one of few community facilities to be set up as 'a sort of *laissez-faire* development', describes it. Donald and his fellow workers are optimists. Their optimism is not dampened by the Québec Ministry of Health and Social Services, which admits that its mental health budget is still focused on hospital beds with only 3 per cent of its 1994–5 budget going to community services including the money used to fund the general walk-in clinics, CLSCs (Ministere de la Sante et des Service Sociale 1997: 4).[6] Neither is it dampened by voices in the local media expressing a suspicion that the money saved by closing beds has been thrown into the project of provincial budget deficit reduction (*Montréal Gazette* 2 May 1998, 'Millions Missing').

Finally, and most importantly, the micro-system of formal community services provides a basis for further exercises in impression management and the building of progressive edifices whose symbolic meaning far outstrips any practical utility. This tiny system has become the focus for lofty and progressive concerns about cultural and ethnic sensitivity and gender equity in the hope that no one notices that the public gaze has been diverted into a tiny crack in a much larger system specializing in neglect rather than equity. I have turned up at many a conference with my tale of neglect only to find myself sat next to a researcher reporting on some wildly innovative and progressive scheme relating to a dozen or so community patients and a temporary set of changes. These are matters of scale. Such systems can become the focus of grand narratives promising social reconstruction through better services. The Association Canadienne de Sante Mentale, an umbrella group of associations and community groups that, while it doesn't deliver services, *connects* services to each other that are not otherwise connected by means of a grand narrative, is particularly good at this sort of thing – political posturing and impression management. It is important to ask critical questions of this kind of arrangement: to discover whether things exist *only* at the level of narrative and intention (and in microcosm) and not in any form of practice or action. The Association Canadienne de Sante Mentale's statements on cultural and ethnic sensitivity, for example, are most laudable, but this concern did not show up in any understanding of clients and services in the community by workers that we were able to discover. It is this kind of organization that feeds the political impression that there *is* a community system delivering services to the mad. In fact this is a simulacrum of what actually exists in practice: a convenient political fiction in which narratives of *inclusion* mask some aggressive forms of *exclusion*. Formal community mental health services are a bad case of the emperor's new clothes.

Cottage industries: adult foster homes

Adult foster-care arrangements, on the contrary, are rather discretely hidden away from the public gaze. They are our second trajectory from the asylum's revolving door and into the city. They are seen by Community Liaison Services (set up in 1993) as a growth area in community provision: a part of a future in which (almost) no one will be admitted to hospital and the re-creation of family in the absence of family. It is a popular option favoured also as a means of dealing with other populations especially the elderly and the mentally handicapped. The Community Liaison Services – one of the three cities distributing mechanisms operating on behalf of six major hospitals – says that it has 675 clients placed in 140 foster homes. The other two will have similar numbers, making it a significant part of the community system. At present, its client base is older, stable and in long-term placement (15 years in one home is common) with little change and turnover. In the future it is seen as a viable shorter-term option for younger people. It is an option deemed suitable for the seriously mentally distressed: Community Liaison Services claim that 75 per cent of its clients are schizophrenic with a further 10 per cent suffering from bipolar disorders. Foster homes occupy a particular niche in the grammar of the city and in the local economy.

As what was once one of Montréal's two major asylums gradually downsizes, so it redistributes its clients around the suburban neighbourhood in which it is located. As the asylum empties, so the spare rooms of local landladies/carers fill up, adding issues once dealt with through public/professional provision to the private troubles of local women. Firmly entrenched in local employment and housing practices, foster homes are a particular form of private enterprise. Montréal's large, municipally controlled, rented housing market is typically composed of accommodation offered by small landlords letting out the upper story of self-contained apartments of their triplex or duplex suburban homes.

Adult foster homes are typically duplex or triplex arrangements that take between

Plate 9   A bedroom in a foster home

one and nine clients in single or double rooms with separate kitchen and lounge facilities in which the landlady/carer lives on the premises and is on call 24 hours a day. This is essentially a rent-plus-care arrangement that is paid for from welfare payments. Carers are typically women (many of them are black) and may have once worked in the asylum in some capacity. For the women we spoke to, running a foster home was a way of earning an income, in a city/province where there are high rates of unemployment, while remaining at home to care for their children. For others it replaced jobs lost with the shrinkage of the asylum or when companies moved their base of operation out of province.

An arrangement used to deal with a number of populations – the elderly, the handicapped and the mentally distressed – foster care is essentially a cottage industry in which home and working life are combined by the worker. It is an arrangement that recalls the work practices that predate the Industrial Revolution, *and* the 'virtual offices' of the future. It is both a nineteenth-century (European) solution in the disposal of madness and a growth area of the future. It is a part of the marketization and privatization of forms of welfare provision noted throughout North America and in Britain (Barham 1992: 110).[7] Goodwin (1997: 99) notes that in the United States there are 1.5 million people living in private nursing home arrangement, three-quarters of whom have a mental disorder of some kind.

A description of how foster homes work provides some important clues in understanding the kind of clients they take from the asylum's revolving door. Liaison Services describe the client base of foster homes as 'adults who are unable to live autonomously in the community, and require social protection and general supervision'. Foster arrangements are an internally diverse regime with some homes offering complete freedom of movement and others working with severe restriction and curfews. They vary in terms of how much support of various kinds the carer is able to offer and their boundaries in tolerating clients' behaviour. Within these parameters they offer a system of supported independent living that, aesthetically and organizationally, replicates some of the character of home and family life. Foster homes are rule-bound environments that place a high premium on peaceful collective living.

As well as being the most home-like living situation, foster homes are also the most medicalized. Barham (1992: 112) describes them as 'hospital annexes'. The Community Liaison Services at the local asylum selects, trains, monitors and generally brokers this kind of placement. Its clients are formally under the jurisdiction of psychiatric services, but contracted out. Each foster home client formally has a psychiatrist and a social worker, forming an infrastructure that the carer will draw upon in managing the client. Phyllis, one of the carers we interviewed, told us a story that provided some important clues to the relationship between the regimes of foster home and psychiatric services.

> Some of them can be a little hostile. Like they would break a cup. I had one before take a cup and smash it on the wall and stuff like that. At that time I have to call the [hospital social] worker and they would have to take him in to assess the medication. And sometimes, most of the time, they would hospitalize them, too, when they do things like that.
>
> (Phyllis)

She goes on to explain that they are told to look for these signs of 'sickness' and that they *have* to be reported to the social worker or doctor. It appears that foster home clients are the most systematically and heavily chemically managed, something that is apparent in their general demeanour. Theirs is a context in which it is possible to enforce medication regimes that are more than supported and encouraged, they are required, by the hospital. Support and chemical management is the unspoken deal cut between psychiatric services and carers in which carers are given a certain segment of the discharged patient population on certain terms. Phyllis, who was an exemplary carer, told us that she didn't take those with a history of drug/alcohol abuse or violence. Rick got into a fight with his foster home carer over the use of his welfare cheque that his carer wanted the provincial government to pay weekly as a means of curtailing his expenditure on alcohol and drugs. He says of this conflict that she: 'pushed me around and I tried to strangle her'. He was rapidly moved to a shelter where his drug/alcohol habit was seen as less of a problem. Foster homes operate frequently as family homes with children as well as businesses and do not tolerate this kind of behaviour.

Foster home clients are a selected group of the ex-patient population being revolved out of the asylum. They are, in medical terms, the most compliant with the psychiatric regimes that manage their lives and their outposts in the foster homes. Like those who use the formal community services they are the most 'patient-like' of the client groups to be directed at the revolving door. In spending time with them, it is clear that they have particular kinds of conversation. Their 'talk' is about comparing different medication and doctors and in this they appear to be the compliant products of the psychiatric system – clients moulded in its own image and priorities. They also demonstrate high levels of dependence on the system – which encourages this outlook in its demand for compliance.

> It's true, if we move into an apartment we have to think about getting furniture, or where do we go to get it second hand? Or can we afford a furnished apartment which is ten times more than usual? These are all factors which are almost prohibitive for people like us to start up a whole apartment on your own unless you have outside help somewhere down the line. It's not easy.
>
> (Gail)

Gail, like the others, is a client who at one time had, and in many respects still requires, asylum of some sort, and it is life in the asylum that provides the comparison with which she defines the foster home as a place of freedom and independence. Most of the people we spoke to were grateful for the 'support' and 'community' foster homes provided.

> But when you're functioning on the level we're functioning on, we don't really have people. We don't have all that excitement in life. We go home to a crummy little room. ... Most of us don't have that many friends and family here ... so we do an awful lot on our own. ... Oh it's fun.
>
> (Gail)

Gail and the others were difficult to interview because they had few stories to tell, as their lives had remained stable and the same for long periods of time. Unlike those who lived in shelters, they had no stories of survival and escape. Having a story to tell requires a shift between past and present, and for foster home clients the past and present were indistinguishable and the future unlikely to hold any major changes or surprises. Generally, these were lives marked by the absence of future plans and in this respect, too, they were unlike shelter clients. They were also highly medicated – as Phyllis's story about the cup underlines. This made them seem passive and lethargic. It is not that foster home clients lack self-direction and social agency. Although the ones we spoke to were generally not the ones who had left or been kicked out, compliance with these medical and domestic regimes, requires high levels of self control and monitoring of behaviour – evidence of the very self-directedness they appear to lack.

Foster home clients also characteristically have a particular relationship to family life and this is another of the means by which they are distinguished from the clients of other arrangements. Many of them have partially active family networks that involve visits and some level of minimal family supervision of their placement. In this, too, they are quite different from the clients of other parts of the community system with the exception of the (elite) client of the formal system. The relationships they maintain with their own families are, however, premised on their remaining contracted-*out* of their family and *into* their foster home. In this respect, too, they resemble some parts of a former asylum population. But their relationship to families is more complex than this. As well as maintaining some contact with their own family outside of the foster home they are also required to 'fit' a type of family model inside their foster home in which they operate on particular terms: 'as children effectively frozen in a permanent state of adolescence'. This means that they must be prepared to live within the varied disciplines of an ordered family and domestic life. Phyllis, who brought up her own family around the group of schizophrenics who lived upstairs, clearly sees her charges as an extension of her own family. She admits 'they have to do what they are told' when it comes to cleaning up their rooms and doing their chores. She obviously runs clients and children alike as a kindly, caring and slightly authoritarian parent. It is her position as a mother in her own family that shapes her view of her clients as large children who need discipline and boundaries in order to operate effectively. The clients we interviewed corroborate this. In interview situations they presented themselves in a particular 'child-like' manner – compliant and generally fitting-in if sometimes with a certain amount of resentment. Occasionally a client (like an almost grown child) leaves home, claiming she is treated 'like a child'.

Clearly foster homes take discharged psychiatric patients who would once have been stored in the asylums – patients who are compliant with psychiatric regimes, dependent, child-like and able to operate in the replacement family contexts of their carers. Foster homes offer pleasant friendly supportive services, but the price of entry is compliance with a particular type of rule-bound environment. In contracting-out this segment of the patient population, psychiatric services have managed to maintain many of the features of the medical regime they are phasing out. In particular, they are able to enforce medication regimes that are a problem in other strands of community provision, stable living environments and some experimentation with levels of independence coupled with a flexibility and home-like atmosphere asylums were not able to provide. Although foster homes operate as an extension of medical regimes, they are private, individually brokered arrangements paid for out of welfare benefits. Those who operate them are not mental health professionals, but women situated in varied family contexts subscribing to many versions of their clients and the meaning and nature of the client relationship. It is a feature of the privatization of care that its social relationships and roles – cut loose from professional training and framing – are reinvented. Private care is also very varied in its quality and difficult to regulate so as to ensure quality. Clients also have poor protection from the demands of landlady/carers and the effectiveness of the system relies on them being reasonable and compassionate people. They are nevertheless people who run their home as part of a business and who have not received any special training in dealing with the mad although, of course, this is not necessarily a disadvantage. It rather depends on how they conduct themselves and the kind of regime they run. Other researchers have suggested that foster home clients occupy a second-class status in a surrogate family in a uniformly lower-middle-class, family-dominated world. As unconventional people they are square pegs crammed into round holes (Segal and Baumohl 1988: 254). Our research supports this view. Foster homes may well be better than asylum, the shelter or the street, but this does not make them the best option for their clients. Scull (1977: 102–3) suggested long ago that, at least in the context of the United States – but his observation has a wider resonance – that levels of neglect, indicated in things like personal grooming, were higher in this kind of boarding house than in asylums. In Vancouver at the end of the 1980s, the City Health Department found that 18 out of 26 boarding homes for those with mental health difficulties 'fell significantly below the physical plant requirements for specialized residential care' (Goodwin 1997: 118–19).

Cottage industries: supervised apartments and rooming houses

The supervised apartment and rooming-house sector is the third route taken by discharged psychiatric patients. It is also the site of some distinctive forms of local enterprise and a quite different set of social relationships from those in adult foster homes. This sector consists of private rooming houses in which rooms are rented out on an individual basis and small, cheap, often shared apartments. Some of these apartments and rooming houses are strictly in the private sector, some operate in the non-profit housing sector, and some are subsidized by the city and are part of the regimes of municipal government and its efforts to provide low-cost housing. They are all minimally inspected by the city for fire hazards and encouraged as a form of cheap housing seen as a viable housing option for a range of socially marginal and hard to house populations who would otherwise be homeless. This sector is the product of the deals cut between municipal government, private landlords and their agents and is aimed at inhibiting the growth of local homelessness. In contrast to suburban foster homes, this type of accommodation is centrally located in the downtown core operating in a part of the urban landscape occupied by a mixture of students, poorly paid city workers and younger professionals living in more luxurious apartment blocks as well as the city's modern commercial centre, its red light district and what is referred to locally as 'the gay village'. From the outside this sector is indistinguishable from other cheap inner-city accommodation, although one of the doorbells in a block will often read *'surveillant'*, which means literally 'to watch over'. This nicely expresses the relationship between this sector's clients and its management. A number of factors mark this arrangement as part of the 'community system' rather than just a series of independent private living arrangements. It operates within a structure set up by the municipal government of the city to provide housing for 'hard to house' welfare clients. It deploys *surveillants* who operate quite differently from the service/guard function of a concierge or doorman. More of this later. And it operates through a direct relationship between the landlord and the welfare system of the state in that landlords of certain kinds of tenants – those who cannot be trusted to pay their rent from their welfare cheques – can receive rent payments directly through the benefits system. These arrangements are 'unofficial' and it is likely that tenants have to 'agree' to them in order for them to be implemented.[8] A segment of discharged patients are directed to this housing sector and maintained there in a network of arrangements that are underwritten by the welfare benefits system and the city department dealing with housing. For these reasons it may be regarded as a part of a 'system' for dealing with those with psychiatric difficulties as well as a range of other welfare clients. Not an ideal set of arrangements, it is a response to local needs exacerbated by the downloading of the mad onto other services, which has occurred with the retreat of psychiatry from its former storage functions. Decarceration has visibly placed a strain on the city's housing stock and the types of tenancy arrangements available, which are not necessarily appropriate to the needs of the mentally distressed.

This part of the system sustains its own forms of local enterprise that connects it with what happens on the streets – loan sharking and drug dealing – as well as the operation of the inner-city housing market and the profits of private landlords. *Surveillants* feature as brokers and suppliers in both of these activities. Those who do not have bank accounts have difficulty cashing welfare cheques and have to rely on

Plate 10   The rooming-house block where Joe and Dominique live

others to do it for them. Those who are permanently short of money need to borrow to fill the gaps between welfare cheques, but they do so at exorbitant interest rates because they are a poor risk and because they do not have other options. Dominique hands all of his welfare cheque to his landlord who cashes it for him but instead of handing over the money supplies him with a half share of a single room, his medication and his monthly supply of crack-cocaine. Dominique eats at the city's drop-in centres and food banks. Like others in his position he cannot afford to do otherwise.

Discharged patients who are directed towards or who launch themselves upon this trajectory at the revolving door are those who are able to operate – unlike those who take other routes – around this kind of street and apartment culture. Many of them are younger. They are not well connected with family networks,[9] but they form their own associations and networks with those in a similar position to themselves. Requiring higher levels of autonomy, they do not fit the rule-bound family-styled environments of foster homes. Often their social/psychiatric problems are compounded by drug and alcohol use and this disqualifies them from both the foster home system and formal community services. Not a discrete population, they also spend periods of time in homeless shelters, on the streets and in jail and well as revolving in and out of the local psychiatric wards. This is a highly mobile client group, compared to the more sedentary lives of those in foster care, a group that rotates through a number of marginal city spaces and are the subject of Chapter 4. It appears to be a client group left to its own devices, but it is in fact highly administered by a number of apparatuses – the judicial system, city housing practices, the welfare system, the health care system – and it is vulnerable to various kinds of abuse and exploitation perpetrated through local street culture. Survival in this sector takes ingenuity and considerable expertise – more of this in Chapters 3 and 4.

Although rooming houses are nominally private and autonomous living spaces, they operate in a particular way in the lives of their occupants who are forced to live rather public lives by levels of welfare benefits that make private eating and even bathing arrangements difficult. These are lives that involve constant calculations about whether to eat, buy clothes, pay bills or rent with the slender proceeds of welfare cheques. Welfare benefits place severe limits on the ideals of self-sufficiency held by those who work in community centres on behalf of their users. They also work against the rooming-house sector, providing a pressure towards homelessness and shelter life. Maisie explained that she normally gets $490 a month because she is not 'on a programme'.[10] When this was cut to $303 (her rent was $385) she survived by eating through food banks and soup kitchens. Occasionally, she says, 'I settled for cat food'. Others told us they moved out of their apartments in the summer and lived on the streets in order to buy clothes, or saved on soap by showering at the drop-in centre. Generally, welfare benefits are only sufficient to pay rent, and living on them is very hard work. Isolation provides an additional pressure to spend time outside of apartments in a search for companionship.

> Sometimes, I dunno, sometimes its boring [living alone], I just sleep throughout, I just sleep, I don't eat my supper, I eat my lunches [at a soup kitchen], that's enough for me, I'm fed up cooking … all the time I'm lying down and waiting for people to call me.
>
> (Myrna)

Those who live in rooming houses and apartments commonly spend the day on the street and in the city's drop-in centres and soup kitchens creating their own version of 'community' and marking time, like Myrna.

Apartments function primarily as places to sleep. They provide periods of privacy away from other people in lives that are otherwise, through necessity, lived in public spaces under the gaze of others. Those who have apartments compare them favourably with the disease, dirt, regulation and religious devotion required of shelter life. Getting an apartment is a mark of success. It shows autonomy, self-sufficiency and the trappings of 'normality' – a successful outcome in a very difficult situation. However, none of this is recognized and rewarded with resources. It does not count as demonstration of 'citizenship' – the undeclared object of community policy – when perhaps it should. Having had, or being in the process of looking for, an apartment was seen as a definite social status used by our informants in this sector to differentiate themselves from the homeless and from shelter users.

> Well, because to look for these things [jobs and apartments] takes a lot of time. Because right now my financial situation is not that good. So I need money to take an apartment. And when you live in this place [shelter], I mean your mind is not always at ease. You always think of the worst that could happen when you're at these places.
>
> (Anthony)

Because those who use this sector are very similar in their daily activities and movements to those who use shelters we will hear more about their daily lives later. What is striking about their lives is their mobility, the precariousness of their circumstances and the lack of services and consideration of their situation as ex-psychiatric patients. Like foster-care clients, their lives are aggregated with others with quite different circumstances.

Human warehousing: homeless shelters

Most of the homeless shelters occupy a particular, and highly significant, niche in the urban landscape. Theirs is an interstitial space between the now chic loft-life of the city and the commercial downtown shopping and restaurant area of the new – a space that belonged to the nineteenth century and its forms of economic activity. Aesthetically, many shelters look like old goods warehouses or disused factory build-ings – square red-brick constructions about five stories high – part of a bleak ex-industrial landscape with no surrounding neighbourhood or much commercial activity to give it life. Most shelters also belong to the nineteenth century in another sense: they are the modern remains of a religious philanthropy that deployed its 'missions' in the salvation of the city's lost souls. In this respect they are a part of a different kind of enterprise than rooming houses and definitely not a cottage industry. Shelters traditionally rescued from starvation those who were lost to a life of usefulness and industry. They are beacons of the past that have found new life coping with what Myrdal (Mingione 1996: 142) called the 'underclass' by which he means those truly disadvantaged by their multiple social problems (which now include madness), and which sets them apart from the rest of society. While there is no analytic benefit to determining whether this is a 'separate' category of people to justify referring to them as a 'class', their multiple forms of social disadvantage are beyond contention. They are geographically separate in their homeless shelters but are otherwise free to roam wher-ever they can or will in the city. In practice they stay close to the shelters where they plan to sleep and where there is to some extent the public expectation (by loft-dwellers and artists) that they, too, *share* the neighbourhood if on specific terms.

Overlying their historical significance are the markings of more recent time, which show up in shelter aesthetics and social practices. Closed-circuit television cameras scrutinize those who hang around outside. Perspex screens and locked doors separate users from workers and users from each other. Entrance halls are high-tension areas – places where policies of exclusion are noisily negotiated and implemented – where police arrive to deposit some people and take other people away. These are generally bleak and forbidding buildings containing sad and abandoned-looking people as well as the oblivious, the noisy and the excitable. Entry is constantly open to re-negotia-tion. Exclusion policies are greatly varied, but drug and alcohol use inside shelters as well as violent behaviour are usually grounds for exclusion. Signs announce the requirement for syringes, drugs and weapons to be left at the door in what one shelter called the 'happy box'. Internal spaces – which favour the architecture of the long corridor with many doors (often locked) leading off them, described by one of our researchers as 'like being on a train' and by some of our informants as 'like being in jail' – are often electronically monitored. It is an arrangement of space suggesting a population whose activities demand constant scrutiny and regulation and, occasionally, heavy handed intervention.

There is no systematic monitoring, but estimates by those who run local homeless shelters indicated that between 30 and 90 per cent of their users have serious and persistent psychiatric difficulties, with many shelters reporting alarming increases in the number of ex-psychiatric patients among their clients. One shelter had responded to this situation by devoting an entire floor to those with psychiatric difficulties. This is consistent with other North American research estimates. Wolch *et al.* (1988: 272) reported as early as 1985 that in Los Angeles 20–40 per cent of the homeless shelter population was mentally ill. Goodwin's (1997: 123) discussion of Wolch and Dear's findings suggest that in the United States as a whole psychiatric disorders are found in 20–90 per cent of the homeless population with rates of 40–60 per cent being common.[11] Similar rates are found in Canada, including Tessler's and Dennis's 1992 study in Montréal, which found that 40 per cent of the homeless (shelter) population of Montréal of 15,000 had a history of 'mental problems' (see Goodwin 1997: 127). Community Liaison Services admit that they use shelters as a regular discharge option for those who cannot live independently and who cannot be boarded out in adult foster care. Shelters, intended as a short-term option for the homeless, have come to resemble the psychiatric wards of the closing asylums. Those who live in them live with their own demons and with those of their neighbour:

> Every night you got one guy, bang nine o'clock he starts to scream. Something in the room is haunting him. I mean, I hear those things. And he's telling, 'Leave me alone'. I don't want to hear it. And I'm thinking, 'Who is this guy talking to?' And he's screaming at the top of his lung. And then the guard comes up and says, 'What is wrong with you?' And he says, 'It's bothering me. It's bothering me.' ... And the guard is rough with him.
>
> (Rick)

> Sometimes it's like living in ***** [name of a psychiatric hospital].
>
> (Paul)

Shelters have no mandate to perform this function of asylum and neither do they have the expertise. Like the city's housing authorities they have acquired by default a role in the social management of madness by responding to needs that have been downloaded onto them by the closure of psychiatric beds. Shelters have become asylums outside of the health care system but without the benefits of its therapeutic strategies or professional expertise. As one shelter worker put it:

> We are not a mental clinic. ... We have no special services for them [psychiatric patients], that is our weakness. We have no specialized services. We are limited. Partly, that's due to that we don't have enough staff to deal with this problem. We know it's there. We are only eight staff ... and so we receive no government funding [some do]. So we are very limited in our resources. We do what we can do but we know we should do more for mental health. But we just don't have the resources and power and money. ... But there is a large number of these guys on the street. Of course you've got to realize from the decentralization of psychiatric hospitals, these people are dumped onto the

street. The theory is that they are supposed to go into group homes and be assimilated in the local communities. But that is a lot of hog wash.

(M. Lecombre)

Here also is a frank admission of the gap between impression and practice when it comes to community mental health. Shelters are, in fact, operating as the new 'mental clinics' of the twenty-first century: an arrangement characterized by new social and spatial relationships in non-therapeutic, non-professional settings. But are these multi-purpose human warehousing arrangements appropriate places for those with complex social and mental health difficulties? In contrast to the highly regulated medication regimes that operate in foster care, medication in shelters is more haphazardly administered – more of this in Chapter 3. Shelter clients with psychiatric difficulties have a great deal of freedom: they can and do regularly 'disappear' from the system and then re-appear months or even years later. There is no system for tracking them or any mechanism to ensure they get any kind of even rudimentary services at all.

Burger King, Dunkin Donuts and the streets

Community Liaison Services do not admit to discharging anyone onto the streets, but this does not mean that discharged psychiatric patients do not quite rapidly end up there. The tenuous and fragile nature of independent rooming-house life and the exclusion policies of shelters mean that people with mental health difficulties frequently end up living on the street. The behaviour of those with severe psychiatric difficulties who are haphazardly medicated or left in charge of their own medication is highly likely to lead them to a life lived at least partially on the streets. In a winter stretching from early November until April when temperatures rarely rise above freezing point, street life presents a problem of finding warm places to sleep and spend the day. Those who are *sans abri*, as it is locally known,[12] search for derelict buildings and heating-duct expulsion points around malls and the metro system, which they share with the rest of the homeless population of the city. Terrance told us he had spent two years living on the streets, including winters, as he preferred this to the degrading and highly regulated life of shelters.

The two things dominating the lives of the street population are a search for warmth – at least for half of the year – and places in which to pass time. These two requirements, set in the context of the available city space, which is focused on private occupation and commercial activity, means that the homeless must rely on being able to use commercial space. There is literally nothing else available to them (or to the rest of the population for that matter) with the possible exception of libraries, where the homeless are not particularly welcome. Brief sorties to the soup kitchen are the only respite from the public gaze of shoppers and office workers and where their right to use space is not questioned. The homeless are forced to use public, city space but they do so on certain terms (discussed more fully in Chapter 4). Their occupation of the 'nooks and crannies' of the cityscape (Estroff 1981) has to be negotiated with other users and with those who, like security guards and managers of fast food outlets, have jurisdiction over space on behalf of its intended uses by clients who are expected to spend money in them. Malls are favoured places to spend cold winter days. But only

Plate 11   The downtown mall where Joe, Dominique and many of the others spend their day

certain malls in the centre of town can be used by tacit agreement with security guards and only certain parts of the mall can be used, preferably those not occupied by other users but used to move from one part of the mall to another like stairways.

It is possible to remain unobtrusive in a crowded food court for the price of a cup of coffee as long as the people involved do not look or smell too bad or draw attention to themselves. Fast food outlets, which pepper the downtown area with their tempting cheap food – a slice of pizza for 49 cents or a burger special for 99 cents – are a magnet for the homeless when they have money to spend. The other advantage of these places is that they have extensive opening hours and are rather anonymous, so it is possible to pass time in them, use the bathrooms and so on. Fast food outlets are where the homeless mad spend their time if they look semi-reasonable and can afford a treat. We met many of our informants in them and did many of our interviews there. Derrik, for example, regularly 'held court' in Burger King, dealing rather expertly with his interviewers and social network alike. During his interview his friends watched and eavesdropped from an adjacent table. A worker at the counter checked that he was not annoying the interviewer, who is identified as a different 'kind' of customer. Dominique recounted for us his rather difficult relationship with McDonalds, which had kicked him out 'cause we're not shaved or the way we look'. These are the city's waiting rooms. They operate quite effectively – among their other uses – as psychiatric day centres. The use of outside space is also negotiated – but mostly with the police and levels of public tolerance. There is one central city commercial street – St Catherine's – where hanging about waiting for the soup kitchen to open or pan handling to earn a bit of money is tolerated as long as it does not harass or annoy others. Pan handling, a highly organized and strategically performed activity and a source of income supplement, is an occupation of certain city spaces with the agreement of the police. The activities and social relationships of these spatial practices are discussed further in Chapter 4, this volume.

Street survival requires enormous personal strength and particular kinds of human capital. Those like Terrance, who live on the streets to escape the 'crazies' at the shelter, spoke of the need to create a tough and intimidating persona as a means of – establishing and maintaining a sitting/sleeping/panhandling patch – survival. Space is struggled over – it is not just there to be used, it is the object of fierce competition. Others, we were told, would instantly prey upon signs of naiveté and weakness. The (fewer) women who live on the street are equally as tough as the men and have been observed threatening to punch out men in a local downtown bar frequented by welfare claimants and homeless shelter occupants as well as prostitutes. (Only certain, cheap, bars in the red light district are used.) Many of the women who operate in this milieu are comfortable in the sexual services enterprises of the streets. Women for whom the streets are more threatening tend not to live on them but in shelters, which are all gender segregated.

Law enforcement and criminal justice

Law enforcement and the criminal justice system are highly significant in the system described in this chapter. They operate as mechanisms for the dispersal and reallocation of people around the system. They offer re-incarceration, a last resort in the daily management of the mad and a catalyst for the recognition and treatment of distress.

The Québéc legal system's hesitance about deploying the legal framework for compulsory admission and treatment under which the mad can be detained in respect of their own and others' safety because of fears about the violation of human rights,[13] rebounds in the form of its use of the police and custody, so that law enforcement agencies, in fact, do play a central role in the social organization of community mental health care. From our findings it is possible to compile some examples illustrating the interface between law enforcement agencies and the mad.

It's lunchtime at the soup kitchen. A woman with a long history of psychiatric disorders throws her lunch tray on the floor and pulls the fire alarm. The place erupts into an uproar. A worker calls the police who remove her from the premises. She will not be allowed back. The worker thinks the woman would like to be in police custody as it guarantees food and a roof over her head. Prison operates as a substitute for asylum. In fact Wolch et al. (1988: 267) draw upon Nickerson's research in the United States to suggest that criminal justice provides the poor man's mental hospital in a context in which asylum has been effectively abolished. Drop-in centres and shelters routinely call the police as a way of enforcing their own policies of exclusion and for sorting out fights between users and in struggles between users and workers when workers are under threat. Those who work in these centres fear users who 'snap' and there are complaints that the police often arrive too late. Homeless shelters adopt a similar strategy using the police to restore order and implement their exclusion policies. In contexts where large numbers of mentally distressed and irregularly medicated people compete for space and resources, disturbances are not uncommon. Police cells function as a temporary holding tank for those whose mental distress plays out as 'public nuisance' in what is a highly regulated society demanding high standards of individual behaviour in public. Clean, safe well-ordered cities are not incidental, they are *achieved* through the work of municipal governance and enforcement policies: strategies that in turn produce a well-disciplined citizenry capable of regulating itself and others. This is a social context in which bizarre, inappropriate or noisy street behaviour is not tolerated for very long. An elderly and disoriented man urinates at a bus stop on the affluent West Side of the city. Within minutes the police have whisked him away. The calm and attractively landscaped ambience of the street and its trendy boutiques is restored in his removal.

Black men are particularly promptly and severely dealt with. Thomas's story of the onset of what he describes as his 'mania' – unusually among our group of informants he was diagnosed with manic depression and not schizophrenia – involved the arrival of ten police cars to deal with him and his brother. The two men, of Jamaican descent, were behaving 'inappropriately' – gesturing in an exaggerated manner and speaking loudly – in a local restaurant when the manager called the police. Thomas was subsequently beaten by the police and later sent to a secure psychiatric unit for assessment: a train of events that inaugurated his psychiatric 'career'. A law-abiding and talented artist, Thomas told us that he had not particularly thought of himself in terms of his Jamaican ancestry prior to this experience and its startling reminder of the local social meaning of blackness and madness. He said: 'I had to discover myself as black.' Other things – particularly the poor relationship between black people and the local city police,[14] coupled with the lack of any mechanisms to bring racially abusive officers to book – began to fall into place for him. In Thomas's epiphany, becoming black is signalled in an abusive relationship between himself and the local police in which he is forced to rethink them and their role in the community:

> I mean, look at these guys in Montréal that got killed [by the police], I mean, they try to go to court and they don't get anywhere so, imagine, you know, you get beat up for disturbing the peace. See, the things is, they [the police] know they can get away with this stuff.
>
> (Thomas)

In Thomas's case there are broader issues raised about the city's racial order that feed its disposal of madness.[15] But there are other dimensions to this and similar stories, too, in which the police serve as an entry to psychiatric referral for someone who had no previous contact with the police or a criminal record. A number of the 'onset' stories we collected involved the police who appear to regularly operate as a conduit between the public, the mad and psychiatric treatment. For others it is crime that prompts a round of testing and the discovery of madness: the boundaries between madness and badness, of course, being a very important issue. Dominique served a two-year sentence for armed robbery after attacking someone with a machete. He was diagnosed schizophrenic while in prison, when the judge ordered tests in response to concerns about his mental health. On leaving prison he was referred for psychiatric treatment. Various writers have claimed that in most states of the United States the distinction between madness and badness has all but disappeared. Whether or not they are right, the interface between madness and badness is clearly shifting, with prisons substituting for secure asylums and punishment substituting for treatment. For some, trajectories through the mental health and criminal justice system work in tandem. Terrance told us: 'I've been involved with the cops all my life. When I was 7 years old I stabbed a foster father in the stomach because I couldn't take the bullshit they were putting on me.' For a system reluctant to use legal force to deal with the detention and treatment of the mad there is a surprisingly extensive use of prison and police officers as a regular everyday part of the community system. This, of course, needs to be set against the liberal rhetoric accompanying decarceration and an apparent respect for the civil rights of the mad. And it needs to be set in the racial politics of the city and the rapidly deteriorating relationship between black (visible, to use the local term) citizens and the police. In the professional void created by the retreat of psychiatry in dealing with this population, other professions have, it seems, stepped in. The use of police officers, judges and prison warders adds to the list of 'general-purpose systems' like shelters and soup kitchens applied to deal with the mad. In other respects, however, as this chapter shows, the trend is towards de-professionalization with foster mothers, shelter workers and soup-kitchen volunteers standing in the places once occupied by psychiatric nurses.

This chapter has provided an account of the administrative mechanisms distributing the mad around the city into a patchwork of foster homes, private rooming houses, shelters and public commercial space with the help of law enforcement and the criminal justice system. The mad are not pawns in these arrangements. Their trajectories are the outcome of the administrative mechanisms distributing them *and* the decisions and practical actions that constitute their lives. The mad exercise considerable levels of social agency and self-determination in making decisions about the kinds of environments they want to live in. They are able to reflect on the kinds of risks and levels of exposure to the public gaze they are able to tolerate; how far they can use and defend their use of public space; how intimidating or passive they feel; and how far they are able to operate in highly regulated living spaces. These, in practice, are some of the decisions that mark the existential-as-active-biography discussed earlier as a combination of inner feeling of self and paths taken. How and on what terms they are both inserted into and compose space within the city, is the outcome of administrative action, existential decisions on their part and the ways in which they are willing and able to negotiate the terms of their use of the multiple city spaces in which they are stored. In their use of city space, the mad also expose the moral and political priorities of city and provincial governance and their welfare regimes. Creaming off a minority elite with the requisite levels of support and self-determination, the majority are left to their own devices. They must navigate city space and facilities intended for other purposes and derive what they can from them. They must do this in a city that places a low priority on non-commercial space and forms of public association. Lacking the resources to participate in commercial life, the mad are squeezed to the margins. In so far as dealing with serious and persistent madness is concerned, any semblance of a modern and professional welfare state has broken down. The mad have been invited to disappear into the family-centred suburban lifestyles of foster homes. They have been induced to disappear into the social practices of inner-city street survival like other precariously socially positioned populations who are inadequately housed, fed and employed. They have been hidden in the homeless population staked out in the city's shelters in the de-industrialized landscapes that once fuelled the city's prosperity. They can use city centre public commercial space but unobtrusively, so as not to disturb its aesthetics and intended uses. Merged with a multiply disadvantaged population, madness as a distinctive range of social and individual difficulties has disappeared except where it responds to treatment and shows the right sort of determination to reintegrate. Removed from the administrative landscape of the modern welfare state madness, like the multi-faceted social problems with which it is merged, is catered for in a residual, de-professionalized way through the monuments and mechanisms of resurrected churches and industrial buildings. The churches and factories designed to extract devotion, compliance and surplus value from the masses find new uses servicing the severely disadvantaged of the twenty-first century. Madness, along with church and industry, is hence simultaneously consigned to its place in history *and* its place in the city. It is, like the sacred, mass production, cottage industry and warehouse sites from which it is serviced, regarded as a relic of the past. The place of madness in the social and political agendas of the twenty-first century is clearly spoken in the text of this and other cities. In societies that aim to do very little for the dispossessed, the reasons for and specifics of their dispossession are of little consequence.

3

INTERIOR SPACE, AESTHETICS AND SUBJECTIVITIES

Chapter 2 traced the mapping of madness in time and space as it was etched into the texture of the urban landscape of Montréal. It traced the movement of bodies and the collage of social practices generating them. These ranged from shifts in the interface between psychiatry, people and layers of governance, to realignments in the nature of welfare provision and the broader regimes in which they are set and to the individual trajectories of those whose lives are shuffled by the system. As the mad think, feel, act and speak in a given set of spatial/administrative arrangements so they write the grammar of the urban text through which their lives are produced. Chapter 2 was an attempt to map the macro, city-wide picture in order to be able to take a closer look at some of the social relationships and practices constituting the key spaces occupied by madness – the streets, the homeless hostels, the rooming houses, the foster homes, the day centres and soup kitchens – which fill the gaps in the day. In tracing the social processes that converged in launching discharged patients on one, rather than another, pathway from the revolving doors of the local psychiatric wards, we were inevitably drawn into indicating some of the social relationships – between clients and their carers/*surveillants* and so on – constituting these spaces. The intention of this chapter is to expand this discussion. The social relationships of space, its aesthetic arrangement and the subjectivities it is capable of sustaining – the texture of the spaces occupied by madness – forms the substance of this chapter. Its purpose is to obtain a more detailed account of the lives and social settings we have embarked on describing. Site and place are used to discuss lives, not as a backdrop, but as a central part in their production. Lives are placed and places are lived in a dialogue that, hopefully, generates a more highly textured account of lives through place, and place through the lives lived in them. It is this set of relationships – between lives and place elaborated in the next chapter, too, that the reader needs to have in mind as the context for Chapter 5, in which we focus on schizophrenia, and for Chapter 6, which specializes in dangerousness.

The texture of space

The purpose of treating space as a text is to generate an account of lives that is not told by other means. Chapter 1 suggests that the analysis of space fills some of the gaps in life-story narrative: that everyday life can be understood through the stories that are told about it *and* through the interpretation of the space in which it takes place. In this chapter we place side by side an account of space as an aesthetic domain in which everyday living takes place. Some of the stories that are told by those whose lives are organized in these settings and some photographs that offer other accounts of the spaces we describe. Each space is introduced through a brief biographical sketch of someone whose life is lived there. These biographical sketches include all of the substantive themes set out in the interviews with each person and their purpose is to correct some of the deficits of filleting interviews for fragments of narrative covering specific themes that are then collected, displacing their biographies. Although the analysis that follows continues to use fragments of interviews because they strongly express certain themes giving a sense of the spaces we are describing, the use of whole stories is intended to restore a sense of the integrity of an individual life and its biographical narrative. Conscious of how the choice of *one* life story rather than another gives a particular sense of the spaces we are interested in, a story is sometimes placed with a contrasting example in order to make the point that the space *is* open to other uses, interpretations and lives. The stories were chosen because they gave a particularly strong sense of everyday life lived in a particular space. And between the description of space and the stories it sustains, a fuller picture of the set of lives we are interested in describing emerges. Understanding the varied everyday life of the mad remains the object of our analysis in this and the following chapters, and a point of access to a more detailed commentary on forms of subjectivity through their mode of being in the world as an active form of belonging to it. The scenes of everyday life provide the substance of social morphology (Lefebvre 1994) and, it is Lefebvre's analytic attention to space that provides a useful starting point in untangling some of the elements that compose the texture of space and provide a means of speaking and writing about it, and the lives comprising it.

Buildings are monuments to everyday life (Lefebvre 1996: 223) and, it is into the buildings occupied by the mad that the composition of the urban landscape unpacks. Buildings and constellations of buildings are manifestations of the lives conducted through them and on which they impose their own limitations. A reading of the visual or aesthetic arrangement of space through observation and photography – in this chapter we refer to the arrangement of the internal spaces of built environments just as in the last we were concerned with the location of types of building within the overall landscape of the city – reveals something of the social codes, behaviour and activities which both shape, and are shaped by, the lives which can be lived there. This line of inquiry is suggested by Lefebvre's (1996: 12) question: 'What occupies space and how does it do so?' The possibilities in terms of the arrangement and movement of bodies in space are also a dimension of spatial texture (Lefebvre 1996: 170). Space is nothing more than the practical and social uses to which it is put (Lefebvre 1996: 8–9). It is the manner of its deployment in human action. Space is also, as we saw in the last chapter, the product of historical legacies, of deliberate action past as well as present, of past and present political and policy choices, of courses of action charted and pursued on behalf of what it is possible to represent as the collective good but inevitably places one set of interests over another. Hence, we can also chart the texture of space by asking – 'by whose agency and for whom was it generated' (Lefebvre 1996: 116)? The spaces etched in the urban landscape by and for the mad described in Chapter 2, clearly support particular kinds of client relationships consistent with significant realignments in welfare provision and its global and local political agendas. But this is only part of the story. Clients occupy and use space in particular ways that are about their life trajectories and their negotiations with those who manage them and with the other clients who use the same spaces on the same, or other, terms. Hence the exercise of human agency over space by those who use it involves a dialogue with space, giving it what Massey (1993: 156) calls its 'power geometry'.[1] The spaces described in Chapter 2 are the outcome of political/policy/professional decisions made about the mad by those who manage them at a distance, and by others who manage and use the urban environment. But these spaces are also worked on by those who use them – those whose lives are the practical accomplishment of space. This formulation of space as a dialogically worked outcome with specifiable power geometry holds for the internal spaces discussed in this chapter. This emphasis on dialogue holds not only for the constitution of space but more generally as a feature of all social action as the product of shared understanding and interaction. Charles Taylor's (1999: 36) argument against the monological subject and in favour of dialogical action certainly points in this direction. How people deal with what is imposed upon them is an important sociological question (de Certeau 1988: 31–2).

In unpacking the texture of space in some of the ways suggested by Lefebvre, it becomes possible to develop a grid of questions that can be used to read the *interior* of the spaces we identified in the last chapter as marked for the use of the mad as a part of an undifferentiated group of dispossessed and socially marginal people. These are questions about social activities, codes and behaviour; about the arrangement of bodies; and the conceptualization of the people for whom spaces are intended. These are questions that make it possible to speak about the social relationships that texture space. They are questions that insist that where and how we live are important in the making of what and whom we are, and what we are able to be and do. They insist that lives shape, and are shaped by, the spatial contexts in which they are lived: that spaces are important in the production of the self and relationships with others. Pitfalls in the reading of space are the same as those operating in the interpretation of interview material. All interpretation gives free reign to the voice of the author and it is important that this is tempered by listening to the voices speaking for the lives under consideration, and by integrity in presenting details uncovered by the research. Space does *not* tell the same story that people tell about themselves. That, indeed, is the point in interpreting it. But in order to be a plausible interpretation the story told by space must make connections with the stories told by people. It must offer a believable account of the lives it sustains, otherwise we fictionalize what we seek to understand.

In revisiting the scenes identified and set out in the last chapter as the end point in the trajectories from the revolving doors of the local psychiatric wards, it is intended to pursue a closer reading of internal space as aesthetic domains of social practice and relationships sculpted by human action, which can be interpreted by means of the grid of questions developed from Lefebvre.

Foster home life

The lives lived in adult foster homes produce distinctive stories when compared to those told from some of the other locations we have examined. Although there is no such thing as a 'typical' story, our brief interview with Alfred shows, in a rather extreme way, some of the characteristics of interviews with other foster home clients providing a context for the analysis of foster homes as living space and the production of particular kinds of client relationships.

Alfred is in late middle age and, like other immigrants of Italian descent, came to Québéc as a young child. His carer has decided that it is all right for us to interview him, but it is not clear what Alfred thinks about this. He is groggy, has great difficulty speaking and is clearly heavily medicated. Although he decides to comply with the interview, his irritation at the questions he is being asked mounts as the interview proceeds. He has no idea why *his* life is of interest to us. As far as he is concerned nothing about it is remarkable or worth discussing. It is simply as it is, for how else could it be? Asked about his first hospital admission, a question that generally provoked some fairly detailed stories from others, he replies 'I don't know'. Asked if he remembers any episode or admission he replies 'Yes, yes', but says in a slurred voice that he doesn't want to talk about them.

> Well I can't say anything at all now. I, they [previous hospital admissions] are all forgot [long silence in which his interviewers panic and attempt to steer him onto a safer topic]. ... How long I've lived with Phyllis? Oh quite a long time. It's around [long pause] it's around 5 years. ... I used to live with my family. With my father and with my sister [he says no more about this and his interviewers try another line of questioning].
>
> No, I have never gone back [to Italy] because I have no money to go back. Because to go back you must have the, you need money and I do not have any money, so I can't go back.
>
> Yes, I see them [his brothers and sisters] sometimes. But not my mother and my father. My mother and father are both dead now. [He doesn't know how long they have been dead but says it is quite a few years] ... I moved out from my sister well before [coming to Phyllis's] I was brought into the hospital, [in circumstances he does not relate] they brought me down from the hospital [to Phyllis's place]. They put me into this place here. [He knows which hospital he was in and that he was there a month. Probing for other hospital admissions leads to a repeated 'No, no, no'. He volunteers the information that he now has an injection from a doctor once a month in his surgery, and that this avoids going near the hospital. He is unable to tell us why he has the injection or what it is for.]
>
> (Alfred)

At this point Alfred yawns, signalling the end of the interview. When the interviewers don't pick this up, he gets agitated. They get the message and leave.

Alfred's interview is filled with long and heavy silences that show the difficulty of remembering the things he is asked to remember. He lives in a medically processed present that he shares with other foster home clients who have conversations with each other about medication, doctors and social workers. Details of lives predating the onset of the schizophrenia most of them have been diagnosed with, are difficult to piece together and seem to be obliterated – or rendered irrelevant – by subsequent events. This is not the case with the clients of other sites, who can give vivid stories about the onset of their condition as well as detail the life disrupted by it. In the medically processed present of foster home clients 'relatives' feature as current visitors or there is little to be said about them.

We can also see – although he says little about it in this interview – Alfred's rela-

Plate 12   A kitchen in a suburban foster home

tionship with his carer. Did he consent to the interview? Or does she regularly make this kind of decision on his behalf? What makes her feel entitled to do this? What *is* her interpretation of Alfred and the meaning of his life? Does she think about these things? Or is she instead focused on her own life and the conditions in which it is lived and on which Alfred imposes? His condition is also heavily chemically managed – supporting Phyllis's story in Chapter 2 about the cup that was thrown – and this in itself limits what can be done in or said about a life.

The limitation medication imposes on lives is highly significant in producing Alfred's apparent passivity and this is discussed more thoroughly in Chapters 4 and 5. Alfred speaks about his life in a passive voice – he is taken here and there – indicating that key events and decisions are not affected by anything he says, or thinks or does. Alfred and his fellow foster home clients, then, live particular kinds of lives. More can be said about these lives – using the grid of questions outlined above to think about their social relationships, forms of selfhood and modes of being in the world – than those who live them are able to say about them. In the silences of what is *not* said, it is possible to read the habitual, the lived-rather-than-reflected-upon and the taken-for-granted shared assumptions on which the regime of the foster home is premised.

Aesthetically and materially the insides of adult foster homes although extremely varied, are indistinguishable from other family suburban homes of prosperous working-class neighbours. Particular versions of family, and not adults/students sharing a house – a perfectly viable alternative model – is evidently the model in play. The unspoken assumption is that some fairly conventional models of family and family-styled relationships prevail in this space. The separate arrangement of lounging/TV, sleeping and food preparation areas organize the activities of the interior and set parameters on the kinds of lives that can be lived within them. These are the individualised, yet homogenised, spaces of mass existence. There is unspoken agreement about the purposes for which these spaces can be used, and there are established patterns for using them, so as not to conflict with other users. All space is communal with bedrooms operating as semi-private domains, unless they are shared as they sometimes are. Most secrets are known and shared, as the space for complete privacy is minimal. All space can be accessed by all residents and by the carer, who enters without seeking permission from her own living quarters via an unlocked door. She is entitled to walk into their living arrangements uninvited and to make whatever adjustments she deems in their interests. Neat well-equipped kitchens, bedrooms and television lounges are not incidental but practical accomplishments that betray a particular sense of the aesthetic of interior space and the regime through which it can be demanded and maintained. Cleaning and tidying are high priorities either shared by residents or imposed by the carer. If this is the priority of the residents, then it demonstrates a mastery over their lives that is not replicated in the world outside, something to which Florence attests in her comments about the use of social workers to accomplish fairly ordinary things.

This arrangement of space, as we indicated in the discussion in Chapter 2 about the kinds of people who became clients of foster homes, replicates some fairly traditional

Plate 13 Joe's and Dominique's rooming-house apartment

forms of family authority and its fictionalised biological ties of living-space-as-community.

Residents effectively live in Phyllis's home and operate as an extension of *her* family, a story that is supported by Phyllis's account of how things work, as well as the unspoken assumptions around which occupants operate. The ordering of internal space – perhaps more latitude is allowed in bedrooms – is the outcome of Phyllis asserting her authority from the position of 'mother' over her resident adult 'children', who are entitled to live within a range of lifestyles as long as they comply with the aesthetic ordering of the home and its routines and agreed uses.

Some residents in some homes, it is true, have jobs, social lives, activities during the day, family and friendship connections. Adolescent children have lives and social arrangements, too – ones that are supervised, and this is the relationship that most closely approximates what goes on in the kindly regimes of foster homes. These are spaces that support degrees of adolescent dependency, permanently frozen on the threshold of adulthood. Autonomies are demanded and struggled over. These are versions of personhood in a permanent process of 'becoming' or 'development' that are not expected to achieve social or personal independence because of the ways in which they are conceptualized by those who live them, and because of the ways in which they are managed by carers and their medical back-up systems.

There are many different versions of this conceptualization of 'personhood-in-process' and its social status, but its boundaries are maintained by the different prohibitions applied to lifestyle and personal autonomy. Some carers have strong views on the use of intoxicants, but for most the bottom line concerns behaviour of any kind that disturbs the household. Much the same conditions – 'my house my rules' – apply to adult and semi-adult children living in their parental home, with the difference that this is not a transitional but a permanent status. An important issue here is how far these social relationships constructing non-adult lives are a feature of psychiatric difficulties or the manner in which they are managed. Or perhaps the two things merge so that uncertainty and lack of confidence following bouts of mental distress are compounded by the levels of dependence and lack of personal autonomy required in submitting to three levels of – foster home, social worker and medical – management.

These levels of social management point to a distinctive feature of the networks of social relationship defining foster home lives. As well as approximating family relationships, foster home lives are also sustained by a network of client relationships – a point that becomes clearer when we turn to consider the disordered nature of rooming house lives considered below. The 'family model' just outlined is over-determined by a client relationship: the 'mother' is in fact the 'carer' of someone she is not related to, and whom she is paid to look after. Her role is not only defined for her in the way in which she draws upon her experience in caring for her own family, but it is also defined by the regime of the local psychiatric hospital, which holds her responsible for the daily care and management of what are effectively contracted-out patients. Although it may be informal, she has a contractual arrangement with the hospital. There are other client relationships, too, in this constellation of relationships: with social workers and medical personnel. Florence was able to say something about these and reveal another dimension of clients' less-than-adult dependence.

We all have social workers. They come on a regular basis more or less. And if you want to see them or have to see them, make an appointment ... anything on paper that I don't understand or anything like that they always help. You know tax, income tax files, welfare. ... I had a bad accident; I was hit by a car. Well where do I start? Well I start with the social worker [laughter]. You need the guidelines and rules of what to do. All those things.

(Florence)

Most importantly, in thinking about the kinds of lives that can be lived by foster home clients, are the contracted-out regimes of 'chemical management' that under-write or even enforce what otherwise appear to be well-ordered family-styled existences. Although he was unable to comment on it, the effect of medication was evident in the interview with Alfred. Medication is the glue that holds together the spatial and aesthetic arrangement of foster homes and the social relationships they sustain – a point that becomes clearer when we look at other versions of mad lives lived in other places in the city. The benefits of medication have to be weighed against its cost in individual vitality. Lauryn, who boarded with her aunt and then got her own apartment, described for us the effects of medication prescribed for schizophrenics on the kind of life that can be lived.

My life became ... I'm much happier and I find that the medication really puts me down, that I'm a dull person. I'm a person that's really capable ... living a life for all your life with medication doesn't give me the hope to become the person that I wanted to become in future. ... The medication stops me from a lot of things ... [she goes on to talk of the difficulty of main-taining intimate relationships, having children and working, the trappings of everyday life for most of the population].

(Lauryn)

Lauryn had, for the reasons she outlined, taken herself off medication. Most accounts of the impact of medication are, of course, given by those who have stopped taking it or reduced their use of it as these are the people who are able, unlike Alfred, to speak.

Lauryn's is a story repeated – with variation – by many of the people we taped, some of whom spoke of it as robbing them of vitality and sculpting their body in particular ways. The heavy mad body is the product of its medication regimes that makes them want to eat and deprives them of the energy to do more than sit around marking time, and many people complained about this.

Foster home regimes and lives involve great variation and individual freedom of movement and those who live them generally present themselves as being content with them. The point of this chapter is to indicate that they are a distinct segment of lives lived in special circumstances and quite different from those lived by other ex-patients who take other routes from the hospitals' revolving doors. These are lives configured by a combination of client relationships and circumstances that shape subjectivities in some of the ways described. This section has shown some of the mech-anisms orchestrating the social scripting of individual subjectivities – an enterprise as old as sociology itself. The subjectivities shaped by foster homes are the product of the requirements of compliance with medical and family-styled regimes. They are the products of (uneventful) lives that do not generate stories, invite reflection or sustain the self-direction and independence they claim to support. One of the more comfortable versions of life available to the chronically mad, these are lives 'parked' in a permanent state of 'becoming' adult citizens.

Rooming-house life

Inner city apartments and rooming houses are the scenes of quite different kinds of lives from those lived in foster homes. Although, as with foster homes, there is no 'typical' life lived in this sector, lives produced in the same kind of space do share some things in common but the biographical details are always unique. Dominique tells us his story in an interview at one of the 'Dunkin Donuts' fast-food chain outlets in the centre of the city and a meeting place he very much favours. We had tracked him through one of the day centres he uses and were later invited to the apartment he shares with Joe to take the photographs that appear in this chapter. Dominique is 36 years old and first came to Montréal from Winnipeg aged 22 or 24 – he can't remember which – to meet his mother 'because I never seen her before. I never stayed with her before'. Having rediscovered his mother who gave him up to adoption at an early age, he then lived with her for 5 years until he began a relationship with a girl his mother did not like 'because she was Portuguese' – Dominique and his mother are of Greek descent. He and his girlfriend then split up 'because *she* wanted to marry a Portuguese' man. From the way Dominique tells the story it is not clear whether he is rejected because of his fiancée's decision or decides to end the relationship because of his mother's objection to her ethnicity. In either version Dominique feels that these events were not of his making but that the women in his life make important decisions for him. He is only passively involved in the various versions of his own life story he relates to us. Dominique was working as a cook in his uncle's restaurant at this time when his relationship with his fiancée ended and his life began to change:

> Then I went to jail [for armed robbery]. ... I needed the money to do coke ... we used to deliver [stolen] bikes to this guy [their fence] ... and I knew he was a crook. So I told my friend I wanted to do him in. So we did him in ... with a machete. ... I put the machete under the throat and I told him I wanted the cash. ... [When this story is retold towards the end of the interview it is *Dominique* and not his fence who has the machete used on him and who is cut on the hands. The police find him by following the] 'trail of blood'. ... I got caught on the third time [stealing from the same man who apparently retaliated] and did two years inside. ... I lost everything ... my friend started me [on coke]. ... The judge, they, they made me take tests ... with a psychiatrist, and they told me I was schizophrenic ... hearing voices.

> [He goes on to say that he takes his medication on week days as it is handed out to him at one of the drop-in centres and he sees a psychiatrist every three months at the hospital.] ... I have to take medication you know. Or else I go back to jail.

> (Dominique)

The lord and the devil still sometimes do battle in his head with machetes. Sometimes they tell him to cut the electricity cables in his apartment block or to draw all over the walls in crayon. The medication he is given has diminished the voices and that is why he takes it as well as to keep himself from going back to jail. Dominique tells us that he rises every day at 7 a.m. As the drop-in where he takes his morning coffee and peanut butter sandwiches opens at 8 a.m., he joins the line of hungry people from shelters and the streets as well as private apartments waiting for it to open. After breakfast, he panhandles – as part of a three-man routine, described in Chapter 4 – nearby on St Catherine's Street for his share of what is usually around $5. This is spent on coffee at McDonalds and on cigarettes, which are shared with the other two panhandlers as well as others in their network of obligation and favours. He then moves on during the late morning to another drop-in centre where it is possible to spend the day just hanging out or sitting around with its other clients. It is here he takes his daily shower, gets some clean clothes and hands in his dirty ones to be washed. He can stay here until it closes at 3 p.m. At night, when there is nowhere else to go, he goes to his shared apartment to lie on his bed and watch TV. Because he has a diagnosis of schizophrenia he gets enhanced welfare benefits of $700 a month. Lacking a bank account he signs over the cheque to his landlord who deducts his share of the $270 a month rent and converts the change into medication and cocaine.

Dominique and Joe, with whom he shares the apartment, met through cocaine. Their association revolves around the rituals of crack cocaine and their income-supplementing panhandling routine. Dominique admits to wanting to move out so that he can give it up. But in giving up his drug rituals he would also forfeit Joe's company, which is evidently important. Besides their apartment, the streets, fast-food restaurants and drop-in centres provide the scenes on which Joe and Dominique's lives are lived. Their apartment tells a story that supplies missing detail from Dominique's account of his day and his life. Aesthetically and materially apartments and rooming houses provide a stark contrast with the bright and ordered interiors of foster homes. Dominique's and Joe's apartment has a small kitchen and washroom opening off the main room, which is so small it barely fits the two single beds that are crammed into it. The mattresses of these beds are covered with an assortment of cloth and clothes in lieu of the bedding they don't have. The entry of an interviewer and photographer, as arranged, fills the room. They are filled with awe and disgust: Dominique and Joe remain comfortably curled up on their beds. The closet has a few old clothes in it, the bathroom one very dirty towel, the kitchen two plates, two forks, and a saucepan. In the main room an upright plastic chair holds a black and white TV and there are the two beds. The room centres on an ashtray piled with cigarette butts and empty cigarette packets are discarded under one of the beds. Another user from the food project where we met Joe and Dominique, surprised that we should want to go to their home, said of it 'all they have there is an ashtray'. The two men spend their evenings and weekends lying on their beds, watching TV and smoking in soporific community. This was not a space for activity: it was a space in which it is just possible to lie down. The kitchen is grey with the grease of meals past, and the apartment as a whole surfaced by a film of dirt and grease.

Anne's place, in contrast, is bright and well decorated with her art, fabric and the bongos she likes to play.[2] It is more spacious, with a bedroom, separate kitchen, living room and bathroom, and she lives in it alone. Her apartment resembles that of a

Plate 14   Detail in Joe's and Dominique's rooming-house apartment

graduate student. It is strewn with books, files, plants, lamps, pictures and framed photographs of her family. She may, as she claims, come from a wealthy background and seems to have good connections. People send her money – she makes the photographer photograph a $100 bill – and her telephone bill addresses her as 'Dr' as, she says, she *is* a psychiatrist. Private living arrangements such as these clearly support a variety of lifestyles and, if Joe and Dominique and Anne are at opposite ends of a material aesthetic spectrum, the majority of living conditions are closer to Joe's and Dominique's than to Anne's.

Unlike foster home clients Joe and Dominique (and Anne) can live as they like. They are free to come and go as they please and lie around all day watching TV on an unmade bed in a regime and set of aesthetics Phyllis could not tolerate for a moment. And there are no prohibitions on their use of alcohol or drugs. The price of this personal autonomy, at least at Joe's and Dominique's end of the spectrum, is a living space that fragments the usual rituals of daily existence – eating, washing and sleeping – and which is highly tenuous.

The contents of their apartment can easily be bundled into a black garbage bag and transferred to the next apartment, to a life on the streets, or to a shelter when next they default on the rent or cause the kind of disturbance which leads to their exclusion from the rooming house. The interior of Joe's and Dominique's apartment tells a story of difficult, temporary, fragmented lives – not at all the key themes in the stories they tell about themselves, which are full of adventure, street wisdom and wisecracks, and show a kind of camaraderie between them. Their getting together, they tell us, was to do with Joe's welfare cheque coming through with the money for a crack cocaine binge and his having nowhere to live and so sharing with Dominique. Theirs is a tale of sharing resources and helping each other out in an emergency, although it is told by Dominique – who moves between tales that indicate his passivity and ones that show he takes hold of his own life and lives in much the way he wants to – in a flat expressionless way. Shabby interiors are the scenes of run-down lives, of bodies draped in dirty poor and ill fitting clothes once belonging to other people: a narrative of poverty and neglect which frames their episodes of adventure lived on the streets.

Rooming-house lives are minimally scrutinized. Joe's and Dominique's landlord/*surveillant* has a window onto the hallway of the building from which he will review and sort out the more active and noisy confrontations among his diverse residents. They describe him as 'friendly and helpful', citing as evidence the fact that he 'fronted' the money for their afternoon's crack smoking without being paid for it. In return, they bring him cigarettes when they have had a good day panhandling. Lives lived in this way require actively being pieced together on a daily basis in some of the ways pursued by those who live on the streets. More of this in Chapter 4. They do not automatically follow on, replicating themselves from one day to the next. They are highly unstable, unpredictable and can change radically at any time. The routines of everyday life have a specific meaning in this context: a semi-automatic series of infinitely varied repertoires constantly adapted to meet the circumstances of the day or the hour. These are lives that are etched by their own agency *and* the precarious circumstances in which they are conducted. They are not what they appear at first to be: they are not in fact passive, but highly skilled and worked around the ingredients of daily survival. Dominique's expressions of passivity are about his sense of the awful power of external events he feels he cannot control. These are lives given shape and

Plate 15   The stairwell at the mission homeless centre

substance by the daily struggle to keep themselves *out* of homeless shelters and local psychiatric wards and *off* the streets. These are lives that mimic other lives lived by the rest of the population, but at levels of struggle and poverty that are difficult for most people to imagine.

These are clearly *not* lives shaped by the network of client relationships that operate in foster homes and shelters. Consequently, there is no formal means of tracking those who live in these arrangements. They may or may not volunteer themselves as clients of psychiatric agencies and they may or may not take their medication. Dominique takes his out of a mixture of legal compulsion and a sense that it helps. Sometimes the workers in food projects, day centres and drop-ins administer medication themselves during the week when they are open. These are rarely the clients of social workers, although informal and supportive relationships are often formed with staff in the soup-kitchens and centres. Dominique sees a psychiatrist and takes his medication because he believes he will otherwise go back to jail. But Joe and many others will see the psychiatrist with their next relapse and entry to hospital. It is most likely the police, called to deal with some disturbance, who will take them to the hospital. The social relationships that compose the apartment/rooming-house sector have little to do with psychiatry and welfare regimes beyond the management of the next injection or relapse or what is necessary to receive welfare payments. Instead, they are to do with the relationships between room mates and those who share an apartment block; they are to do with the regimes and rackets run between residents and their *surveillant*; they are to do with what goes on at the drop-in, the day centre and the food project between users and between users and workers (more of this below); and they are to do with a certain segment of life on the adjacent streets, its bars, hang-outs and panhandling patches – things that are explored further in Chapter 4.

Shelter life

The lives lived in shelters are both highly regulated in the sense of being 'time managed' and they contain high levels of autonomy. This is because the jurisdiction of the shelter over lives is part-time – confined to the period between late afternoon and early morning when its clients are disgorged onto the streets.

Michel's story foregrounds many of the elements of shelter life. He is a long-term resident with his own room who lives on the 'second floor', which everyone knows is the psychiatric wing of this particular shelter. Being on the second floor brings the privilege of not being sent out to wander the streets all day as is the case at other shelters, and it brings slightly higher welfare benefits, although after paying for his room

Plate 16 Bathrooms at a homeless shelter

Michel is left with very little money but with all of his basic needs of food and shelter catered.

Michel is a lively 59-year-old francophone, who has lived all of his life in Montréal.[3] He tells us that he was studying to be a priest when he became 'sick in the head' aged 17, something that coincided with the ending of an affair he was having with an older married woman. He has 'never had any ordinary day since'. His subsequent episodes of 'sickness' are also co-ordinated with the ending of other relationships, also with older women. It is one of these co-ordinated episodes/affairs that ends his working life in an office when he is 23 years old. Clearly it was difficult for him to manage the daily routines of work in his state of heightened emotional turmoil. He tells us that his Catholic faith remains 'something precious' to him, and one of the more permanent features of his life. He notes that in this he is out of step with key shifts in the basis of social organization as the churches have been emptying over the last 25 years. He tells us that he is happy to be interviewed because 'people tend to put me aside you know' because 'I'm psychiatrically sick'. His sense of neglect extends to his relationship with his extended family network living locally who, he says, are too occupied with their own lives to visit him. This is what he has to say about his life in the shelter:

> I was surprised that they were having that, this service you know, to helping people personally, not only about things to give up and that sort of thing ... it's the first time I saw service so open ... respecting the liberty of individuals. You know, not to put, put them in ... [pause] to leave them quite free in fact ... not asking you certain things in regard to you're ah, to the fact that you're staying here. They leave you free com-plete-ly [emphasizing each syllable] ... you can sleep during the day ... you can uh not dress. ... Because we, we are supposed to be sick you know, ahh, on medication, and sometimes people are feeble you know. ... [Asked what he does with his freedom in the day, he replies] I'm not a good example, I do sleep a lot and live rather at night. It's because we make friends along the line you know of ... you know psychologically, or the ones that are more alert ... at night there are more people that do the same as me [he refers to them as] the 'patients'. [Asked later in the interview to expand on what he means by this he says:] They are quite alert you know, by their mind. So they are not satisfied, they don't find enough stimulation here. A newcomer comes ... he has his mind, so at least I'll make a friend of him. That's how it operates here. The ones that are quite sane you know they tend to be together. [These are his friends and not people 'outside'.] Me, I don't go out often, no. But I do go out because I make errands for others. I go to the restaurant ... and that sort of thing ... that's one reason I go out often ... it forces me to go out.
>
> (Michel)

Michel's account of the freedom of the shelter is in contrast to his 23 years in psychiatric hospital. For Rick, who feels he is 'shut away' in the evening when he would otherwise be out partying, shelter life is unbearably restricted. Rick was reallocated to the shelter following an altercation with his foster carer referred to in the last chapter. At 36 he is much younger than Michel and feels he should be out enjoying

Plate 17   A sixty-bed dormitory in a homeless shelter

himself and not stored away. We will meet him again in Chapter 5 over his account of the meaning of schizophrenia, but this is what he has to say about the shelter life:

> The *** [name of the shelter] do try to control you as well. They have this procedure that they should control the patients' money because patients can't control their money. But what people should do is mind their business and give people their money. That they go back is not anybody's fault but themselves. I mean you got to learn to go through life suffering because you make yourself suffer. So that makes sense. ... Because when the money runs out they go crazy and they're trying to bum some money from someone ... to budget their money ... they will learn to control their money. ... And operate by themselves. ... To be controlling their own lives and spending their own money and doing the things they want to do by themselves ... if you don't let people do that then later on in life when the *** [shelter] is not around and the hospital is not around ... they will tell you, 'No you have to do it for yourself'. And then you will be frustrated and you might develop a mental relapse.
>
> (Rick)

Rick, for reasons which will be clearer when he reappears in Chapter 5, uses money to discuss the things that have happened to him in his life and he uses it in the extract above to discuss the shelter regime and his feeling of being controlled by the bureaucratic apparatus through which he sees his life as being managed. In fact in the broader context of his story it is evident that he makes a great many decisions himself about the conduct of his life. He also has extensive knowledge of the medication regime through which he is managed and trades and combines substances freely. He also controlled the (six) interviews we had with him: he would sometimes arrive with an agenda and behave like 'a professor giving a lecture', according to the interviewers, and other times was relaxed and laid back, always smartly dressed, always apparently in control of himself and the way he looked and spoke.

Michel's satisfaction with the shelter is connected with his status within it as well as the asylums with which he compares it. His comments above concerning those with whom he sees himself associating are revealing of the ways in which he sees himself. Asked what is 'wrong' with him Michel searches for the word in English and then in French in which he says that he is insufficiently aware of '*de la realité sociale*' and that he needs to '*recouvrire ma sante tranquillement*'. In English, he settles for the phrase 'a light mental handicap'. He is, in his own assessment, just sick enough to be on the second floor, 'behaves' himself (like others accepted at the shelter) and takes his pills. He is ideally just mad enough to be the recipient of higher welfare benefits and in a position to socialize with others who are alert enough to provide him with companionship. But this also has a downside.

> I am left alone, maybe a little too much … they take care more personally about others that are more sick. [At this point the ex-Russian army doctor who is in charge of health and hygiene in the shelter enters and Michel addresses him.] I feel a little left over, because you, you are, you have a limited personnel here and you take care of the people who are more sick than me.
>
> (Michel)

Others, especially those who have moved out of, or been excluded from shelters are far more critical, like Anthony whose views on the shelter appear later in this chapter. Paul also told us that shelter life was like living in a 'mental hospital' – by which he refers to the fighting, the arguing and the arrival of the police to deal with those who refuse their medication.[4] The regimes of the shelter enter lives in no predictable way. Many of those we interviewed viewed moving 'off' the second floor as a marker of success indicating that madness added further dimensions to the stigma of homelessness. The narratives of shelter clients provide important details of the variety of lives lived in them. A slightly different and rather striking story however is told by the internal arrangement of shelter space.

Aesthetically shelters present themselves as human storage facilities allotting space to only those activities – such as eating and sleeping – that are central to human survival and, perhaps, matters of entitlement. For most of their clients – except in the one shelter with a psychiatric ward floor – they offer a half-life covering the non-working day of the late afternoon to early morning through which a certain regime is worked. Industrial-strength kitchens produce evening meals and breakfasts served to several hundred residents. Dining rooms service waves of hurried diners, who eat and move to make room for the next batch. Eating is frequently used as an opportunity to extract the gestures of religious observance – prayers for sandwiches, as one informant put it – and shelter space is often staked-out with a smattering of religious icons and other gestures of religious observance. Sleeping space is arranged in large dormitories in beds closely placed in rows. The 'Mission' divides sleeping space on the basis of the age and condition of its users. Seniors – with pension benefits that are far superior to welfare payments – are placed together in ordinary single beds on a separate floor so that younger men do not harass them for money and cigarettes. The men prey off each other seeing each other as one of few resources in a difficult life. The image of the 'bricoleur' (used by Lévi Strauss in 1962, cited Harper 1986) piecing together an existence from the meagre resources available, structures relationships between shelter clients that are inherently predatory as well as a source of camaraderie. The rest of the Mission's clients are arranged in large dormitories in bunk beds with no room for personal effects or to do anything but climb into bed and rest. Sleep is widely reported to be very difficult in these conditions and those who suffer from sleep walking and nightmares are especially unpopular. Side rooms with mattresses on the floor – hosed down in the morning – offer sleeping space to those whose drug and alcohol habits make it difficult for them to get into a bunk. Other shelters specifically exclude clients in this kind of condition. Tiny cubicle-like private rooms are provided for long-term residents who hand over most of their welfare cheque in exchange. The internal arrangement of space is such that the private activities of sleeping, waking and dressing take place in most public settings. Space, then, is divided according to the principle activities it sustains and the categorization of its clients by gender, age, circumstances and their drug and alcohol habits.

At the 'Mission' and in other shelters the narrow corridors and stairways that connect eating and sleeping spaces are painted in bright colours. These are often scrutinized by closed-circuit TV from the reception, presuming a client group whose activities demand close observation. The client relationships in shelters are not of the kind that exist between foster home occupants and social workers or between psychiatrists and their patients. Those who work in shelters have a slightly benevolent 'siege mentality' towards their clients, which is tinged with a genuine desire to 'help', 'understand', 'redirect' or 'save' – depending on the importance placed on religion – the lives in their charge. All shelters have spaces that are off bounds to clients and occupied only by staff. These usually house things like money and office equipment that might be stolen, and also things that are not for public consumption, such as record cards containing information about clients' history and circumstances that provide staff with a better understanding of their clients. One particular shelter had some elaborate rituals for locking staff in and out of areas designated for client use and when interviewing there, we were locked up with clients in small rooms that had a telephone for emergencies! Entry into shelters is guarded by Perspex screens and locked doors with security systems that resemble prisons. Unlike the emptying asylum, it was impossible to wander around these shelters with their heavily guarded entrances that maintain policies of exclusion. They may be the last resort of the desperate, but staff still pick and choose their clientele with behaviour and habits being key grounds for exclusion. These architectural arrangements were designed to deal with a volatile client group – a point that was substantiated in interviews with workers who were concerned with keeping the lid on shelter tensions: 'one person starts running around it disturbs the others' (Mr Radditz) – and who saw medication as the key to a calmer life. Social relationships between clients and workers in shelters, although often cordial, are charged with a certain amount of anxiety and tension on both sides. Trustees – known as 'linemen' – who work for extra welfare payments and fringe benefits, bridged the gap between clients and workers, augmenting the work-force.

Operating inside a shelter as a client is clearly a daily scramble for beds, food and space: social relations between clients are necessarily about competition rather than co-operation and fellow feeling. Little space is given to residents for socializing with each other. Although there are TV rooms, these are usually small compared to other spaces and there is also little time provided for socializing as residents are locked out during the (working) day. The lack of space and time given to client interaction indicates that developing camaraderie is a lower priority than basic survival and there is an implicit reluctance to support days spent in apparently purposeless activities such as 'hanging out', even though there is little else for clients to do. This particular story told by the shelter's spatial arrangements is expanded in the stories of informants.

> You have to be there by 3.30 because the amount of beds are limited right. So when you come by 3.30 you have your bed. And then you come and tell the guy that is your bed number so if you come later than that then they won't cross out your name. That will give you an assurance that you have a bed to stay in for the night. ... At *** [name of the shelter] you could only stay there for 15 days. And after 15 days they throw you out. It's like a bad marriage went wrong ... no time for socializing. I mean who can socialize?

Plate 18   A drop-in centre in a church

You need a place to stay [and that has priority]. ... You cannot think of making friends at that time. Unless you make friends at the Mission. These are the only friends I have. Friends I made while staying at the Mission. Some of them have girlfriends outside the Mission. ... It's like being in the army and you have to be on time. If you miss the train you miss everything.

(Anthony)

As Anthony points out, the shelter is both the only source of friendships *and* it militates against friendships in constructing a life of isolation and struggle for survival. It is not that shelter clients do not form alliances with each other. They do, but they do so in difficult circumstances. Many of the stories we collected amplified the individualistic and defensive attitude of shelter clients towards each other implied in the internal spatial arrangements. Clients frequently spoke of each other in terms of disgust and fear that focused on contagion and dirt.

You have to be there by 3.30 in the afternoon. And I don't like to be there because most of the people that were working were like ... they're not working to help the people but they working as if to get extra points with god ... maybe they're trying to get a point to go into heaven. So I didn't like it there. So I went to *** [another shelter] and I didn't like it there either because most of the people that were there they are sick, they are dirty. And the people that are working inside most of them are dirty. They give you food without plastic on the hands. When I was there I learned that two of the workers were HIV positive. ... And he's still there giving food to people. He has this kind of rash coming out on his skin and he scratches, scratches and puts the fork and spoon in his hand. ... And the bed they give you to sleep is hard, kind of hard and thin ... very uncomfortable there. And everybody has to use the same bathroom, the same toilet.

(Anthony)

The degraded state of other clients offers constant reminders of one's own social position. Living in a shelter is highly stigmatizing, It is not a place from which people are likely to forge and sustain a broad range of social contacts: quite the reverse. Anthony is acutely aware that the shelter also cuts him off from finding his own place and getting a job, so that shelter life becomes *all* of his life.

You tell people when you are going for a job that you are living at the mission ... [laughter] it would take a really good person to give you a job. ... I mean all sorts of things can go through that person's mind. He thinks either you're a gambler or a drug addict, not a good person. I mean no good person really stays at a Mission. So you think of all these things as you go for the job.

(Anthony)

In social terms shelters operate as an enclosed world cut off from other aspects of society, symbolically located in a part of the city that has lost its former social and economic importance. Places and people, like old books, are remaindered when circumstances change.

Some shelters have responded to the increased demands placed on them by the closure of psychiatric beds by dedicating space to those with psychiatric problems as Michel describes above. Others have responded by incorporating the chemical management strategies of psychiatry into their own, highly pressured, regimes and their own fears about the volatility of their clients. On one of our visits to the Mission – which reports the highest number (90 per cent) of clients with psychiatric difficulties – medication was being dispensed from the office during one of our visits. Having run the gauntlet of the Perspex entry screens and the security system, we were ushered into the office where the young man who had been left in charge was sitting with a stack of plastic drawers containing names and the times at which medication had to be administered. He was transferring pills from bottles, matching their labels with the names on the plastic drawers in preparation for the evening medication round that he would incorporate into his supervisory tour of the dormitories. As he determinedly, but haphazardly, transferred pills, we talked about how he came to work at the shelter. He was an ex-soldier, a member of the Canadian Peacekeeping Forces who had witnessed worse human tragedies (genocide) in other places (Bosnia). People as well as places are recycled! As we talked, his narrative kept switching between his experiences in Bosnia and the shelter so that it was obvious that for him they were closely connected. The connection, it transpired was the smell of human flesh, unwashed – the dominant smell in shelters – and burned – the dominant smell in Bosnia – which no amount of personal scrubbing would, he told us, remove. The soldier's expertise in human suffering may have made him an excellent and sympathetic shelter worker, but it didn't guarantee the accuracy of his 'medical round'. This required him to match doses, types of medication and (transient) faces at the same time as deal with the police who arrived twice to interrupt his tour of the dormitories on which we were allowed to accompany him. There is no way of enforcing medical regimes in shelters, as attendance is voluntary and exclusion not infrequent. There is also only minimal psychiatric monitoring in shelters. Some have a psychiatrist visiting once a month, but attendance is voluntary and relies on the client to recognize and act on their needs, which may be difficult.

Shelters are monuments to the lives that can be led in them – lives that are highly circumscribed by what is on offer and the spatial context in which it is offered. These are lives that are minimally warehoused: fed and rested bodies disgorged onto the streets each morning to return later in the afternoon to secure a bed and eat supper. These are lives lived in a scramble for food and beds, imagined as volatile, and requiring constant supervision. These lives belong to the clients of philanthropists who implement versions of psychiatric intervention with little expert knowledge of how it works or what it is meant to do. And yet these regimes do not wholly prescribe the lives that can be led within them. We found examples of shelter resources being deployed in a number of ways to sustain quite different kinds of lives. Some people, who had another daytime life that they kept separate, used shelters only as a place to sleep. Some used them to support a different kind of life lived predominantly on the streets and had to be abandoned in the coldest part of winter or when they felt in need of a break from the streets. Terrence, for example, – who says he 'hates' shelters – is able to compare one with another from Québec to British Columbia, and is proud of the fact that he spends only the three coldest nights a year in any of them. Others, who live predominantly in the private apartment and rooming-house sector, use them to save on rent payments so that welfare cheques can occasionally be diverted to other uses such as clothing or entertainment. Still others disrupt shelter life and get themselves excluded for a while. For some, shelters are a place where they can prey off others or trade and experiment with cocktails of legal/illegal drugs. Shelters may be, as one client referred to them 'high school for the crazy', but they also provide rich pickings for those who live in the interstitial space between medication and illegal drugs. Shelters are spaces in which lives are lived and which produce certain versions of lives over others. But they are also deployed as part of a strategy in the living of a life on terms that allow considerable freedom over how that life may be conducted in the context of very limited resources.

Life in drop-in centres, food banks and soup kitchens

Although drop-in centres and food projects attract high numbers of ex-psychiatric patients, they also cater for a broad constituency of working and non-working poor. Their ex-psychiatric patients come from a variety of living circumstances of which Paul offers an example in his testimony below. The position of these resources in the lives of their clients is consolidated by the available housing arrangements and the relationship between rents and welfare benefits that make it impossible to eat and pay rent – as referred to in Chapter 2. There are different kinds of drop-in centres. Some focus on providing food. Others provide a range of activities – such as art, pottery, and exercise classes and others offer 'hanging-out' space for those with nowhere else to spend the day. Some cater specifically for those with psychiatric problems and some have a broader clientele. Some give out groceries for people to take home. Some centres offer showers (or even demand that people take them as a condition of use) and clean clothes. Dirty clothes can usually be dropped off to be washed and clean ones borrowed for the day. Some centres offer referral or advocacy services around welfare rights. They are mostly closed in the evenings and at weekends and often consist of a single room or a couple of rooms with a locked office that is out of bounds to users.

Paul uses one of the centres – a soup kitchen – serving breakfast and lunch and this was where we interviewed him. Aged 40 and having come to Montréal from Guyana as a teenager, he lives in a shelter temporarily and strategically because he has just given up his own apartment in order to save rent money for clothes for himself and his sons aged 9 and 16 who live with an ex-partner. He expects to get another apartment soon and meanwhile leaves his clothes and takes showers at friends' houses, where he will occasionally stay the night. His 'breakdown' (he has a diagnosis of schizophrenia) prompted by the fact that he 'was too much stressed out' accompanied the loss of his job and the subsequent break up of his 6-year marriage. Unlike shelters, drop-in centres, he tells us, have few rules, and this is why he likes them.

> The only rules they have is that … no smoking inside of it. Rules like that. Times that they are open and stuff. … there's no problem with that. You know they tell people, breakfast and what time supper is served and stuff like that … some shelters you go to, shelters should be free. … You shouldn't have to pay for a place to sleep. Some people don't get a cheque some people come from Vancouver and some people come here and have no money whatsoever and they go to places like that and you have to give them $5. … These

people live on the street, that's very hard. Half of the time, people sleep on the street because they don't have that $5 to get into a shelter to sleep.

(Paul)

Paul is working at this centre, on the 'extra programme' and this demonstration of effort on his part boosts his welfare cheque, and seems to be a job that passes back and forth between him and his sister, who also uses the centre and has a diagnosis of schizophrenia.

You work a year and then you finish and someone else gets a chance to work for a year. And then you stay off work for a year. And then you can come back if you worked good ... it's an extra programme on welfare for a year. ... Sometimes it gets so stressful [working at the drop-in] and that's why people sometimes want to run away. That I don't like, I don't like, some of the people that go there when they don't take their medication, it's very, very stressful. ... I don't like to be fighting I just like to be peaceful, easy going, I try to get along with everybody. ... [As for the social workers who are employed to work there] I see them as my friends. They are social workers but they are not mine. They're just my friends ... they would give me a job any time.

(Paul)

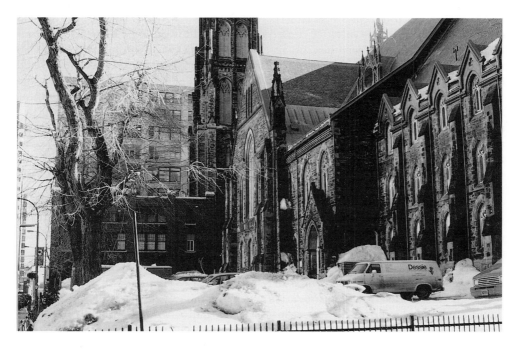

Plate 19   A Montréal church with a soup kitchen

Centre venues are frequently parts of churches – often attics and basements – peripheral spaces. Sometimes relations between centre clients and declining congregations, who do not like dishevelled people hanging about at the side door of their place of worship, are conflict-ridden, indicating divergence over the legitimate uses of sacred space, as well as resistance to the new uses to which spaces designed for quite different purposes are now put. Sometimes there are historical arrangements between individual philanthropically inclined clergy and drop-ins, which secure the use of high ceilings and disproportionate, divided rooms for lounging or pottery classes: space recycled with new uses for which they were not originally designed or intended and that require minor adjustment. One centre serving breakfasts and lunches, where we were regular visitors and often helped out serving food, occupied a church basement and had an uneasy relationship with the congregation, evidenced in some officious-sounding signs outside prohibiting spitting, peeing and loitering. It consisted of one room with a locked office and had a window from the kitchen at one end, where staff could keep a watch on the toilet and whatever might go on in there and shouldn't, while serving lunch at the same time. A cheery band of (largely ignored) touring Mennonites on one occasion sang happy songs at the other end of the room, while the clients queued up for soup that they would eat hurriedly at the tables that were set out for them.

Lunch – a pot of soup that on a good day contained meat – was served from a hatch where clients lined up in an orderly fashion. There were strict codes of practice involved in getting food. This place opened at 8 a.m. when there would be a line outside waiting for breakfast. Lunch was served at midday promptly, and the tension in the room rose in the run-up to it. Clients could return for soup as long as it lasted and everyone had had something. Deserts – a very popular item – were served only on alternate days as a treat. Only two desserts each were allowed and a dispute broke out on one of our visits over whether this rule meant two per visit to the hatch or two in total. Precedent was cited in order to settle the dispute. 'Twinkies' – chocolate-covered cakes that have an astonishingly long shelf life by virtue of their chemical content and yet were covered in mould – were handed out one day as a 'treat'; 'Wagon Wheels' – in much the same condition – were handed out two days later. Beyond shelf life – a mechanism for consumer protection – there is the half-life of marginally edible food regarded as suitable for the hungry. Food that cannot be sold and no-one else will eat – leftovers from hospital dinners, old airline meals and so on – is distributed to those whose lives are clearly not the object of food health and hygiene regulation. Uncooked food is also given away in some centres having been collected at the end of the previous day from street markets, or donated by agencies, companies, individuals and fast-food distributors who dare not sell it. Crowds gathered around a box of radishes on one of our visits to the breakfast and lunch drop-in: prized items were struggled over, and unwanted items traded for other items.

Relations between clients in drop-ins and food projects are highly territorial. People have their own seats to which they return each day. The use of someone else's seat is an occasion for fights, intimidation, insults 'it's like someone walking into your home' (Samuel). Occupying a seat at a table among others does not mean having to interact with them: these are not voluntary associations entirely, but associations structured by necessity. People frequently sit in silent proximity to each other. These are spaces in which men operate more easily than women, and those women who use them sit on the margins with black and ethnic minority (visible) men.[5] Relations between clients and workers/volunteers are more informal and less defensive than in shelters. Workers will lend money to the desperate, help them make telephone calls tracking their welfare payments, pay for their medication, dispense medication, ask after children, and so on. There are limits to trust and cordial association: anything valuable or removable is locked up in the office. A sense of relations between worker and client is given in this interviewer's notes.[6]

> John was in the back; there always seemed to be no one in charge up front. ...
> We said our hellos to John and Nina in the clothing room only to be told that
> it was early and already seemed to be a slow day. There wasn't anything to do.
> John was handing out bags of chips. But Nina asked me to stay in the room
> and make sure that each of the men took only one of each thing [clothes] they
> needed. She also made us put our things in the office. 'Things disappear.'
> Later we folded clothes, straightened up the hangers and swept. Between all
> this men filed in for everything from shirts to underwear and socks. Two even
> got shoes. ... The users were generally very selective but few preferred shorts,
> yet most wanted short sleeves. When we got there, there was a tall black man
> trying on a jacket. He was well dressed but could not find a shirt that fit.
> After some haggling Nina agreed to wash and dry his shirt while he waited,
> 'just this once'.

Workers can, however, have quite antagonistic relationships with each other and with those who work as volunteers. Giving away the more unpleasant jobs like sorting dirty clothes or threatening to make them supervise the showers is a way of sharing the horror of their work with occasional volunteers, as some of us became, and valorizing it at the same time. Shadowing the fears of shelter users, workers admit to having (not unrealistic) fears about catching TB and often make obsessive use of disinfectants in washing up and washing themselves.

In spatially unpacking the concept of the 'psychiatric client' – a label that, like mad, clearly confers a false unity of circumstances – we have in this chapter been able to map some of the divergent ways in which the mad self is produced at the existential/administrative interface in the community at which lives can be lived only in certain ways. Who the mad are and what they are able to be are matters determined between the spaces producing them, the management of those spaces and the life courses that are charted by individuals within the range of available options. The mad are able to live as semi-autonomous adolescent children with limited capacities for independence. They are able to be itinerant homeless in need of monitoring for potentially volatile behaviour. They are dealt with in terms of the basic functions to which they are as human beings minimally entitled – eating and sleeping. They are able to be poor rooming-house tenants connected – along with others – with the seedier side of life on the urban landscape. They are spatially separate and cut off from other lives conducted in the same city in their warehouse buildings, foster homes and soup kitchens. Their social/spatial isolation is compounded by the difficulty of developing social networks *inside* – never mind outside – these spaces because the manner in which they are organized militates against forms of co-operation. This is not the isolation of the asylum. Far from it. It is the isolation of the world outside that results from particular forms of poverty, social exclusion and the fragmentation of the habits of everyday existence and survival: things touching on some of the boundaries of the human condition itself.

4

LIVING IN TRANSIT

I didn't grow up with a black family ... a black neighbourhood ... going
to a black school you know. I grew up in the city, in the system.

(Terrance)

The 'placing' of lives and the 'lived-ness' of place, the threads connecting the trajectories of mad lives with the grammar of the city and its implied mapping of the administratively/existentially generated self, has anchored lives in place more decisively, more firmly, than intended. What appears to be placed is about the moment in time – arresting lives – at which the sociological reading was made. The purpose of this chapter is to disrupt what has been placed. Lives are not static, fixed in place, but in the process of many journeys from one place to another. Biographies – which are not the living of a life but its telling – are also, like the lives they seek to represent, journeys. In this the mad, like the tourists and refugees whose lives have been conceptualized as emblematic of globalized post-modern city life, are no different from others. What marks their difference is the nature of their journeys, the scenes on which they are set, and the character of the processes and relationships connecting them with the social.[1] Their lifestyles resemble those of refugees, except that they are expatriated by different political processes and realignments: of welfare regimes and moral agendas, which differentially value lives and construe forms of entitlement, rather than shifts in the meaning of community and ethnicity in the broader schemes of history, which traditionally displace refugees. To present mad lives as stationary would involve airbrushing-out their mobility, anchoring them to the spaces they use and move through, rather than inhabit, and this would seriously distort their situation. These are, in fact, lives in various forms of interconnected transit – global, national and urban, as this chapter will show – and they should not be understood in place but in transit between places connected by the mad in the varied living of their lives and the diverse movement of their bodies in space. Those who live in shelters, in rooming houses, and on the street and who graze from food banks, soup kitchens and day centres generate (a version of) the city – not as overlapping zones of occupation – but as a series of nodal points (identified in the proceeding two chapters) connected by the movement of people between them.[2] Lives are not lived in place but in the threading together of places as sequential scenes in their trajectories. It is in the activities of lives and bodies connecting places that the grammar of space is written, configured through the agency of lives. All of those featured in this chapter, with the exception of Terrance who claims to have delusions but not schizophrenia, carry a diagnosis of schizophrenia. It is worth reminding the reader of this, a point, which might otherwise get lost in the analysis of space.

The conceptualization in sociology and social anthropology of lives in motion *between* places and not *in* place has prompted radical reconsideration of the character of human association. If people live in the rituals of movement between places instead of in places, then traditional concepts like community demand revisiting (Rapport 1997). Terrance captures the substance of this line of thought and of this chapter in his comment above. His version of family and neighbourhood is over-determined by the interface between the welfare and city regimes that gave substance to his early life, and through which he measures the distance between his own and other lives. To see Terrance as the product of the city's black community is to misunderstand the social processes through which the self that is Terrance is written. Terrance is the product of various forms of transit: around the child welfare system that supervised his childhood, and around the city in which his life was, and is still, lived. Early forms of personal dislocation in the disruption of family relationships are continued in his later journeys around the city as a discharged psychiatric patient. Are these in fact forms of dislocation or contemporary forms of location? At least, are they not so in a particular segment of lives? Are not 'family' and 'community' fictionalized snapshots of forms of human association that are organized by myriad administrative apparatuses and always in process? What makes Terrance's childhood different from others is the character and composition of the administrative apparatuses supervising it – the relationship between these apparatuses and the 'family' and 'community' and the various families through which Terrance was passed in his journey through childhood. In Terrance's case all of these processes are configured through the modality of race. In presenting himself as a 'Jamaican Mohawk from British Columbia', Terrance's personal genealogy spells out other forms of movement. It combines the global migrations of Caribbean people with the aboriginal occupation of the Americas disturbed by European settlement. Terrance (literally) embodies the three levels of movement discussed in this chapter – global, national and urban transit. His life and its narration were both product and producer of these three forms of trajectory. Lives are hence best framed and understood as multiple journeys from place to place and not as the processes occurring in *one* particular place. Time and space intersect each other and give each other form and substance.

Jacques and Samuel

The journeys and collaboration of Jacques and Samuel provide a way in to discussing a group of lives lived in a particular set of circumstances-in-motion at the interface between welfare regimes, city, national and global space. Their journeys intersect in Montréal when Jacques, who is 31 and of Jamaican heritage but who has lived all of his life in the city, takes on a mentoring role with Samuel, who is just 18 and, having recently arrived from Toronto, needs to know how things in this city 'work for someone in his position'. This connection with the way things work is one of the many connections between the two men. Another is Jamaica. Neither of them has ever been to Jamaica, and Samuel has one Dutch as well as one Jamaican parent, which makes him look white, while Jacques is unmistakably black. Skin, of course, has a privileged place in construing race as a category of social recognition tied to place and the politics of belonging. And although Samuel looks white, he does not – demonstrating the plasticity of even these categories – think of himself in these terms.

The two men have a rather common living situation. They are mostly based in one of the city's shelters. But this is a day-by-day arrangement. If they don't get a bed for the night, Jacques has a mental list of disused buildings in which they might sleep. And they are about to move into a small apartment together: a thought that sustains them through their current difficulties. Like others in their position they eat from the city's soup kitchens and food bank and make use of its day centres to fill the gaps in the day when they are excluded from shelters. Against the odds, the two men have formed a very close friendship in which they have developed strategies whereby each of them makes it easier for the other to operate in the shelter, and then to move on to a better life in an apartment of their own. Samuel says of his relationship with Jacques: 'If I'm not with Jacques something's wrong'.

> That's just the way it is. Like in the showers or when you go in to eat, that guy is cutting in, in front of ya. I don't care if someone's cutting in front of ya anyways, but there's other guys who will do it, who will throw ya aside, and that's why with Jacques behind me I'm pushing through the crowd and he's watching my back, stopping me from falling down the stairs and *both* of us get through.
>
> (Samuel)

Plate 20   Samuel (left) and Jacques (right) playing pool

They are able to move in together because 'we think the same way', and because Samuel is used to 'hanging out with (other) Jamaicans'. He knows exactly how many days – eight – until moving day. Their new apartment is, highly significantly, located in 'little Jamaica' in the Côte de Neige area – a place that smells of curried goat and sweet potato pie and reminds Samuel of his grandmother's cooking. Côte de Neige is the corridor between two parts of the mountain that sits in the middle of the city and otherwise separates the two most expensive areas of the city, Outremont (French) to the northeast and Westmount (English) to the southwest. These are the places associated with the founding ethnicities of Canadian nationhood, the foundation of official bilingualism and the local racial and ethnic politics in which Jacques and Samuel are forced to operate. Côte de Neige contains the world in microcosm – a little of everywhere – because it is traditionally an area where global migrants first settle and from which they move on to areas with higher rents and better neighbourhoods as their fortunes improve. To Jacques and Samuel it is 'little Jamaica', but for others it is 'little Vietnam' or 'little Haiti' – home from home in a rich tapestry of lives woven around global migration.

Both men present themselves as being in control of their lives – a claim that is supported by their story about where and how they live and conveys the impression that they manipulate city space rather than allowing it to manipulate them. Similarly, Jacques' cogent account of his 'mild schizophrenia', which deploys social explanations of 'stress' following the birth of his first child as well as biological accounts of 'chemical imbalances' in the brain, gives the impression that he manages his condition rather than allowing it to manage him. There is no acknowledgement from Samuel that either he or Jacques has suffered psychiatric distress. Both men take pride in 'managing' and refuse to see family networks as a source of support. Jacques repeatedly refers to himself as 'independent'. Forceful and determined characters, they draw strength from their association with each other and for the feeling of control over their lives this sustains.

On one of their Sundays spent on the streets while the shelter is closed to its residents, Jacques and Samuel agreed to take two of our researchers out with them for the day. Weekends are special in that the day centres are closed, which means there is no where to eat or sit down in the warm during the day, and so they must insert themselves into the city in a different way from weekdays. The 'rich silences and wordless stories' (de Certeau 1988: 106) revealed by their trajectories around the streets of the city to some extent undermines their narrated story of self-determination. Ejected from the shelter, they hit the streets at 7a.m. having had coffee and doughnuts for breakfast. They begin the day complaining that they are tired having had a very disturbed night's sleep in the shelter dormitory. It was a cold winter day but Samuel has no socks, having had them stolen at the shelter the night before. As the day progresses they get hungrier and their mood more fragile. The researchers feed them in cheap restaurants, but normally they would go the entire day without food. First, they take the researchers to the city centre mall nearest the shelter where they usually spend the first part of the day. Many of the 'regulars' from the centres and shelters they use were already in the mall wandering around 'acting crazy' as Samuel describes it. Jacques and Samuel do not interact with them because of this. Instead they position themselves on the stairs: a place most people move through rather than spend time in! Although the mall is patrolled by private security guards, they are only asked to leave when they begin to smoke. They then move to the door next to the car park in order to smoke and linger there a while admiring the cars. They stay at the mall for more than four hours. Most of their time is spent around the food court where, in a charade agreed with security, they pretend to be drinking coffee – in fact it is water – from a polystyrene cup. Bored, they borrow Dabert's camera and, through the window, they take pictures of cars and women they like the look of. Eventually leaving the warmth of the mall they walk down the city's main shopping and panhandling street. They are increasingly bored and tired as they wander about the central part of the city, staying in the shopping district not far from the shelter zone. But apart from the time they spend at the mall they stay nowhere longer than half an hour. Jacques greets the many people he seems to know, also wandering about the streets of the city centre, and they drift to Burger King and then from Burger King to a cheap pizza joint for yet another small meal that doesn't seem to satisfy their hunger. Being able to eat like this is not typical, but is a product of their contribution to the research. When they eat, they eat quickly and lick their plates clean. In the early evening they leave the researchers and return to the shelter to eat supper, reserve a bed, go out again briefly, line up for a shower and go to bed. If they don't get a bed, they go to an abandoned building they know of to sleep for the night.

The day spent with Jacques and Samuel tells us quite a lot about their (version of the) city and corroborates the stories others tell about it concerning the use of space that is not really 'public', but commercial. In spending the day with Jacques and Samuel, it becomes clear that there is no indoor public space – that the city is comprised of commercial space that is privately owned and rented to retailers. In the winter especially the underground city and its miles of tunnels connecting one commercial area with another, become significant. The city's architecture is 'taking the place of the political, the processes by which public space is constituted and configured' (Caygill 1997: 25). This is a city built for consumption. Other activities and the lives attached to them must be fitted around the edges of these higher priorities and the versions of the self they sustain. The use of city space is importantly contextualized as the outcome of broader, global and national, pathways and it is to this that we now turn.

Global pathways

Like Jacques, Samuel and Terrance, many of our informants or their recent ancestors had arrived in Montréal through globally configured pathways. This is mentioned for two reasons. First, it forms the bigger picture of which their local/national migrations are a part. And second, for some people these forms of belonging, which are displaced and relocated in the city – as in Jacques' and Samuel's 'little Jamaica' – are important sources of personal anchorage and versions of the self that impact on ways of using the city. Recent and imagined immigrant origins and their reconfigured family relationships of proximity and distance organise the conduct of lives lived in local space. Many of our informants had well-dispersed family networks connecting them with the Caribbean, various parts of Canada, the United States and Britain. Others operate from a substantial family base in other European countries, especially Italy and Greece, or South America or the countries of the Far East. Many of them move back and forth between Canada and the Caribbean; some came to Canada to visit family, overstay and need to regularize their immigration status. Although proximity reactivates some family relationships and abandons others, there were often quite complicated systems of obligation between family members spanning continents. Anthony, who carefully guards his Dominican passport, explained to us why he came to Canada in the first place:

> This is why I came to Canada because I got laid off from my job. And they had, it was a special price, it was like an excursion going to Canada. Excursion, when you go on an excursion the flight is cheaper [he has an unused, return portion of a ticket back to Dominica]. So I called my friend in Toronto and said I'm coming to spend a couple of weeks because of the special. You see that every year in my country they have specials to England, to New York and to Toronto. So I thought, well, I just got laid off my job so I had that price [of the ticket], so I thought I could start a new life. Since Canada was the cheapest one, so I hopped on the plane and I came to Canada. ... I didn't like Toronto. Because the apartment there was really too crowded and it was like a disaster waiting to happen ... I think this city for me was too fast. You know back home it's a completely different place. It would have taken me two years to get accustomed to life in Toronto ... where I was living, even while I was living there, they [he is referring to the police] killed somebody there. So I thought that person could be me. ... I had to leave that place. And my destination was Québéc City. ... [Why?] Because I read in a brochure, I did some research on Canada. And I read in a brochure magazine because I went to a travel agency and they gave me that magazine. And I was looking at it, and they showed me a picture, and they show you it's beautiful. It's very beautiful there during the winter – so beautiful that I wanted to go because I never saw winter in my entire life before.
>
> (Anthony)

For Anthony, Québéc and its snowy landscape is exotic. His narrative reveals the 'discovery' of the tourist edged out of home by the collapse of his economic prospects. Paul accounts for his move to Canada in the context of the post-colonial collapse of Guyana.

> Well ... yeah ... everything just went, and now everything just went ... when Britain was there [Guyana] and we were ruled by the Queen and it was nice, we had everything. Everything, we had everything. Because everything used to come from England. Most of the stores there were owned by the British ... all the clothes that we used to wear, all the T-shirts, the sweaters, the running shoes, everything used to come from England. By the way we really had a whole lot of gold and diamonds and sugar and rice. The government went away, it just went down because [of] the country [England] that's keeping everything that's there, they want to take the diamonds out, just leave everything.
>
> (Paul)

It is unsurprising that Montréal, an attractive city in one of the key receiving countries as far as global migration is concerned, should feel the local effects of global restructuring in the demographic movements from poor to rich countries. Some of the lives we describe are global lives in transit. Others are more locally produced in a globally configured city. To some extent, then, globalization impacts on *all* lives, even those that first seem left behind by trauma and circumstance.

National pathways

The city is also the product of national population movements, which have as much to do with the established pathways of internal migration in search of jobs and lower living costs as with differences between welfare regimes. We commonly found people who had moved to Montréal from smaller cities and from rural Québec to make use of the city's facilities and be with others who were in a similar position. A number of people had taken traditional migration pathways from the Provinces to the east in search of employment and 'big city life'. There was also a notable 'drift' from the cities with higher living costs to the west, especially from Vancouver and Toronto, where housing costs are considerably higher. Those who come in search of lower living costs must not also be in search of jobs, as Québec has a high rate of unemployment, although not as high as some of the provinces to the east, which traditionally source the out-migration of the young. The gap between welfare benefits and rents was very much larger in Toronto – reflecting the city's higher rents – even before the (Conservative) Government of Ontario reduced welfare payments in the mid-1990s. This is the reason Samuel moved to Montréal from Toronto. Derrik tells us that with recent welfare reforms, it is not possible to be poor in Ontario. Montréal is a better place to be poor. These differences between provinces have produced internal welfare migration. Another informant, Pras, combines the Vancouver – Toronto – Montréal axis with movements back to Haiti to visit his family.[3] And Derrik's movements span the eastern half of the continent: a native Canadian born in Nova Scotia – traditionally an area of out-migration – he moved to Toronto (like his friends) to find work.

> In the last 10 years, I've just been travelling in the provinces – Nova Scotia, New Brunswick, Ontario and Québec. ... I want to settle down somewhere you know. It could have been Québec City. It could have been Halifax. It doesn't really matter. All cities are different to me. I could find something interesting in all of the different cities. Montréal doesn't have any preference over any other city. [He moves between cities by bus.] You know – I was, I was like Jack Kerouac. So to live between cities is nothing for me. It's life you know – to be on the road, to travel. But city is life. It's the thing I do.
>
> (Derrik)

Certainly Derrik is not 'displaced' by his mobility, but 'placed' within the genre of the American road novel/movie, which underwrites in being used to explain his life in motion around the country. He is, however, displaced in another sense he does not mention. He is displaced in the negotiations between government and native land claims, the failure to acknowledge the veracity of aboriginal land tenure, the summary resettlement of aboriginal communities in the siting of hydroelectric dams and the aggressive assimilation policies that established the residential schools in the sixties to which natives like Derrik were taken, having been summarily removed from ('unfit') parents in a series of moves designed to erase aboriginal identities. Abruptly reversing these policies of ethnic erasure and reinforcing the containment of aboriginal peoples on 'reserves', the governments of the 1970s produced a raft of entitlements accruing to natives – as *natives* and not as *citizens* of the nation state – which led to establishing the Department of Native Affairs to administer them, and to having to subscribe to 'biological notions of race' in delineating 'pure blood' natives from 'half-breeds' like Derrik. Nowhere else, outside of South Africa under apartheid, were these things so diligently attended to! The upshot of this complicated chapter of racial history is that people with some aboriginal ancestors – like Derrik – wander the country, and thousands of other mixed-race and pure natives live in ghettoes (reserves) – often without the benefit of running water and electricity – as a 'fourth world' adjacent to one of the highest urban living standards the world has to offer.

Pathways through urban space

Pathways through urban space are etched within (national) pathways within (global) pathways: triply configured and intersecting. These are lives in transit: lives whose mobility constitutes the city and the community system as a patchwork of partial and disconnected facilities that are not connected by other means. Individuals make use of *ad hoc* and fragmented facilities in ways that suit them and the system itself demands

Plate 21   A church with a drop-in centre

constant movement. Movement between shelters occurs because one regime is preferred over another: shelters have different levels of tolerance of behaviour and rules of exclusion. Movement from shelters to the streets occurs because of a lack of money when beds have to be paid for or because of policies of exclusion. Movement from shelters to apartments is considered to be upward mobility, but these are fragile arrangements that often lead back to the shelter or the street. Movement from apartments to shelters and the streets are often about the collapse of personal finances or the need to temporarily redirect expenditure. Jacques and Samuel are in transit between all three of these forms of accommodation and this is not atypical. The separation of living and eating arrangements sends people around the city in search of acceptable soup kitchens and the best food banks. The limited opening hours of most places cuts people adrift on the streets and in the malls of the downtown core. Other, more cyclical movements are about the trajectories of chronic psychiatric conditions and the movements in and out of the revolving doors of the local asylums following periods of relapse and treatment. Hospitalization frequently leads to the loss of tenuous housing arrangements when rents are unpaid. These fragile systems have a temporary air about them but are, in fact, permanent solutions to long-term circumstances. People grow up, grow old and die in this system.

Stitching together a life in the community system requires a detailed grasp of what is locally available; and the navigation of facilities creates its own trajectories in assembling a place to sleep, clean clothes, food and showers as Anthony points out:

> Most of the people bounce from one mission to another. ... [Asked about where he goes he checks.] Do you mean to sleep or eat? ... Well, I go to I don't know the place. ... It have a name but I cannot remember. I go to the Old Port to eat. Every, well I just got to do that every last Sunday in the month we can go to the place in the Cathedral. We have a good meal there but it's every *last* Sunday of the month you can go and eat there. And I've been to that place but I cannot remember that place. I, I, its like ... it's in the area, they have a lot of warehouses in that area. But that place you go every Wednesday for a meal. Like for me, every Wednesday I come there, my name is there, so I am entitled to a meal. And you have people that would come every Thursday and you have people coming in every Friday. But those that come on Wednesday, they cannot come of Thursday and Friday and vice versa. [These are just his lunching arrangements, as Anthony lives in a shelter.]
>
> (Anthony)

Jacques' and Samuel's Sunday showed a similarly complex piecing together of the day. What is routine for most of us requires work for Jacques, Samuel, Anthony and the others. Because living in the 'system' demands expertise, it has produced its own experts. Jonathan, for example, is a street musician with considerable expertise born out of his extensive experience of the city's shelters, day centres, food banks, soup kitchens and so on. He is so adept at working the strings of city philanthropy, he even knows where to get free dental hygiene services for the annual spring-cleaning of his teeth. When it comes to matters of daily routine he takes us through the various places he has to go in order to get food and, indirectly, points out the expertise of others who are forced to work the system:

Where else have I gone for food? [He lists the church basements and other venues, and pauses at one place in particular.] That was pretty grim. The food was ahh the vegetables and stuff were all slimy, the bread was just all ... fighting old ladies ... big fat old ladies for loaves of bread [laughter]. Seriously, there are these two women who look like they need a food bank right [said with irony], they are like this [gestures with his arms to show how large they are], and they are in there and they are not even waiting, they are just going through all these big piles of bread, all of the best loaves, and all the buns, and all the Danish just everything they can find yummy looking and they're leaving all the broken bread, the squished breads, they're filling up bags and bags, and they're rushing off to all the other food banks.

(Jonathan)

Jonathan's entertaining (if rather disparaging) account (of women) doesn't mask what is clearly a highly competitive scramble in which the women he describes have learned how to feed their families without an adequate food budget. His façade of street wisdom covers his humiliation in 'begging for some Spam and some ... snack noodles'. But it is Terrance, who was reared in the system, and not Jonathan, who is the 'real' expert in Jonathan's estimation. He provides reverent testimony of Terrance's expertise:

That guy grew up in the system, his parents ... I know a couple of guys who grew up in the system too ... as an infant his parents drop him at *** [he gives the name of a group home] kind of thing and him and his brother, Terrance's brother got murdered a couple of years ago, and Terrance went out and killed the guy who murdered his brother when he was a 10-, 12-year-old boy. He's been growing up in the system his whole life, so you're talking about a guy who knows places to go. He knows every food bank in the city, he used to use it as a business almost ... he'd have a few places to crash and show up somewhere with about two big bags of groceries and say, 'Can I stay here for two days?' you know ... or he'd sell it for a bag of weed, and he could do a food bank a day and walk away with a bag of groceries, *serious* groceries, too, and then he'd show them his 'I've been through the system card', so that he could show them that 'Montréal really screwed me you know' [the demonstration of entitlement] and they would say, 'Well we have this ham and we have this turkey'. Me, I go there and we have a bag of hot dogs ... they were frozen you know, they say 'Don't worry', although the air seal is broken.

(Jonathan)

Pathways through the city are a matter of accumulated knowledge in assembling the basic ingredients of daily survival. They are also a matter of the terms on which public space may be temporarily occupied.

Those who operate through the street, those for whom it is a nodal point connecting a fragmented life, do so on certain terms. When Jacques and Samuel are followed by our researchers, they *move through*, rather than *occupy*, city space. Their use of space, in fact, also provides a commentary on the grammar of public space in the city, revealing its nature, its meaning and its politics.[4] St Catherine's street, the commercial heart of the city that runs east to west connecting the French and the English side of the city, is the main city corridor where homeless and other people can sit and panhandle. With the disused forum, that once housed the 'Montréal Canadiens' ice hockey team before they found better premises, at one end and the fringes of the red-light district and the gay village at the other, St Catherine's is a collage of empty stores, boutiques, shopping mall entrances, disused churches, video games and peep-show parlours. It is the place where the police turn a blind eye to loitering by those of unkempt appearance and tenuous circumstances. Symbolically, this street runs a line through the binary system of French- and English-Canadian heritage, otherwise observed even in the provision of two television rooms in homeless shelters. The street is the place where these allegiances – dissecting all others cast by national belonging, race, ethnicity, language and ancestry so that 'allophones' must cast themselves on one side or the other – are played-out. It is where these allegiances matter most – and least.

Panhandling, which is tolerated on St Catherine's street, is a key reason for occupying the street. It fills some of the gaps in the day and in the *ad hoc* system of provision by providing extra cash for coffee and cigarettes. It is a highly organized, routinized and territorially based use of street space. Most panhandling pitches operate as 'time shares' so that certain people have what is generally acknowledged to be a certain pitch or space at particular times. Different pitches have different values depending on 'location' and 'yield'. Asserting the right to a spot involves intimidation of would-be invaders and takes certain strength of character.

> This old guy was panhandling on my spot, so one day he give me a little spit like this, and I was like 'What's this about?' so I just went [makes a gargling noise] and it went splash across his face ehh. So he comes over to me and gives me a little poke in the chest, so what am I supposed to do? It's like an old man, I can't just go boom, so I give him a little kick in the shin, and no one's seen anything, so I tell him that, 'There's more of that if you hang around old guy'. It's pretty competitive out there. Street musicians are calling the cops on one another if they don't have licenses, I know it's kind of stupid – they call the cops up on you to try and get rid of you. I've done it to one or two guys because I don't like them and they were in my spot.
>
> (Jonathan)

Panhandling is not an activity for the faint hearted. And it is a way of being on the street that is not particularly favoured by women outside of the sex industry, although this general point is contradicted by Jonathan's description of Madeline's panhandling routine:

> I'm singing the other day in front of the Faubourg [a small indoor market on St Catherine's Street], I'm singing 'Bridge Over Troubled Water' and she knows all the words. [He mimics her singing.] … Oh God, it just goes on and on and then she's panning, at the same time she's panning she's doing her little sexy dance. I mean she's not just crazy, you ought to meet her sometime – after she's panning after just finishing smoking two or three rocks and she's panning out there and she needs another rock and she's scary man – she's

assaulting people man – literally. She goes up to them and she goes [shouting], 'Come on gimme more, you, you mister gimme money. I'll blow your job for only $2'. – She scares the hell out of people, man. She scares me.

(Jonathan)

It can be very dispiriting and dangerous.

That's why I wouldn't go panhandling. I mean, I deal well enough with rejection, but having 300 people a day telling you [screaming] 'Get a job you fuckin' asshole', or just 'NO! NO! NO!' Two or three hundred 'Nos' in a day you start to twitch – you know, and then you have to deal with all the people who say like, 'Would you like to come over to my place?' That's it, it's seedy, seedy, crappy ... this city is around here sometimes. That's all it boils down to, everybody wants sex, money and drugs, you know. ... The city is full of them [the lonely]. You're going to get the people who go to McDonalds with machine guns, they're like, 'I'm lonely. I need a friend [mimics machine gun fire].' The city is full of them, I mean it seems to me that most street people are on a hair trigger right now, it's like they're borderline. ... [He makes an interesting use of a psychiatric term to discuss broader personal and social circumstances.] You give them a little push, you know, you say the wrong thing to a lot of street people and I think that you could just flip 'em right out, and have violence perpetrated against yourself.

(Jonathan)

As well as being territorial, panhandling is also highly organized, involving the calculation of earnings and routines and forms of co-operation with others, which are highly scripted and considered. Terrance, for example, calculates what he makes every hour so that he can identify the times of day on which to maximize earnings and hence concentrate on his efforts more efficiently. Each hour he transfers his takings into separate pockets so that at the end of the day he can make his calculations. He talks about the gimmicks he uses. He has routines with devil sticks, and various ways of making people part with their money using the right combination of assertiveness and manipulation. His street performances are highly thought out. So are Jacques' and Samuel's. They often operate as part of a three-person routine that involves softening up the approaching public with a show of pathos, knowing that it will take them to the third person in the staggered pitch to find the appropriate amount of change and part with it. The three men share their proceeds. Panhandling involves considerable insight into how the street with its flows of people works, and how to work the crowd deploying the appropriate combinations of performed tragedy, cheerfulness or need. Jacques, Samuel, Jonathan and the others are insightful social analysts, philosophers and students of human nature.

But living on the streets has to include ways of staying *off* the streets, at least for six months of the year because of the harsh winter climate. There are basically three kinds of indoor public spaces that our informant could use – the mall, fast-food joints and churches – and they use them on certain terms.

Many different kinds of people spend time in the mall apart from determined shoppers. The mall offers indoor space for mothers, baby sitters and children who would otherwise be housebound. It is a place where the elderly congregate for social interaction, people watching and cups of tea. And it is a place where women spend time planning future consumption as well as attending to the current consumption needs of their families. Malls are not intended for hasty purchases – indeed this is infuriatingly impossible. They are places in which to pay homage to the 'idea' of consumption and secure its place in North American lifestyles as a legitimate avenue of human gratification and way of spending time. Our informants are not potential consumers and consumption of the kind offered in the mall is *not* a part of their lives. In fact they live in a domain of social activity that is beyond the segment of lives addressed by the mall and these are, in fact, the terms of their exclusion, rather than the fact that they have no money to spend there on any particular occasion. Because of this, and because they need indoor shelter in the absence of other options, they must somehow 'insert' themselves into this space of commercial activity along with its other users. The use of downtown malls is contingent on the largesse of its security staff – a delicately negotiated operation. Mindful of this, Jacques and Samuel place themselves in the stairway and at the side door leading into the car park – the rather grimy, functional concrete areas other people pass through on their way to somewhere else. They occupy the food court discreetly and play the game of sitting with what looks like a cup of coffee but is in fact a cup of water. Remaining 'invisible' is the price of using public space. It is important not to disturb the aesthetics of what is a space intended for contemplating and validating private consumption as a way of being in the world. When they spend money our informants are much more likely to be customers of smaller corner shops known as *depanneurs* and their consumption revolves around food, cigarettes and beer. Jonathan provides a striking example of the relationship between a *depanneur* and one of its homeless customers.

> This guy was so bad [he is smelly and talks to himself] they wouldn't let him in any of the stores around here. There was a store, Jimmy's, you know Chez Jimmy's? They used to sell beer there and they had a big long bagel flipping stick, and they used to put the pole out, and he'd put his money on it. ... Yes, it's true, and they would bring the pole back in, and they would balance [his] beer on the stick ... and then they would stick the pole back out again. He would take his beer, open it up and pour it into a big McDonald's cup, he would then stand facing the wall like this [demonstrates] at the Seville Theatre, and he would drink it [mimics the man talking to himself], to the wall.
>
> (Jonathan)

Fast-food outlets, especially burger joints and doughnut shops, are favoured commercial spaces, because they are cheap and anonymous (see Chapter 2). Elijah, whose welfare cheque has just arrived, sits in Dunkin Donuts munching his way through a list of 99-cent breakfast 'specials', oblivious to the fact that he is not the object of their marketing strategy. This is a system in which doughnut shops are as important as day centres. On welfare cheque day (the first of the month) the tension of waiting and wanting is broken and the cheap bars of the city's red light district are bulging into the night. Here the mentally distressed and precariously housed rub shoulders with drug dealers and sex workers over large bottles of cheap beer. On a warm and heady night in the city the problem of where to sleep is less pressing than in the depths of winter.

Churches are the third form of public space to feature on the maps of the precariously housed, but these too, like commercial space, have their own conditions of entry. They are good places to warm up in winter:

> I used to like go there in the morning ... and to sleep for a while and to warm myself up. ... Sometimes they have a service and I go to the service and they have a Holy Communion and I take part. And I receive the communion. And when the sun comes up bright and I go.
>
> (Anthony)

They are also:

> a cool place to grab lunch. They have a bunch of smelly people though. St [name of the church] on the first Sunday of every month that's pretty cool because all you have to listen to is one prayer, you know, it's like 'blah, blah' and 'God thank you, blah blah', and then you dig in.
>
> (Jonathan)

Even if they are as mired in bureaucracy as local social services. Jonathan describes the process involved in getting a Christmas basket, along with a line-up of more than a hundred others 'with their little vouchers' from one of the local churches which checks the credentials of the needy:

> Well you uh have to make an application through some other social agency and they will write you a letter. You need a ton of documentation. You need everything [in order to benefit from this religious organization] ... ID, a letter of reference from one of the associations, and even then they try and talk it down, they say 'Well we can't give you all of this but we can give you this and that. Will you take it?' You know you take it because it's free.
>
> (Jonathan)

The demonstration of need or token expressions of religious devotion is the price of using church space. Access is any way temporary and for specific events and purposes. Once a key provider of the health and welfare services of all kinds to the local population, displaced by the brief appearance of a modern welfare state, the church is once again an important provider of refuge, hot meals, clothes and groceries to the local population. This produces its own forms of client/provider relationship that is not based on entitlement but supplication and the demonstration of sufficient need or religious observance.

The particular forms of urban mobility and precariousness described in this chapter raise two key issues among the people we interviewed. The first concerns the contribution of mobility in deepening a sense of fragmentation and lack of belonging, adding further layers of distress to compound existing distress. It is not that mobility itself inherently produces uncertainty and distress. Like other people, the mad tread global, national and urban pathways in making their lives as a sequence of places in time. But

the nature of the urban pathways they tread and the purposes of survival for which
they tread them cannot do other than add layers of stress, uncertainty and dislocation
to already difficult lives. Jonathan's theory is that street life itself produces its own
forms of mental illness. He illustrates his theory with the story of another street musician whose sense of precariousness was accelerated by life on the streets and:

> who was going mentally ill. Lack of nutrition, smoking too much cigarettes –
> uhh sleeping two hours here, and hour there, uhh, and then not sleeping for
> days on end, this guy is going mentally ill like he's talking that the Rock
> Machine is trying to blow up my apartment, and that my gas stove is leaking.
> Go look at my gas stoke ... it's electric! There is no gas in the building
> [laughter], and uhh, I told you what happened to him right, he woke up in
> the middle of the night and he walked out onto the balcony and went aah
> boom. Four floors bounced, hit another one, bounced down again and didn't
> break a bone in his body. He fractured his skull and they had to take a bone
> out of his brain and uhh ... but he's out and walking around again and he's
> going to hit the streets again soon. But no umm ... mentally ill people I try
> to shove them on.
>
> (Jonathan)

A life spent treading the particular urban pathways described above raises important
sociological questions concerning the kinds of subjectivities sustained in a life
textured by this particular kind of transit. These questions are accentuated by the
mental distress suffered by those whose lives they address. The lives in question are
anyway punctuated by personal crises and uncertainties as Chapter 5 will show. What
kinds of being-in-the-world are formed by having no place in which to spend time?
Having to keep moving. Having to use the edges of public space and remain unno-
ticed. Being accepted as a consumer in a society that prizes consumption only at a
distance. Having to hunt for food and shelter on a daily basis. And having to beg for
money in order to eat. What are the minimal forms of personal anchorage necessary to
avoid the kind of personal disintegration noted by Jonathan? These are particular
forms of transit that are as much a part of global society as its other forms of transit in
pursuit of business and family connections although they are rarely identified as such.
This is connected with the second issue raised by informants and is to do with
personal baggage in its literal and metaphorical sense. The transit of the precariously
housed raises significant problems for them concerning what to do with the minimal
trappings of civil life – forms of identification, important documents, photographs
and memorabilia – the things which connect people with the social, the minimal
social bonds connecting one human life to the collectivity of human lives in a locale
and with a personal past and means of official recognition of being a person. Should
these things be left somewhere or hauled around the streets? Living in transit significantly reduces these trappings to a minimum. But are they not particularly significant
given the severance of life from place and other forms of social participation? If people
are not connected to spaces but to temporary associations with particular configurations of spaces, are they connected to other things? Are these personal effects the
minimal conduits of personal anchorage? Norma, who rotated between cheap apartments, a women's shelter and the streets, offered some insights into these questions as

Plate 22   Baggage stored in a drop-in basement

she relates the story of the loss of her bag from one of the temporary storage basements of one of the local churches:

> I got my whole life taken away. I had a travelling bag with all my photograph albums, of all the years that I've been here [Canada, she came from Jamaica], and pictures, documents, my daughter's birth certificate, some of my expensive clothes, n' stuff like that. I leave my, I used to leave a lot of clothes there for a month and they put it down in the basement and I would come an' pick it up. 'Cause I was not there, I was running around crazy. And, um, once I leave some stuff there and I think somebody stole the bag, with – my big travelling bag like this, and all my, I have some silk, nice clothes, all my nice clothes, and I think somebody walk out with everything. But all my documents, all my lifeline was in that bag. And because they didn't want to pay me for it, they told me: 'Oh you were a week late, we threw it out'. And I

know that was crap. ... I've been leaving things there for years and I knew somebody take it. ... So I knew somebody took the travelling bag. And because they didn't want to reimburse me, they told me they throw it in the garbage. The same thing happened with my apartment the year before.

(Norma)

These are lives in which shelter and things are constantly disappearing: lives which are inserted into the grammar of city space and lived in transit between a complex pattern of spaces. Spaces are used and passed through. There is no leave to remain, except temporarily en route to the next place. This is the meaning of transit in the context of these mad lives and it is this that marks their unique peculiarities, their mode of connection with the fabric of the social domain and their mobility. As de Certeau (1988: 103) says: 'To walk is to lack a place', and places are important sources of personal anchorage. The mad live a life of 'walking exile' (de Certeau 1988: 103, 106–7): their few possessions deposited precariously, often on a weekly basis in church basements. It may not sound like a very impressive arrangement, but its ramifications are clear in Norma's distressed revelation. Visually these are arrangements that invoke the image of a refugee transit camp in one of the world's border zones: the internal boarder zones in the *centre* of the city where space is used on particular terms. The image of this baggage serves as a motif for the processes that are described in this chapter. The mad form a part of the 'crazy theater of the streets' (Estroff 1981), where lives are lived in more or less permanent motion.

5

'SCHIZOPHRENIC' LIVES

I'm fine, and she's fine. They're the crazies.

(Dave)

I have a little cinema-scope inside my head and I turn it on and it starts reeling fast and I can literally, if I close my eyes, I can see pictures going by. ... I can project from my brain (pornographic) stories onto the inside of my eyes and have a good time doing that.

(Evan)

The lives finely etched by space, time and the regimes dealing with multiple forms of displacement and poverty, and which form an inseparable, if unseen, part of the city's rhythms, are also etched by the private terror of madness. As Lefebvre (1996: 8–9) says, space *is* its deployment in human action. The human action in contention in these pages has to deal with the infinite variety of personal and social circumstances collectively referred to as madness. The preceding chapters have described some of the ways in which mad lives move through and etch social space. They have shown how people are assigned and assign themselves to the different spatial arrangements composing the local geographies of madness. And they have described the different kinds of client relationships which mark these spaces. They have shown that spaces are important, as Lefebvre suggests, in the production of the self and relationships with others. All of this, most particularly in the segment of lives described in these pages, is mediated by the impact of madness. And so it is to the various forms of private terror embedded in lives and the social processes through which that terror is produced that we turn in this chapter to explore some of the personal conceptions of schizophrenia with which schizophrenics navigate their world. Personal conceptions of schizophrenia are concerned with its meaning, its underlying causes, and its overall place in the grammar of a life. What is wrong with them? Why they are so afflicted, and the resonance of their condition with the other aspects of a life, are matters on which our informants had much to say. The significance of their conceptions lies in their contribution to the theorization of madness as schizophrenia. Schizophrenics occupy a central place in the lived production of the meaning of madness on the streets of the city, and in the various places where it is acted out and socially managed. Theirs are practically based conceptions of madness: conceptions that have a force in actions and modes of being in the world. In this respect they play a highly significant part in the production of the community system and its city context explored in previous chapters. Schizophrenics' conceptions of madness form a part of the public regimes for disposal of private terror. It forms a part of the ways in which they walk the streets of the city. More than a backdrop against which the scenes of madness are played out, the streets with its routes, centres, shelters and rooming houses, and the versions of madness that are lived and acted on are interactive social processes. We have occupied many of the preceding pages with discussion of the 'scenes' of madness and so it is to madness itself that we must turn.

The stories we collected contained highly personal versions of schizophrenia finely tuned by the social circumstances in which they were embedded. Fragments of these stories show through the stories related in previous chapters depicting individual social circumstances and uses of space and available facilities. This chapter brings these fragments into the foreground and explores them. Schizophrenia's 'rage' (Gail), its pain, its proximity to 'living in another world' (Louise), its approximation to 'playing a video game' (Scott), in which you have to anticipate the actions and reactions of others, are inadequately captured in identifying the meaning of schizophrenia – as we do in this chapter – in a series of overlapping narrative themes. This is, of course, one of the problems of trying to discuss highly individual experiences and feelings that are anyway 'wrenched' into narrative. The themes to emerge most clearly in individual narratives, and which have a bearing on the meaning and causes of schizophrenia, are attempts at theorizing it by those whose lives it shapes. These themes are: popular theories of schizophrenia as 'split personality'; the idea that schizophrenia involves entering a parallel reality; medicalised notions of schizophrenia as a disease; the loss of an authentic sense of self; religious-based notions of schizophrenia as spiritual suffering; and conspiracy theories. These themes-as-theoretical-reasoning will be illustrated below and set in the social and personal circumstances that constitute mad lives. These are not neat, discrete and self-contained theories. Many stories combine what appear to be contradictory or incompatible themes in an attempt to make sense of schizophrenic breakdown in the overall context of the life rendered as narrative. In pillaging stories for themes, their constellation in lives is inevitably disrupted, depersonalized and disembedded from the context in which they have meaning. Although these theories are not unique but shared with others, their meaning and impact is differently drawn through the lives they touch. Schizophrenia is personal. But it is also socially drawn, and our identification of themes is another attempt to discuss this personal/social interface, developing earlier observations of the existential administrative interface involved in the placing of mad lives in the grammar of the city. There are also other aspects of schizophrenia apart from themes – mechanisms – which are socially drawn and revealed in schizophrenics' stories. Examining the stories it is evident that schizophrenia has a dynamic, a trajectory, set in the life in which it has imposed and which schizophrenics are able to describe. It intervenes in a set of social and personal circumstances that it disrupts and reformulates. It involves a trigger – a series of identifiable events or processes that set it off – and which are accounted for in the context of the life on which they impose. And it always involves forms of accommodation and coping, so that life goes on in some reformulated way. These mechanisms are, of course, revealed in schizophrenics' narratives and they significantly shape the narrating of the stories from which our accounts of the meaning of schizophrenia are derived. Accounts of schizophrenia, then, are highly personal but also contain common constellations of themes that are individually worked. They also impose certain patterns on the life they disrupt and reformulate. Conceptions of schizophrenia are both personal *and* socially worked. They contain the existential writ large: crises of the nature of individual existence, which never the less contain (social) elements shared in common and processed by the administrative apparatus of community mental health care and the broader social and political context in which it is set.

The place of psychiatry in formulating these personal, socially and administratively worked versions of madness is worthy of attention in passing, given the claims that have been made about the ubiquity of psychiatric thinking in framing the lives of the mad. Do schizophrenics' versions of madness as schizophrenia deploy psychiatric thinking? And if they do how do they do so? Or is schizophrenia understood by other means? Do schizophrenics 'borrow' from psychiatry in making sense of themselves and their lives? Psychiatry alone is professionally concerned with the definition and treatment of madness: what is the contemporary place of professional thinking in formulating versions of madness? Although we have noted in earlier chapters the retreat of psychiatry in engaging with the seriously and persistently mad, having ceded its spatial dominance in the asylum in organizing the daily affairs of the mad in the community system, might not its hold on the production of knowledge about madness outlive its strategic retreat in providing professional services and space? Does psychiatry, as its critics contend, operate as a mechanism for self-knowledge among schizophrenics? Or are their lives theorized by other means? Because the theorization of lives is a practical, interactive, activity we also want to take into account the versions of madness operated by those with whom the mad come into daily face-to-face contact – those who work in informal community provision and who have replaced the attentions of those who once worked within the orbit of professional psychiatry as nurses and orderlies. What versions of schizophrenia do those who work with the mad operate? And, most importantly, what are its sources and points of connection with the conceptions of schizophrenic clients? All of these questions form a part of two broader questions – what *is* schizophrenia in community settings? Or, put another way, what (hybrid) versions of the nature and meaning of madness operate in the community? And, second, how are these theorized and embedded in strategies for social management? We noted in Chapter 3 that spatial contexts contain implicit versions of its clients written in the internal arrangement and aesthetics of space. This chapter follows up this claim by taking a closer look at workers' versions of their clients as schizophrenics.

In addressing the influence of psychiatric thinking an immediate problem presents itself. The social sciences in general, but particularly sociology is guilty of simplistic renditions of psychiatry in making it a target for its critical and, implicitly, superior moral stance. The diversity, disagreement and controversy surrounding psychiatric accounts of schizophrenia cannot adequately be discussed here, and has been extensively reviewed by others better qualified to do so. In place of this discussion and acknowledging the necessity to say something about psychiatric versions of schizophrenia in order to gauge their impact, it is possible to identify some key points that establish the basic outline of psychiatric thinking on schizophrenia. Psychiatric conceptions of schizophrenia generally stress its chronicity and incurability, strongly indicating it as a condition to be managed rather than cured (Barham 1984: 8–21). It is described as manifesting itself in a range of behaviour that includes hearing voices and seeing visions, hallucinations and disorganized speech and its diagnosis 'involves the recognition of a constellation of signs and symptoms associated with impaired occupational and social functioning' (*Diagnostic Statistical Manual of Mental Disorders IV*, American Psychiatric Association 1995: 280). Delusions are:

> erroneous beliefs that usually involve a *misinterpretation* of perceptions and experiences. Their content may include a variety of themes. ... Persecutory delusions are most common; the person believes he or she is being tormented, followed, tricked, spied on, or subjected to ridicule. ... The distinction between a delusion and a strongly held idea is sometimes difficult to make and depends on the degree of conviction with which the belief is held despite clear contradictory evidence. Although bizarre delusions are considered to be especially characteristic of schizophrenia, 'bizarreness' may be difficult to judge especially across different cultures. Delusions are deemed bizarre if they are *clearly implausible and not understandable and do not derive from ordinary life experiences* [my emphasis].
>
> (American Psychiatric Association 1995: 281–2)

Disorganized thinking, speech and behaviour are also symptoms of schizophrenia which, at least in the regimes of *Diagnostic Statistical Manual of Mental Disorders IV* (DSM IV) focuses on the reading or diagnoses of underlying states from individual presenting behaviour – a concern that is, understandably, far removed from those whose lives are shaped by schizophrenia. Its underlying causes operate on a continuum with organic factors at one end and social causes at the other with most interpretations positioning themselves at some point upon it. 'Although much evidence suggests the importance of genetic factors in the etiology of schizophrenia, the existence of a substantial discordance rate in monozygotic twins also indicates the importance of environmental factors' (American Psychiatric Association 1995: 289).

Schizophrenia is the object of wide professional disagreement as to its symptoms and causes and an ongoing area of psychiatric research.[1] More than any other diagnosis, schizophrenia carries the accusation of 'misdiagnosis': for incorrectly reading the behaviour of racially and ethnically defined minorities as symptoms of schizophrenia, something that DSM IV acknowledges but provides no mechanism for dealing with in the context of individual consultations.[2] A large and important body of research spearheaded by Littlewood, Fernando and others from the 1980s indicated the over-diagnosis of African Caribbeans in the UK with parallel findings among African Americans sustained suspicion of psychiatry's racializing practices. No such claims are made in respect of Canada where a lack of ethnic monitoring of the distribution of diagnoses would make such claims unsupportable.[3] The accusation of misdiagnosis rests on the application of western diagnostic principles and assumptions about behaviour in which decisions about normality and pathology are cast. Ethnic personhood – or so the argument goes – is improperly understood with normal habits being mistaken for signs of underlying mental pathology. Consequently, transcultural psychiatrists attempt to understand culturally framed idioms of mental distress and frame their therapeutic encounters in terms of individuals' cultural context. Misreading cultural context is strenuously avoided by prominent local psychiatrists, who display high levels of cultural competence and sensitivity in their work. Psychiatrists like Carlos Sterlin, Jaswant Guzder and Laurence Kirmeyer have

Plate 23 Anne's world

generated the best possible therapeutic regimes in this respect. But their expertise has not transformed the regimes of mass disposal and we may legitimately suspect local psychiatry of the same racializing practices that are in evidence in psychiatry in the United States and Britain. Precise connections between diagnoses of schizophrenia and its social and political context are a complicated business and difficult to pin down in any concrete way. It is, however, evident from DSM IV that schizophrenia is an 'interpretation' of particular forms of social divergence from the norms (and their political regimes), which are assumed to hold in place the behaviour of the non-mad, as well as being a description of the behaviour manifestations of particular forms of private terror and distress. Because the terror is real in its capacity to terrorize, it does not follow that its interpretation and means of disposal are *not* politically scripted and manipulated.

Narrative genre and performance

Personal versions of schizophrenia are socially worked by being told as stories, as well as by being told as specific kinds (genres) of stories. The capacity to order episodic and traumatic events surrounding schizophrenic breakdown in narrative form is a truly astonishing, reflexive and theorizing activity. Even after hearing hundreds of stories of schizophrenic breakdown its quality as an experience is still impossible to imagine. An art exhibition at the University of Edinburgh in the mid-1990s, containing the work of people with various disabilities, shows a painting by a psychiatric patient with schizophrenia showing a human face in sequence in various stages of ever more jagged Picassoesque distortion was an attempt to describe visually one person's descent into schizophrenia. Verbal rendition of this vivid visual – but equally partial when compared to living through this kind of experience – representation of experience would inevitably be a flat and pale version of what had occurred. Schizophrenic breakdown is likely to be unrepresentable, so that attempts to render schizophrenia in narrative inevitably reinvent vivid, disturbing and disordered experiences as sequential, understandable events like the others that make up a life. And yet they cannot be this. The stories schizophrenics tell about themselves also involve the reassertion of meaning where meaning has been systematically eroded, a point that Skultans (1998: 124) makes about illness narratives in general. As well as having to be partially invented by the demand that they be told, schizophrenics' stories are highly rehearsed. Our questions about 'what is wrong', 'how *it* happened' and 'how you came to be here' inevitably unleashed stories of 'breakdown' and 'recovery' set in the broader context of a life and had been told and retold in the psychiatric hospitals, the homeless shelters, the day centres, the foster homes and the other places where accounts of the schizophrenic self are required and demanded. Versions of these 'stories' operate as part of the therapeutic and social management contexts of contemporary madness, which must negotiate workers' conceptions of who the mad are and what is wrong with them in the contexts of the services they make use of.

Schizophrenics' stories are stories of personal struggle in the face of various forms of compounded difficulty. It is precisely these compounded difficulties that bring a certain kind of material to the story. The lives we describe are highly troubled. They are structured by multiple forms of individual adversity, such as the lack of love in personal relationships that Rhona describes below. Or (and as well), they are structured by social problems such as racism, or poverty, or a lack of opportunity. Benny portrays his life as a struggle against shortage of money, the difficulty of getting jobs and trouble with the law over his marijuana use. In discussing 'what is wrong' in his life he persistently returns to his financial troubles, which dominate his life and threaten to make him, his wife and child homeless. Most stories describe a complex cocktail of individual and social suffering and the individualized struggles required in order to get through each of the days structured by these difficulties. Each struggle is defined by what it is that is being overcome in the context of an individual life, such as a deficit of love or lack of money – a point that is sometimes buried in examining the overlapping themes that constitute the meaning of schizophrenia.

As well as working with a particular kind of material, schizophrenics' stories are structured by a 'before' and 'after' in which a former life is disrupted by the appearance of madness. Within this basic formulation, and working with a specific kind of material or content, only certain kinds of stories can be told. Narrative genres operate as templates that affect the sequence of stories, the selection of details to disclose and the possible outcomes. There are stories of personal decline from a former state of 'happiness' or 'normality' to the depths of 'despair' and 'disintegration'. Stories of decline generally provide an account of how this is overcome or accommodated in the truce that makes it possible to 'carry on' against the odds. There are other kinds of stories too. There are stories of personal progress from an original state of despair and degradation culminating in schizophrenia as one of a list of personal and social difficulties, to a more acceptable and happier life. There are also stories of escape, of somehow working the system and moving on to another more comfortable life on the edge of the system. This is the kind of story that Craig, the 'asylum historian', told us in Chapter 2. It is also the story of Jonathan, the street musician who lives on the fringes of the system and provided such eloquent commentary on it in Chapter 4. And there are 'survivor stories' describing how the territories of the self are maintained in the most difficult of circumstances and foreground the activities of constant struggle. The survivor story is the genre most commonly used by published versions of schizophrenics' stories such as *Cry the Invisible* and *Shrink Resistant*.[4] In these published accounts, they have survived the terror of schizophrenia, the attention of psychiatry and the forms of social exclusion that come with it. Rhona's survival is that of overcoming a series of obstacles in a highly troubled life.

> I consider myself lucky that I survived. I survived the last war, World War II. I survived that. I survived two children [she had to give up for adoption], I survived four [alcoholic, abusive] husbands and I survived all the beatings from everyone that I got. I survived it all and I am still here to live to tell the tale. I survived. There was no love in my household growing up, from day one 'till I was 14; there was nothing there. I survived a mother that hated my guts because my father was, pardon my expression – 'black'. I grew up in a racist family. I survived it. I don't give a damn if my father was green. He was my father. ... [Long heavy pause.] You wouldn't believe the shit that went on in my house with my mother. That's where the hatred came from, my mother. Physical abuse, okay. I was abused by my own mother because she hated me because my father was black. My mother [who was Jewish] hates black people – [yet she married a black man when] she found out she was pregnant. ... I survived, I survived everything. – I'm a holocaust survivor ... and I'm 51 years old.
>
> (Rhona)

This – detailing multiple forms of survival in the face of adversity – is the only part of Rhona's heart-rending narrative delivered in a serious tone. That it includes some personal forms of racial antipathy is instructive. In this case forms of betrayal and breakdown of personal relationships are described in racial terms. Issues relating to broader social and political struggles regularly 'walk' into emotional landscapes. She delivers the rest of her narrative as stand-up comedy in which we were encouraged to laugh with her at the series of disasters and the catalogue of abuse that constitutes her life story. Each new set-back is met with humour and sheer persistence to continue – to survive. She was performing for us in the interview itself the key mechanism in her personal survival kit – her ability to laugh at herself and the situations in which she finds herself. Her life is tragedy played as comedy: a routine for personal survival. Stories like Rhona's – stories of decline, progress, escape and survival – form the substance of age-old traditions of storytelling replayed as film and television plots *and* used to convey the details of individual biographies. For there to be a story to tell, there has to be a shift from one state to another, hence the lack of stories told by foster home inmates referred to in Chapter 3 who lived in a continuous medicalized present.

Performance, as we noted in Chapter 1, occupies a central position in narrating (and living) schizophrenic lives. Interviews were performances staged for us that echoed other performances staged in other social arenas and connect with versions of social/individual identities attached to the meaning of schizophrenia. Being schizophrenic was not necessarily *the* major component of social or individual identity, but it does *enter* the calculation of identity through performance. As Evan, who earlier described himself as an 'Irish Catholic' growing up in a 'middle-class Westmount family', puts it: 'I'm gay and I'm schizophrenic and I'm an alcoholic too'. Not all informants put it this directly. Identities can be performed without this kind of explicit narrative. Our informants frequently conveyed a strong sense of themselves in terms that were not centrally focused on the meaning of schizophrenia, but in which versions of schizophrenic identities featured in some way. Not a central part of identity, schizophrenia is certainly one of the filters through which it operates, and this is evident in interview performances of the self. The photographs in this chapter are Anne's performance of herself through the meanings she attaches to schizophrenia – a visual commentary of what it *means* in *her* life. Anne's hijacking of an interviewer and photographer, her directing the camera's lens (in place of an interview) gives us a visual commentary as powerful as any verbal one of the things that were significant in her world. The abstract and traditional Chinese water colours she has painted, her tablet dispenser, her psychiatric records in the filing drawer, her cluttered dressing table, her neat bedside table, her desk area and her Mohawk flag are the items she offers for us to see and record. She directs the camera onto herself, marking the different characters that make up what she presents as her multiple identities, and hence offering a particular version of schizophrenia as multiple personalities, with wigs, hats and facial expressions. She directs the camera onto a former version of herself – the self in a photograph of her wedding, and onto photographs of her daughter and her husband with whom she occupied a particular social role that was different from those that she now occupies. Anne is many people – a popular version of schizophrenia – with a life 'before' – the life we are invited to witness. She performs what she cannot or will not discuss and her performance offers a narrative to the *camera* instead of to a tape recorder. The images she offers invite a multiple interpretation of schizophrenia by those who see them. And they sustain a version of schizophrenic life that comprises a multiple and complex fractured collage of past and present – a life that cannot be rendered as narrative.

Other interview performances are less striking and visually manipulated, but

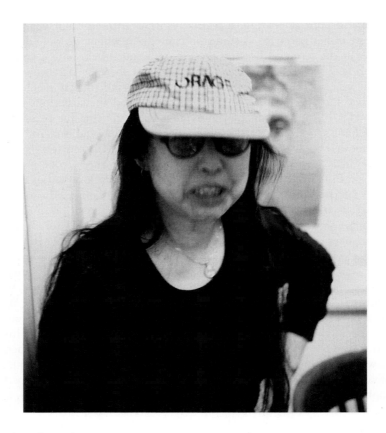

Plate 24 Anne 'storm'

nevertheless intended to convey an image of the schizophrenic self as 'dangerous', as 'unpredictable', as 'victim of circumstance', as 'really normal', as 'better', or as 'rational'. Sometimes interviews were evidently used to test the plausibility of these theories – positioning the meaning of madness from bizarre/dangerous to indistin- guishable from 'normality' – on the interviewer. Craig checked with the interviewer off tape if he *looked* like a 'mental patient': 'Can you tell? You can tell can't you?' Looking like a 'mental patient' in the social arenas beyond the interview had serious consequences: 'You are labelled. You go out for a job and they think you could accom- plish one and I never mention mental illness on the application form unless it states: 'Have you ever been in a mental institution?' (Louise). The issue here is less *being* schizophrenic than being *seen as* schizophrenic and what that entails – matters of performance. Schizophrenia can be invisible. If it has to be declared on a job applica- tion, then it is *made visible*. These are matters of public recognition, social identity and the social consequences associated with madness and they are well recognized by those who deal with them on a daily basis.

Schizophrenia involves certain 'modes of being' that may or may not be declared in public performances. Important distinctions were drawn around performances that acted out internal states and those that concealed them. Dave, who is quoted at the beginning of this chapter, distinguished the private suffering of his own version of performed madness as indistinguishable from normality, from the public exhibitions of others who display forms of personal disintegration through unkempt or bizarre behaviour. The DSM (American Psychiatric Association (1995) also recognizes these as signs of impaired social functioning – a view Dave clearly shares or at least acknowledges in his presentation of himself. Those who show dignity in their conduct, and those who allow the pain and turmoil on the inside to be transparent from the outside, are clearly distinguished in many of the accounts we collected. Dave is one of a very small number of schizophrenics with a place in the highly provisioned formal community sector. He presents himself as outwardly calm, serious and controlled and hence deserving of respect (and resources). He does not stage 'crazy', foolish, angry or bizarre performances like many of those who live in shelters and who, by implication, deserve to live in shelters. This distinction – with its implied spatiality – between the 'normal' and the 'crazy' in the performance of madness is an old one that recalls seventeenth-century versions depicted in Breughel's engravings of the fool (Gilman 1982: 33). Terrance, who lives in a private rooming house, also distances himself from the 'crazy', unhygienic, behaviour of shelter inmates, whom he refers to as 'hard core schizophrenic(s)'. He means 'people that never wash, people that are sick, people that are fuckin' nuts'. Fearful of being stuck in a shelter with the unclean crazy, he prefers to sleep on the streets when he can't afford to pay his rent. This, too, recalls earlier versions of madness that stress a lack of personal hygiene and grooming and now occupy new social contexts in homeless shelters and life on the streets. Unkempt performances of madness display a lack of self-determination and self-control. And, as we saw in Chapter 4, they enter the calculations concerning the use of commercial city space. In Terrance's calculations, to act crazy is to discount yourself. Performance and space are intricately connected.

> And if I'm able to get myself off the streets and off the coke you know, and fuckin' wash and shave, and put on clean clothes every day then fuckin' make them do it too. And if they don't want to do it that's fine because it's not for me to sit here and get down on their case alike that, but I ain't gonna put up with it. And you know I refuse to be around and that means I gotta sit on the streets.
>
> (Terrance)

Versions of schizophrenia that involve not 'acting crazy' demand self-discipline and strength of character. Performance then invokes important distinctions in the meaning of schizophrenia, which have implications for personal and social identities. Performance is the connection between private states of being and their public performance as versions of madness. It is where versions of madness are played out and stress appearance and behaviour – two very visible items in the presentation of the self in the scenes through which mad lives are lived. Performances are sometimes rendered in narrative, but sometimes they have to be read by other means – by observation or by visual representation. Those who operate these distinctions in their versions of madness have learned the psychiatric game and *its* distinctions. They have learned to be mad while not presenting themselves as mad in any overt, disquieting and disturbing public displays.

The place of schizophrenia in lives

'Why me?' was the central, unspoken, question addressed in interviews. The ability to ask and reflect on this question involves the sequential ordering of a life – spoken as autobiography – in which the circumstances surrounding the arrival of schizophrenia are noted as being connected with it. Being able to reveal the (autobiographical/ circumstantial) point at which madness makes its entry into a life is in effect an exercise in positioning it within its broader context and an attempt at answering the question 'Why me?' Positioning schizophrenia within a life also contains implied theories about its nature and meaning – also prominent concerns in interviews. The place of schizophrenia overall in the sequences constituting a life is therefore highly significant in locating its meaning, its underlying causes and the reasons why it imposed itself on a particular life. And in the stories that people tell, these three things – meaning, causes and reasons why – are intricately interwoven. The place of schizophrenia is most evident in 'onset stories', which concern the moment at which schizophrenia appears. Hence, whatever theories people have about the nature, meaning and causes of schizophrenia – even organic theories – it is always also biographically (and hence socially/spatially) located. Onset stories were graphically told and easily collectable. These involve highly memorable events, sequences and scenes. The exceptions were those who had no real sense of there being anything to discuss because they were not aware of having passed from one state or set of circumstances to another, but had some sense of themselves in vaguely medical terms. For example, we found one or two cases of 'itchy scalp' and 'sunstroke' in those whom, we were assured by workers, had diagnoses of schizophrenia. Others who had difficulty with onset stories included those who subscribed to conspiracy theories, in which schizophrenia operated as a (false) reason for detention, regulation or punishment. Those who subscribe solely to conspiracy theories – in practice these are often held in tandem with other theories that admit the 'reality' of the schizophrenia, which is simultaneously denied – instead tell stories about the onset of oppression and persecution. These are factors presented as external to themselves and for which they are not responsible rather than factors that are about the onset of some change in their personal internal equilibrium. Because onset stories are located in the other details of a life, they are presented as being consistent with a pattern of events and themes in a life and the spatial modalities through which it is lived. The onset of schizophrenia can be associated with any series of events, but is commonly linked with the experience of stress/overload surrounding the pressure of work or study or problems with significant relationships. Becoming a student, taking on a new job, the birth of a baby or loss of significant relationships through death or abandonment are frequently cited as social factors precipitating the onset of symptoms. This is so even in cases when individuals' theories of schizophrenia hold it to be biologically based.

Rhona,[5] one of the people whose story is threaded through this chapter, sets the onset of her own difficulties in her family circumstances – something that was quite common. She tells us that her mother decided to move away from Montréal and *her* mother to make a life on their own. Rhona is 14, and it is at this point that things begin to fall apart in the absence of a grandmother who has provided care and a counterpoint to her daughter's (Rhona's mother's) cruelty and physical violence towards Rhona. These circumstances culminate in Rhona's admission to psychiatric hospital

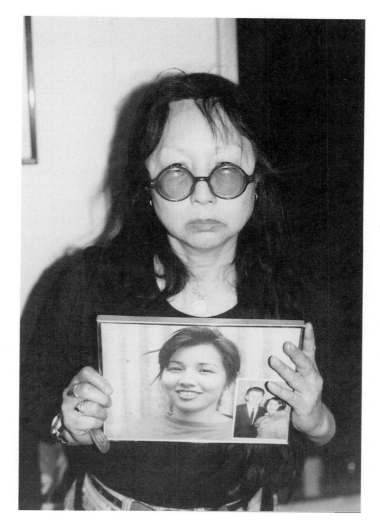

Plate 25   Anne as a child with parents

for four years in the late 1950s when such things were still possible. Further questions uncover the context of this trigger in a broader tapestry of social and life difficulties. Leaving her grandmother – a relationship dislocation expressed in spatial terms – is one of many, or one *too* many, difficulties in Rhona's life. Norma, who featured in the last chapter on the subject of having lost all of her personal possessions when the church basement in which they were stored decided to get rid of them, also details the onset of schizophrenia in the context of other events in an equally difficult life. Norma's story is one of sequential abuse by men and she discusses her present relationship in these terms, too – as part of a pattern – which sets the personal context (of vulnerability coupled with a lack of support) for the onset of her schizophrenia. Her current partner and his new girlfriend have managed to use Norma's condition to have her 11-year-old daughter removed by the courts, pointing to one of the more dramatic consequences of schizophrenia in the lives of mothers.

> I was a person, like trapped inside you know and screaming out for help, and then just putting on a good front for everybody, like everything was okay, for the longest time. And nobody don't know like the hurt and pain and the regret and the remorse, that's like, inside me ... like livin in fear, walking in fear, that sort uh thing because I didn't have no, at first, you know I didn't have anybody constructing around me when it happened to steer me the right way really – there was none in my life, so, from that my life just became a total disaster.
>
> (Norma)

Her account of schizophrenia, of being 'mentally confused', we will see below, involves inauthentic forms of personhood – based on her assessment of her failure to operate effectively as a mother – which resulted from her taking the 'wrong road in life'. Personal vulnerability to abuse and isolation provide the social context that allows schizophrenia to 'take hold' of a life in a state of stress overload, and drive it in the wrong direction. A false displacement is again expressed in spatial terms. Isolation or withdrawal from social contact with others – retreat from the world, the emptying out of the social content of a life – is the other set of social circumstances (apart from stress overload) commonly associated with the onset of schizophrenia. These are indirectly spatial displacements in which a person disappears without leaving. Most onset stories are located at the threshold of adulthood (late teens or early twenties) when other important changes are also taking place, but there were also some 'child' schizophrenics among our informants.

Turning from social circumstances to the 'manner of arrival', there are two kinds of onset story and elements of these, too, are expressed in spatial terms. Schizophrenia either arrives suddenly, without warning or it is worked up and worked on. Florence, whom we met in Chapter 2, where she outlined her dependence on the regime of the foster home in which she was living, details the sudden arrival of her schizophrenia in the following terms: 'I was home and I used to work and I was going up the stairs [this is very precisely located] and I started to have a nervous breakdown and shaking'. Even though it arrived suddenly and she is unable to give a very full account of it and the reasons why it might have happened, Florence's schizophrenia had a social context. She was walking up the stairs of her home as she had done so many times before. It happened during the period of her life in which she had worked. And, it was the mechanism that radically shifted these social/life circumstances. This constellation of circumstances contains an implied account of *why* it happened. It was connected with living at home and doing a particular job, even if no direct connection between these things is made in the narrative. Daniel's schizophrenia may not have arrived suddenly, but it was 'activated' suddenly by (stressful) social circumstances, although he also believes that it has an organic basis Daniel says: 'Schizophrenia is something you are born with. You have it for life. ... It becomes apparent when you're about 14, 15 ... I guess as the stress levels increase in your life.' Here, there is no contradiction here between organic and social factors. They simply act in tandem reinforcing each other – the possibility is there and it is activated by circumstances.

For Rick,[6] whose story is told more fully below in the section concerned with theories of schizophrenia that foreground the issue of 'reality', it was not the 'symptoms' that arrived suddenly but the 'system' that had suddenly converged upon him. He was at school in his final year and in the middle of an examination. He was, most precisely at question 59 when the principal arrived:

'You have to stop your exam and go home right now.' I said, 'What for?' He says, 'Your mother says you're very ill ... and your mind is not very functioning very properly.' I said, 'At least let me finish the exam'. [He went home] ... She [foster mother] said, 'The doctor has a court order, that you're supposed to go to the hospital ... because they need to test your blood, they need to check up on your mind, they need to see if you are delusional.' ... He [the psychiatrist] said, 'You're a schizophrenic. Schizophrenic people can't study, they can't read they're delusional ... and they're liars, and they tease and they're drug addicts and boozers.' I said, 'You think that about me?' He says, 'That's the information I got from your foster mother.'

(Rick)

This cavalcade of unwanted attention was prompted by Rick's insistence that a woman had arrived the day before with a suitcase full of money for him from his birth mother in Britain. Social services and his foster mother in Rick's version of this story are part of a plot to take his money away from him.

For others, the onset of schizophrenia is worked up and worked on over a period of time. It is earned and can be described as a process in time and place, as part of the ongoing nature of the life in which it is set. The contribution and responsibility of the schizophrenic as the *agent* of his/her suffering is more readily accommodated in this kind of onset story. When schizophrenia is sudden, it is more in the nature of an accident that strikes randomly and indiscriminately. Its *victims* of the intentions of others and random diseases and misfortunes are struck down suddenly. Craig vividly describes his own descent into schizophrenia as an accentuation of certain processes in his own life for which he is accepting some responsibility.[7]

The whole thing was a nightmare, from beginning to end it was a nightmare, for me. I was out of school, I was unemployed, I was seeing a girl at the time, not even seeing a girl, I was just speaking to her on the phone. But for me with my, illness, my illness took over and kinda hid in a little world for me. And in that world I was seeing her, more than just speaking to her on the phone. As for the phone conversation, she was calling me three times a day at a certain point, but for me my head got carried away with the whole thing, and um I found myself, getting obsessed with the idea of thinking that the girl was a girlfriend ... but not stalking her. What happened was, the radios and stuff and the TV because I was schizophrenic, seemed to be talking to me and telling me things.

(Craig)

Craig's contribution was that he colluded in allowing things to get out of hand and out of proportion. He is, by extension, responsible for getting them back into proportion and so his schizophrenia is something over which he exercises a certain amount of control. It is also connected in his telling of it with a budding relationship and the circumstances in which he lived with his family and had no job to go to.

Onset stories are also charged with identifying what it is that marks the appearance of schizophrenia. For most people, and for Craig, this meant hearing voices, although in one case it involved seeing visions, and in a few cases it involved only incidents of bizarre or otherwise inexplicable behaviour leading to arrest or detention in a psychiatric hospital. Voices occupy an important place within accounts of the nature and meaning of schizophrenia in lives. From the accounts we heard, they clearly terrorize those who hear them. What the voices say can usually be linked with themes, problems or general social circumstances of the life in which they intervene. They are highly contextual. God instructs those of religious faith, mothers and grandmothers issue the usual instructions and warnings and television sets give directions that make sense in the overall context of the life in which they occur – hence their capacity to terrorize. Thomas who, as we saw in Chapter 2, first recognized his social position as a black man with the onset of his 'mania' and 'delusions' and the arrival of the police in force, hears voices that are about the symbolism of blackness in a particular kind of racial politics of counter-assertion advocated by the Nation of Islam and its claims concerning early black civilization.

> I was greater than Bob Marley. … I saw myself as an Egyptian person, like my face was really big and everything and I had a body like I seemed I was around 10 feet tall and just this giant. But I was black. I looked like an Egyptian, something that you'd see in those old Egyptian photos or, um, rocks, carvings.
>
> (Thomas)

Thomas's delusions involve biblical images of King Solomon and Ahab, whom he says are high priests. This particular set of images is supplied by the political rhetoric of the Nation of Islam, which mobilizes a racial politics of counter-assertion that reinserts black people – whom it conceptualizes in terms of notions of biological race – into the history of Egyptian civilization. Race does not respect the boundaries of public and political life. It is a social category used to refer to people like Thomas and draw attention to their social marginality. So what is it doing in Rhona's mother's relationship with Rhona's father and why has it become part of Thomas' delusion? Clearly emotional relationships and delusions are socially mediated by the local racial order and the imagery and tensions it supplies. Voices also serve to convince (sufferers as well as psychiatrists guided by DSM IV (American Psychiatric Association 1995)) of the 'reality' of schizophrenia: proof if it is needed that there really *is* something wrong, because hearing voices is widely regarded as 'not normal'. Voices are also the most commonly cited reason for taking medication, which is otherwise unpopular and provides its own forms of additional difficulty and suffering. Voices are ameliorated, if not controlled, by medication and the fear that they will return and take over is strong enough to overcome the disadvantages and unpleasant side-effects that come with medication regimes. Onset stories also contain graphic accounts of first contact with systems of psychiatric referral. They contain accounts of how referral was initiated – frequently by the person themselves, by close family, friends and neighbours – by those in close social contact and not outside agencies. Onset stories contain certain clues about what schizophrenia is, why and how it works itself into lives, and the kinds of social and personal racialized circumstances with which it is associated. Further discussion of stories in which the meaning of schizophrenia is more clearly indicated through certain themes and combinations of themes, provides further insight. These themes also allow us to trace any connections with psychiatric frameworks and say something about versions of psychiatric thinking that prevail in community settings.

Popular versions of schizophrenia

Schizophrenia is formulated in popular thinking so as to stress conceptions of the schizophrenic as the bearer of a 'split' or 'multiple' personality and as potentially volatile and dangerous (Philo 1996: 45–81). Parker *et al.* (1995) note that popular versions of schizophrenia are not separate from psychiatric versions, which subscribe to popular demonology in admitting that the schizophrenic subject is an object of public fear. As dangerousness is dealt with more fully in the next chapter, we will mainly be concerned in this section with the idea that schizophrenia is about split or multiple personality. Anne performed this version of schizophrenia for our camera. It also surfaced in some of the stories we collected. Sometimes it was combined with other versions of schizophrenia that made use of medical discourse, or with versions of schizophrenia that stress its behaviour manifestations.

Plate 26   Anne at the drop-in centre

Split personality, I hear thoughts, you shake your foot. You know, smoke a lot of cigarettes ... seizures ... craziness ... madness ... maybe I say stupid things you know, but I don't mean it, I just say it because it's there to be said.

(Wycliff)

Wycliff's version of schizophrenia combines popular conceptions with fragments of lifestyle, muscular responses and a loss of control over narrative.[8] These elements are apparently discrete, connected only by their impact on him and his life. The rest of his story does not elaborate on, or in any way demonstrate the split-personality theme he repeats in this list. Popular versions of schizophrenia frequently had to contend with the fact that they are not born out by the *experience* of schizophrenia. For Rhona this cast doubt on the veracity of her diagnosis:

I was diagnosed with something. I think it was schizophrenia. But I never quite understood why they categorize it as schizophrenia because the schizophrenic person I had seen, like on the 'Oprah Winfrey Show', or something like that [was] somebody who has twelve different personalities. But, uh that was my diagnosis. Because I told them I was feeling sick.

(Rhona)

She deals with this apparent contradiction by 'working' her story so as to sustain her psychiatric diagnosis – and hence the authority of her psychiatrist – *and* the popular thinking on which it *must* be based because it was played out on television – the ultimate test of reality.

I'm a schizophrenic [she continues with more certainty] because I take fits, I mean I could be sitting here talking to you and the next thing I could go across the room, or the table could be flying [alluding to her unpredictability or even dangerousness]. I'm a schizophrenic – dual personality, more than one personality. Sometimes I do [agree with this diagnosis] and sometimes I don't. You know it depends on me, or who ever I'm talking to. If they feel inside themselves, yes, she really *is* a schizophrenic – [so it is also a matter of others' versions of her based on certain kinds of performance]. There's a side of me. [Pause, and then she hits on how it all fits together – her situation and the people on the 'Oprah Winfrey Show'.] Do you know about the film work here in Montréal? That's what I do. I'll take an extra part in a film. *That's* the other side of me, so there you are, I would say I'm a schizophrenic because I could do all this – the minute I get a phone call to do a movie, I'm a different person. My personality changes automatically.

(Rhona)

Popular versions of schizophrenia are for Rhona, as for Wycliff, anchored in muscular spasms and the temporary loss of consciousness and control over the body – described as 'fits'. The issue of multiple personality is resolved by Rhona in recounting the job she is periodically able to do as a film extra. Multiple personalities are shifted onto multiple parts: the dramatic possibilities of multiple performances in films. There is extensive work available in the large number of Hollywood and other films shot in

Montréal. Ironically Rhona was often used to play parts she might well occupy in real life. She told us she had played drunks and homeless street people in background shots. She is able to list the films she has worked on, tell us how much she has earned, and produce an album of photos taken while she was working, which operate as trophies and evidence supporting her story. Jim also wraps popular understanding around his own experience. Less imaginative than Rhona's account, his elides the two characters comprising him with the voices he 'imagines' hearing.

> Having one character that says one thing and another character that says another … having two different, especially when I talk to myself, that's sort of my schizophrenia. … I imagine people talking to me, I just *imagine* I don't *hear* voices … sometimes I hear *society* talking to me, yea, which is not normal [laughs].
>
> (Jim)

In being able to distinguish reality from the 'imaginary' voices and run a commentary on the 'normal', Jim is pursuing the theory that he is 'better'. He manipulates fragments of psychiatric understanding in order to do this, implicitly addressing (in search of confirmation) those (psychiatrists) who have the authority to confirm his recovery. But he does so in a way that does not disturb the popular conception of schizophrenia as 'split personality'. Andrew's version of schizophrenia pivots on erratic and unpredictable behaviour and is arranged by a classic film representation of madness narrated as bedlam comedy. 'One day, it was Christmas and I freaked out, like *One Flew Over the Cuckoo's Nest*. I started running in the hall ah! Ah! Ah! All over and through the tunnel upstairs, and I smashed the door, the Christmas tree' (Andrew). The failure of popular conceptions of schizophrenia to square with experience does not lessen their hold on the explanatory frameworks operated by schizophrenics to account for their situation. Experience and biographical detail *can* accommodate this kind of dissonance. Behaviour, organic (muscular) factors and notions of schizophrenia as a 'sickness' or as volatile multiple personalities coexist in the same explanatory framework without disturbing each other. The popular is embedded in a framework of explanation, effect and cause, *and* it operates as a test of the veracity of diagnostic categories.

Entering a different reality

For many people schizophrenia involves living in a different reality where the 'normal' expectations and social relationships and social rules do not apply. Accounts of schizophrenia that invoke 'reality' have a number of layers. Concern with reality makes fleeting appearances in a number of stories. But it is most insightfully and centrally discussed by Rick, who exposes some of its layers. Rick, who is almost 30 and who came from Jamaica as a 10-year-old, lives in one of the city's homeless hostels. Because he liked being visited by us when we were at the hostel and enjoyed telling us stories, he was interviewed on tape six times. He sometimes repeated bits of his stories word for word in more than one interview so they were either well rehearsed or well remembered. We became temporarily part of the way in which he dealt with the painful experiences we had asked him to recount: 'I got a lot off my chest, and that's about it. … And so I keep it all bundle up inside, I said, Oh, I got to let you know.' In the process of these many interviews we learned rather a lot about his thinking and circumstances that helps us understand his version of madness as a configuration of theories that centre on parallel realities. His stories contain diverse theories of the schizophrenia (and manic depression) that he variously owns and denies. He owns these things most often in his theories of reality, and denies them most in the context of the conspiracy theories he uses to connect and make sense of otherwise disparate events he needs to remember. We return to some of these in the section on conspiracy theories.

Asked to tell us about his 'problems', Rick comments first on others: 'There's people that's missing from the reality section … ', and then on himself: 'Only problem I have is that I missed out on a few years of … you know, reality with the public.' The reality invested in the public is the first of several strands of the reality lost in schizophrenia. Rick says: 'I have been *out of society* for a long time … I haven't been *around society* for a long time'. By society he means a particular slice of public life – bars, restaurants and movies – city places for the consumption of entertainment. These are spaces other people use because they have jobs and can afford it. He doesn't have a job and can't afford it. But not having a job is not the only reason he can't afford it. His story is about being cheated of money that is rightfully his: money accumulated from unused welfare benefits, money he thinks his birth mother sent from Britain but he did not receive. In fact he does not have control over his financial affairs at all because he is not deemed responsible and so they are in public curatorship. But there are other reasons for his particular form of social exile: 'When I walk among people, I get the interpretation that … somebody spread the news already this … guy is a mental retard schizophrenic' (Rick). Schizophrenia *is* the unreality of social exile and social exile is the consequence of the real or imagined reactions of others to schizophrenia in public spaces that, for Rick, operate as arenas of public judgement. Space is constituted in this instance by the social relationships invoking stated and imagined forms of public judgement. There is still a further, racialized, layer to the unreality of social exile and connects and explains other things that have happened to him, which he needs to remember. This concerns his experiences from the age of 10 within the local education system. He was, he says, put back two grades because he came from Jamaica where the education system could not be as good as the one to which he had moved. His father, with whom he lives, loses custody of him to local social services: the outcome of *their judgement* of his capacities – mediated by their assumptions about black masculinity – as a parent. His mother, for reasons he does not explain, lives in Britain. Consequently, he is processed through the child welfare system and juvenile justice system. He trails through a series of foster homes and into contact with the local police, whose interface with the black population is rather aggressive. His account of schizophrenia, it seems, must also be able to accommodate these experiences of being black. The unreality of social exile shifts from one spatial context to another connecting the events remembered as 'Rick's life'. These are the sum of the accumulated social judgements, actions, agencies and processes supervising the passage of this particular black child into adulthood in a white society. This incremental racism is embedded in the network of systems administering his life. Individually insignificant, these things have consequences that accumulate to affect his life in highly significant ways.

Two further layers of unreality – also connected with this theme of social exile – appear as he describes his experiences of hospitalization.

> I saw a uh 18-year-old girl came into *** [name of hospital]. She got pregnant, she had a baby ... and then she doesn't know where to go no more. ... She comes back to the hospital every day to visit her friend, because, she doesn't, she's lost herself from reality ... she don't have no more friends, the friends she had they dump her because she ended up in a mental institution. ... She don't want, they don't want to talk to her, they don't want to hang with her, they, she, they think she's a basket case.
>
> (Rick)

Rick stumbles over whether the source of the information that she is a 'basket case' comes from the girl or her friends. He stumbles because he recognizes himself and his own confusion. He thinks others see *him* as a basket case and he suspects and fears they might be right: in practice these two things – seeing yourself in certain terms and being seen by others – are interconnected. He is describing the unreality of her (and his) 'lost self': a direct acknowledgement that a kind of unreality is embedded in the grammar of schizophrenia itself and the scenes on which it is played out. Another unreality compounds this unreality: the unreality of hospitalization – a world closed off from a lot more than a few bars and cinemas.

> When you go to the hospital, the hospital life is like, you don't know reality no more. ... You don't know what reality is, it's hard to function like that. Basically I live on my life from when I was 1 year old 'til I was 17. [When he was diagnosed schizophrenic. This has another significance too. It was his last year of a childhood. At 18 his wardship ended and he was passed on to the adult mental health care system and public curatorship.] That's the basic life I live on. That's the reality I live on.
>
> (Rick)

The parallel reality of madness fades into the parallel reality of its therapeutic solution. In the practical contexts of lives, the problem and its professional/administrative solutions are all part of the same thing.

Rick's narrative shifts between several layers of unreality and forms of social exile, dissecting the spatial arrangement of his life, that give substance to his view that schizophrenia is a parallel reality – a distinctive plane in which he lives alone and with those who share his situation. In this formulation schizophrenia correctly registers his own experience of social exile, and is erroneously applied to him in yet another conspiracy. The disavowal in schizophrenia in conspiracy theories is supported by recourse to accounts of schizophrenia as organic and rooted in maternal health. Rick tells us that 'real mental illness' comes from alcohol and drug abuse in pregnancy. This involves a set of circumstances that do not apply to *him* and sustain the view that he is *not* schizophrenic. ' I was a healthy baby.'

To claim to have been erroneously placed within the reality maze is one route out of it. It raises the prospect of the mistake being recognized, rectified or challenged. There is another route out – a form of accommodation that recognizes to some extent the

Plate 27   Versions of Anne

validity of schizophrenia and its parallel reality. Rick tells us that the erosion of reality means:

> [Being seen as a] mental retarded person, I mean your whole family, your friends gone, the people you talk to is gone, they don't deal with you no more. And if you have money they come and grab your money from you and they take what you got and then they're gone, and leave you in a hole ... so it goes. ... I mean this is something I've been through.
>
> (Rick)

The solution is:

> I live my reality from 17 backwards [onset of schizophrenia] till I'm the age of 1 – and that's why I don't freak out, because my life is based on church ... my life is based on church and based on Royalty [the Queen is the Canadian Head of State], and my family and cookin' and cleanin' and givin' me bath and taking care of me and things like that. These are, my life, is based on Jamaica, 'til I'm 17 years old in Montréal. ... Since I was 18 I went to the

hospital, I live then that life backwards. I don't try to focus on the life ahead of me, ahead of 17, cause I never got the chance to be there, I never had the chance to look at it, a chance to focus on the reality of it. ... [Do you think you will ever live forward?] I cannot live forward; it is too late for that.

(Rick)

The reality that can be relied upon, upon which the self can be anchored, lies outside of the schizophrenia, in the past, before it struck. Significantly, the healthy earlier, pre-schizophrenic Rick is located in Jamaica – the place of his birth (right). This sustains the view that there is an authentic self that is unafflicted by the distortion of reality that is schizophrenia and that his new (schizophrenic) 'immigrant self' is doubly pathological. It is both sick and transplanted. If the authentic self can be remembered, then another more authentic reality can be established as a counterpoint to the present. This is one of several anchorage points on an otherwise moving land-scape. The others are the solid rituals of everyday life – the symbolic reality invested in the Queen as the (colonial) sovereign of both halves of Rick's heritage and the head of state of the jurisdiction in which his birth mother lives, and the church. Mother, Queen, country and God – the symbolic heads of quite divergent territories – attest to the real, early version of Rick and the possibility that he may again recover the authentic self. The 'symbolic' and the 'quotidian' stand in for the 'really real' when reality is placed in question by schizophrenia.[9] Rick's is of course a much more complicated and highly textured account of reality than that offered in DSM IV (American Psychiatric Association 1995) as plausibility.

Conceptions of schizophrenia utilizing notions of disease

Accounts of schizophrenia make extensive use of biological conceptions of disease. This does not necessarily align them just with psychiatric thinking, although certain psychiatric interpretations of schizophrenia are more rooted in biological disease, than social, models. We found that notions of disease travelled rather freely and fluidly between body and mind without respecting the boundaries of specialization in medical knowledge and practice between psychiatry and general medicine. Psychiatrists and other kinds of doctors are not necessarily distinguished, and the generic term 'doctor' was often applied to consultations with psychiatrists despite wide recognition that some doctors had (because they are backed by) legal powers. Conceptions of schizophrenia drawing upon biological models of disease were very common, and held in combination with other theories as we saw in Rick's narrative. Schizophrenia is frequently referred to as a 'disease', an 'incurable disease' or a 'mental infection'. Myrna thinks her 'mental infection' was triggered by sunstroke: 'I had a mental infection for a long time since I'm a young girl. ... Infection, it goes in your head like its right in your in your system. ... I don't know how that happened ... it grows in your system'.[10]

Joan also thinks it is a disease.[11]

Sickness, schizophrenia is a sickness to me. Is like something that, no matter what I do I wouldn't get helped. I wouldn't be cured. So it's bothering me to know that I have this disease and there is no cure for it. Even though I prayed.

Even though I go to the doctor. This is something I have that can't go away. … If you're schizophrenic, you have to go to the doctor. You're not free. You have to. That's, that's mandatory. … He can call the police.

(Joan)

Joan echoes aspects of psychiatric framing in which schizophrenia is incurable, and has therefore to be accepted and accommodated. Daniel, who has had electroconvulsive therapy (ECT), thinks schizophrenia is a disease like others, but caused by 'chemical balances in the brain', most likely *one* of many possible psychiatric formulations that stress organic factors. In it the brain operates as the site of a 'real' physical or organic problem.

Being schizophrenic means, um, well, it's just, it's just like being diabetic or epileptic, or any of these types of things. Um it's just an illness. It's just a chemical imbalance in my brain. And in my body, that has different kinds of symptoms. And I have to deal with it. And the lessons of the whole stigma attached to it, and the lessons of the dramatics, and the trips of schizophrenia … in the morning I'm going to wake up (groaning) like this from medication … walk around all day half stoned out of my head. That's about it. It doesn't mean I can't be successful.

(Daniel)

Encouraged to expand on this, Daniel reveals that it is his diabetes/epilepsy that *caused* his schizophrenia. This is not an accidental or idiosyncratic connection but one commonly noted (along with sunstroke) in interviews in London as well as in Montréal. Daniel stumbles and stalls when he is asked what he thinks schizophrenia is. Either he suspects that we know and we are testing him, or he thinks it is obvious and not, therefore, something that demands discussion. Daniel's version of schizophrenia as a disease is underwritten by what he perceives as its hereditary nature in his family. His uncle, Craig, is diagnosed as schizophrenic. And his cousin, he concludes after cataloguing a series of seemingly unconnected defects, is also schizophrenic.

Well my whole family. … [He backs off and qualifies, although he thinks his whole family suffers from poor mental health if not schizophrenia.] There's a cousin who was born with the cord round her neck so she had her air chopped off, so she's brain damaged and she's also schizophrenic so she has to take medication … she was hyperactive and they gave her Ritalin. … I had an aunt that just died of diabetes, and diabetes has some cultural aspects to it.

(Daniel)

Bernard connects mental with physical sickness.[12] 'Your emotions are tentacles in your brain, doing different things'. Tony, who was given ECT, shows how medical narratives work in offering minimal explanation to those who are unable to give an account of themselves and what has happened to them. Tony has a sense of himself in vaguely medicalized terms: he suffers from 'itchy scalp' and 'painful wisdom teeth', and these things stand in for the various psychiatric treatments he has received but which he is unable to recount. Unusually among our informants, schizophrenia, its meanings and implications, does not impinge upon his account of himself and his life, which is 'written' by other means.

Medical versions of schizophrenia rarely stand alone. Although firmly committed to the idea of disease, Daniel concedes that schizophrenia is also a 'type of lifestyle'. The disease entity combines with its social impact as we saw in onset stories. This is another version of a similar elision made by Rick's account of reality. The lifestyle Daniel refers to incorporates the difficulty he has living independently and the effects of the medication regimes on which he reluctantly relies. Twenty years old, he lives with an uncle, which makes him unlike most of the people we interviewed who are without active family connections and support, and perhaps this accounts for his optimism about the future.

Those who subscribe primarily to versions of schizophrenia as a disease are less questioning of medication and less reflexive in their stories about it. Medical explanation serves to close out further reflection. Medicalized versions of schizophrenia absolve the patient of responsibility for causing their condition and encourage them to submit to medical solutions that involve prescription medication. Thus, psychiatric conditions are absorbed into the routine medicine outside of the hospital and its regimes of occasional contact with doctors; a system already fitted to community contexts. The regime of the psychiatric hospital survives its abolition as a place. The use of medical idiom often coexists with other kinds of explanations. Medical versions of schizophrenia as disease are compatible with popular conceptions or with conceptions of schizophrenia as the loss of the authentic self, and they are frequently framed, as we saw in some of the onset stories above, by the social spatially configured circumstances in which they occur. We may think of versions of schizophrenia as overlapping and drawing simultaneously on more than one source of information and understanding.

Loss of the authentic self

Conceptions of schizophrenia as the loss of more real, authentic, versions of the self are typically combined with the disease models, again displaying the social nature of medicalized constructs individuals use to explain their lives. In these accounts it is the self (and not just the brain) that registers the impact of the disease in its functioning and in its social relationships. The ill, inauthentic self operates as the basis for a new social identity with a new set of social circumstances and social relationships, which in turn ensures both its perpetuation and consequent further loss. The 'real' self in this dynamic becomes ever further away – hidden in the inner recesses of a life. Joan, whose conceptions of schizophrenia – as we saw in the last section – lean also on disease models, notes the gap between the 'real' private inner self (this corresponds with our earlier discussion of the existential as a felt inner self) and the false (ill) self of the disease and its public (popular/administrative) representation. It is her 'disabling public self' that stands in the way of realizing the inner self, which is somehow resilient to the disease, and which prevents her leading what she thinks of as a 'normal life' in which she gets married and has children.

I think that other people think of schizophrenics that you are crazy. You're crazy and you're not capable of maintaining yourself as a respected person. ... It bothers me a lot being schizophrenic because it is like a disease, like cancer. And living a life where all your life [is] on the medication doesn't give me the hope to become the person that I want to in the future.

(Joan)

This is another version of the complicated 'reality' accounts of schizophrenia examined above. As in reality versions of schizophrenia, the disease or problem is elided with its treatment – the medication – which exacerbates the disability of the disease in placing the authentic self even further out of reach. Norma (who also thinks schizophrenia is a disease) sets her authentic self (by which she means the self that was deserving of her own and others' respect) in the part of her life that predates the disease in which she lived with her daughter and husband in Jamaica.[13]

The way I was when I leave Jamaica when I was 21. I was a proper person, I used to travel, I've been on the US naval base in Cuba with all my friends, all of them, all over. I was a totally different person; it's all night and day now. Like I lost my own self, my own self-esteem, when you lost your self-esteem, and your self-respect ... how am I and what I have been through?

(Norma)

Norma lost her real self, her home (with husband and child) and her homeland at roughly the same time, and it is likely that these things are connected. The self is lost – to madness (and prostitution) – at the same time it is cut free from two senses of home as hearth and land. As with Rick the authentic self is sited in the homeland, also coincidentally (?), Jamaica. Again this appears to elide the immigrant and the sick self as dual forms of in-authenticity. As Norma's story proceeds, it is clear that there is another loss – the loss of the self that is moulded by moral and sexual codes. The (inauthentic) schizophrenic self survives by adopting further forms of 'in-authenticity' – by becoming a prostitute. The inauthentic self is uprooted from household and homeland, its moral and sexual codes and the regard of others. Norma's story is a story of multiple loss of multiple senses of the self, which are evidently gendered as well as raced.

Spiritual suffering and punishment

The place of spirituality in making sense of schizophrenia cannot be overestimated. We collected numerous references to spiritual suffering and experiences even when these were not centrally placed in accounts of the meaning of schizophrenia. Religious faith offers a way of coping with schizophrenia, biblical explanation accounts for the reasons why some people get schizophrenia and not others, and religious experiences feature in giving substance to voices and visions experienced by schizophrenics. This is sustained by the central place of religious groups in this most ex-Catholic city in providing venues and services in the informal community mental health sector. For Dave, who also subscribes to the idea that schizophrenia is a disease, his experiences of episodes of spiritual suffering and punishment explain why he has this disease. It is a divine punishment for a life misled. 'God made me schizophrenic to punish me ... for wasting my youth, for the things I did as a child.' Religious imagery also provides the content of his delusions – he was convinced he was a prophet – and a church-run homeless shelter provides him with a place to live. For Tina, schizophrenia was a medical/spiritual problem.[14] 'So, it's a big complicated personal story why I'm sick ... a lot of people wouldn't understand it. They would just say, "Okay Tina, you have schizophrenia and that's it." But it's spiritual problem for me.' Derrik's account of schizophrenia is particularly insightful as it combines all of the possible contributions of spirituality – the content of his delusions, the reason why he has them, and a way of coping with them.[15] In a parody of biblical reasoning his delusions and visions are responsible for his conversion to Christianity. He also demonstrates the combination of scientific rationalist accounts with the spiritual. His schizophrenia is quite precisely a 'chemical imbalance in the brain', which results in him hearing (not thinking he hears) angel's voices. This is not so bad, he explains at the soup kitchen where we speak to him, as some people hear Satan and develop a 'persecution complex'.

> Other people go the other direction. I'm hearing angels and just as bad you know. And there's no experience with these voices. You can't understand the experience. You could never, could never tell somebody what this experience is like. You could never explain it to them. It's too deep. I've tried everything to lose it. The first voice I heard was Jesus Christ. This was when I became a Christian. So how do you feel when someone tells you, 'It's the biggest blasphemy I've ever heard'. ... You have to deal with the things that people say. The voices say things to you and they are so direct with it you know. It'll sound like truth, whether it's truth or not. ... It's a very terrible experience. It's a virtual reality. It's a virtual reality, you can touch it, you can feel it. ... [He goes on to admit that this situation, and the brain in which it is sited, is more complicated than religion or psychology can deal with. But this only serves to affirm his belief in God as creator.] He [God] created something incredible when he created man and woman ... and someone screwed around with it [the creation] ... and we're paying for it. ... Freud wouldn't treat schizophrenia ... you know he treated neurotics ... so all the psychology may be in a lot of ways coming at it from the wrong direction. I think in a lot of ways, as a Christian, I believe it is an unclean spirit ... we really don't know enough about the mind to know what it is. ... I think it was stress – the stress of the university, the stress of my adolescence. [Derrik's onset story is set in his university career. He is a native Canadian, brought up – like other native children – by white foster parents as part of an aggressive assimilation policy, having spent his early life on a native reservation in Nova Scotia.] ... You know what adolescence is like. It's a terrible time for everybody. Especially when you're fat.
>
> (Derrik)

Spirits fill the deficit in the chemical imbalance theory of psychiatry and therapeutic failure by providing both explanations for schizophrenia and clues about coping strategies. Psychiatry provides neither. Unclean spirits are activated by a chemical imbalance in the brain and its social context in the stress of adolescence terrorized by pressures of body image and more. And another highly imaginative multi-dimensional theory of schizophrenia is set in the social/existential context of a life.

Conspiracy theories

Conspiracy theories were a reasonably common explanation for a *diagnosis* of schizophrenia. Conspiracy theorists, of course, either deny the veracity of schizophrenia or consider it erroneously applied to them as a social management strategy. In this respect they are different from the theories of the meaning of schizophrenia discussed so far. The difficulty for those who subscribe to them lies in their elision with psychiatric formulations of schizophrenia as involving various forms of paranoia. Conspiracy theories lean on more sociological accounts of madness as deviance requiring social control, developed by what is often referred to as anti-psychi-atrists. The conspiracy theories we heard were importantly sustained by two sources: the local history of psychiatry's involvement in the CIA drug experiments referred to in Chapter 1, and the experience of being 'dealt with' by psychiatry and other agencies from an early age. The history of Montréal psychiatry quite reasonably sustains the local belief that psychiatry continues to experiment and test new drugs on the live human bodies of the mad. Rick was one of the many people who told us he had been used to test new drugs: 'I went to hospital and they told me they'd pay me to test medication.' Although this may refer to legitimate drug trials – which are now highly regulated and covered by ethics certification – (can the mad give informed consent?) this is clearly an issue on which there is a great deal of misunderstanding between psychiatrist and patient. These fears of violation were most potent for those who subscribed more generally to conspiracy theories and in which a large number of appa-ratuses, and not just psychiatry, converged upon them. In some conspiracy theories psychiatry operates, not on its own account, but as the agent of 'government'. In these, the government acts as a central point in a web of conspirators connecting otherwise discrete encounters with different agencies into a major theme in the telling of a life.

Vincent's story combines these two sources of conspiracy. He offered the most vivid of all accounts of madness as an *excuse* for intervention and social regulation. In order to understand Vincent you have to imagine him as I often saw him outside of inter-view situations, passing through the area where I lived on his way down town. Neatly dressed in sports clothes and travelling at high speed on a drop-handled bicycle, deter-mined, self-directed, head down, he yelled at others (like myself) also using the cycle path in a slower and less determined way to 'get out of his way'. Vincent told us that he was put into mental hospital not because of his madness, but because of his rebel-liousness, as someone who does not (in a highly regulated society) 'go along with the show'. Vincent – one of the child psychiatric patients in our group of informants – and (he suggests) other children (aged 9–14) were 'locked up' in a 'mental hospital', 'just to keep their mouths shut'. It was here that he was 'used as a guinea pig' as the authorities tried out drug treatments on him. This is what he had to say:

> One day – sudden without warning or context – the *schooling system* said, 'We'll put Vincent in a mental hospital'.
> It was a good place because I did interesting things I never did in High School ... and then there's those mental patients, you know. They're like

everybody else. Somebody's good at some things and somebody's not. Somebody can pick up things if they went to school or read books on it and can pick it up like that [snaps his fingers]. And then there are people that are slow at some things and fast at some things and don't have a mental problem classified in society [he says he was seen as 'retarded' a common complaint], you know ... so they're no different from anybody else but ... [they are] like everyone else and that's what it is about. We cannot train this individual like they've done with 99 per cent of society ... so we're talking about 26 million people, 28 million people in Canada and we're talking about 28 million people who've been trained to walk in Frankenstein, Dr Frankenstein's foot-steps, and 100,000 refuse and they don't know why ... I wouldn't go about training. And another thing ... we're not here to condition people's minds.

(Vincent)

Having been dealt with by the child welfare system, child psychiatric services, the juvenile justice system, adult psychiatric services, the adult welfare system, and the *ad hoc* arrangements of community mental health provision, Vincent has an acute sense of the regulatory apparatus organizing his life as a *black man* and he is used to doing battle with it. These apparatuses converge in a particular way on a black man feeding his conspiracy theory with the experience of being dealt with in a particular way. Being poor and homeless (he moves between the rooming-house sector and homeless shelters) is both hard work and a highly administered condition. It is not therefore unreasonable for Vincent to see himself as the centre of multi-agency attention. What unites this apparatus – apart from its focus on Vincent – is its 'game of control'. In this formulation the mental health system is indistinguishable from the welfare system or the justice system or the electricity company. In Vincent's experience, utility companies fade into highly empowered social agencies and all other aspects of a highly regulated public culture, from litter wardens to mall security guards. Vincent has been told what to do by others for his entire life, and yet he cuts his own track, unimpeded along the cycle path – evidence that the conspiracy has failed because he has outwitted it, which is, of course, his version of his story.

Rick, whose account of schizophrenia as a loss of reality was detailed above, also believes that he – and his father – were the victims of a multifaceted conspiracy. His story is included here because it details another kind of multiple conspiracy and because it coexists with another version of the meaning of schizophrenia that both admits and denies its veracity. The ambivalent admission and denial of schizophrenia is fairly common, and Rick shows how conspiracy does not necessarily entail the denial of schizophrenia, but can cohabit with it. Admitting his schizophrenia by providing cogent accounts of the loss of various levels of 'reality', Rick then denies it by saying that his only 'problem' is the way he has been 'used and abused by doctors and by public curators' (who have taken over his money). The problem is hence both a genuine loss of reality and the administration of his affairs as someone who has been unjustly diagnosed as schizophrenic. Such ambivalence is not uncommon and reflects the telling of different versions of a life and its inherent unevenness: the combination of lucidity and coping with despair and confusion. At the centre of the conspiracy that dogs Rick's life is the Canadian Government: the fulcrum of a set of all-controlling tentacles. He encounters the government as a young immigrant to Canada from

Jamaica; he encounters its child welfare system when he is removed from his father's custody by social services; he encounters its police force as a young black man on the streets of Montréal; and he encounters its adult welfare and health system as a psychiatric patient. Being black or Jamaican is a matter of which spaces operate in the networks of governance and on what terms. He thinks the *system* has stolen his money. The financial dimensions of the conspiracy are compounded by the medical: medical mishandling killed his father, and medical experiments were conducted on him while he was in hospital, almost killing him too. This is a version of genocide.

> They just brought me to the hospital to test the new medication that came out on the market, on me just to see how it works, I just see if that – if the medication can be used, for other patients also. They tested lots [lists them] ... they test all these things on me. ... They went to court to get a court order for me to take medication, the court never saw who I was, the court don't even know who I am, and they give order for the doctor to give me medication, they almost kill me five times ... the doctor overdose me and I have to go take a cold shower.
>
> (Rick)

Psychiatric diagnosis and handling is embedded in versions of agencies as indistinguishable from each other and united by their convergence on an individual. Conspiracy theories tie together and make sense of otherwise disparate aspects of a black life. And they position the individual as victim *or* as victor in the struggles they involve. Vincent triumphs, but Rick is a victim of multiple adverse circumstances. They both admit *and* deny the veracity of mental distress.

Psychiatry and the meaning of schizophrenia

Accounts of schizophrenia utilize and combine many different strands of thinking in establishing the meaning of schizophrenia in the context of a life. In the accounts we have examined we catch glimpses of psychiatric thinking, explanation and encounters. These are set in the geographies of the city described in Chapters 2, 3 and 4 and not in their former sites of hospitals. Schizophrenia is set in the context of life events, notions of disease and chemical imbalance in the brain. Set the problem within broader medical discourses, conceptions of disease and chronicity combined with accounts of spirituality and reality, and stories are told in ways that re-live their telling in therapeutic contexts. There is evidence that psychiatry provides, not a framework, but bits of knowledge that are drawn upon and combined with other bits of knowledge in 'working' versions of schizophrenia. Psychiatry is neither irrelevant nor a central source of understanding in a schizophrenic's accounts of what schizophrenia means. It is one of many resources to be drawn upon selectively to provide the required bits of information, but it is generally no more significant a source of self-understanding for schizophrenics than popular or religious conceptions.

Interactions between psychiatry and its patients are anyway fraught with misunderstanding over the use of medication. People remembered their encounters with psychiatry as periods of time spent in hospital and set a good deal of store on whether they were treated kindly or not. But just as important were relationships with other patients. Periods of hospitalization, especially for multiple re-entry patients, all merged into each other leaving an overall impression. Sometimes the names of special doctors or nurses were remembered and sometimes there was continuity of care under a particular psychiatrist, but most often there was not. Evidently some entered into negotiations with psychiatrists, even over the issue of diagnosis. Jim describes what is clearly a negotiation with the psychiatrist to re-route his diagnosis away from schizophrenia towards anxiety, a much less serious condition:

> Well, they say, 'How are you?' and this and that and I say 'Fine', and then we start to have the same talk ... but it would go in circles really. A big circle, they don't stay on one basic line, it goes round this circle. I think there's one thing wrong with me and they think it's another. ... They are not very strict with the, about the, you know, what went wrong. ... I enjoy that because I'm not sure myself, you know what's actually wrong with me ... we hope to get to a compromise ... you know, is it anxiety (him, he thinks he lacks the confidence and security which comes with working) or is it paranoia? (them).
>
> (Jim)

Jim is one of many who are prepared to negotiate with psychiatrists on the rare occasions that they get to see one. There are others who are far more compliant with psychiatric stories about who they are and what is wrong with them, although, as we have seen, medically worked accounts are threaded through biographies in their broader social contexts and narrative genres.

Medication regimes, which as we saw in earlier chapters were rather haphazard, formed the main conduit between psychiatry and their schizophrenic occasional patients. The prescription, although not the enforcement of medication regimes, remains firmly within psychiatric jurisdiction. Most of the people we interviewed were managed either through regular injections on a weekly, bi-weekly or monthly basis, or by taking medication in the form of pills on a daily basis. Medication is a major reason why schizophrenics come into contact with the health care system, and it is highly significant in mediating relationships between workers and users in the informal sector as we saw in the last chapter. Medication is deeply unpopular among those who take it. It is often accepted as the lesser of two evils because it assuages the voices. We collected many stories complaining about the medication, the manner in which it is administered, its side effects, and the feelings of dependence and powerlessness it induces. 'They can dope you up sometimes, you're just like a vegetable. ... It takes years ... to get rid of that dopiness' (Rhona). Less common are accounts of medication as a solution to the 'problem': 'As soon as I get my shot, I'm cool man ... everybody as soon as they come in and get their medication are back to normal' (Wycliff). Wycliff replays the views of those who *work* in drop-ins and shelters. Some people take their medication, others refuse it and some customize it as we saw in Chapter 4. This also describes the various possible relationships with psychiatry. People decided what they would take and when they would take it and what they would combine it with to get the best effects. One shelter user recommended marijuana with lithium to us. Daniel adjusts his own medication, trading controlling the voices with feeling too tired. He speaks knowledgeably about 'maintenance doses' and the 'build-up of toxicity in the brain', the source of his problems. Medication *is* a direct conduit to psychiatry, but it is one over which considerable social agency is exercised.

> Well sometimes I skip the medication, for example, I'm drinking, for instance, I'm going to the bar. And taking the medication and drinking is like. I never tried it, but I heard it's like taking cocaine. And I don't want to indulge myself in that, in cocaine, because it's a killer.
>
> (Joan)

This is not true of those who live in foster homes where medication regimes are very rigidly administered and rarely customized. Place is very important in implementing psychiatric thinking and solutions.

Always problematic, the status of medication in the lives of those with serious and persistent psychiatric difficulties is further complicated by the newly implemented drug insurance plan that leaves even welfare claimants with substantial medication bills. Aside from the arguments about whether medication is the best option, this new policy is making things worse. As a worker in one of the drop-in centres told us:

> One man, he'd been taking his medication for quite a few months. He was doing really well on it. But he decided he was going to stop taking his medication cause he couldn't afford to pay for it anymore, so he stopped for about one month, and he didn't feel well. So he decided, on his own to start taking it again. ... So often we're having to buy the medication for them, and then be reimbursed like at the beginning of the month.
>
> (Sarah)

Given the ambivalence towards medication in the first place, the amount of medication used by those we interviewed – the side effects of medication are managed with further medication – and the poverty of those who use it, this is a most ill-conceived policy that further exacerbates individual ambivalence to medication.

Workers' conceptions of madness and schizophrenia

Workers in the informal sector, rather than trained psychiatric personnel, interface with schizophrenics on a daily basis and this confers significance on the theories of schizophrenia of the workers themselves. It is *they* who are responsible for the day-to-day management of madness in the community and for this reason their formulations of what schizophrenia is and the impact of psychiatric thinking on their formulations are clearly important in judging what kinds of care contexts they provide. Do they in fact operate hybrid forms of psychiatric knowledge in their informal contexts? And if so, what do these consist of? Workers' conceptions differ from those of schizophrenics in some ways that merit noting. They obviously have no basis in personal experience of mental distress and their theories are hence less textured and richly elaborated than those of schizophrenics. Workers' conceptions are less multi-dimensional: they are more simplistic and more likely to draw upon some aspects of psychiatric thinking. They are, unsurprisingly, rooted in their daily experience of *dealing* with schizophrenics on the scenes of their daily employment and so are very much focused on behaviour and ways of managing behaviour in particular contexts. Rhona gave us some insights into the kinds of behaviour drop-in-centre workers – with no special training – have to deal with on the 'front line' of the community system. Although Rhona deals with acute episodes herself: 'when I just can't take life itself and it sends me off my rocker', others, she says, take them to the centre with them, where workers have to deal with them.

> I don't really know if they could handle mental illness downstairs [at the drop-in centre where she spends her day]. There is no doctor or medical doctor or psychiatrist or psychologist, only a social worker coming in twice a week, but that's about it. I don't think they are really prepared to handle. ... A lot of the people that do come to *** [name of the drop-in centre] for lunch have very real problems. Most of the time they come and take it out at ***, at the people, and I feel that's wrong. If you have a problem go and see a medical doctor or psychiatrist a psychologist. I see my doctor. I don't bring my problems here ... [unless, she explains, she] 'turns it into comedy'. If I left it alone it eats away at me. ... I either do one of two things, get locked up into a hospital like the *** [name of hospital] or I lock myself at home.
>
> (Rhona)

Workers' versions of schizophrenia that prominently feature behaviour – the thing they actually have to deal with – are textured by their fear of volatility and uncontrolled behaviour by their clients. Phyllis, who runs a foster home and who, as we saw in Chapter 2, watched out for aggressive behaviour and reported it to the local psychiatric hospital said:

> I can't comprehend it [schizophrenia] you know. I try so hard to, I had a client before, just two months ago, had to be admitted to the hospital permanent because I really couldn't cope any more.
>
> (Phyllis)

This underscores the severely limited capacity of foster-home workers/carers in understanding the schizophrenia of its clients. Lisa, who worked in a drop-in centre, said that aggressive behaviour 'came with the turf', it was in the nature of schizophrenia, adding, 'but I find that more recently though that it is getting a little scarier'. She is referring to the increased pressure of numbers and the difficulty of persuading people to take medication when they can't afford it or remember to take it. Jane, who worked in a lunch drop-in centre said she thought that schizophrenia meant 'one minute they're in this world and the next they are not' but also gave examples of people who were 'big and menacing' and 'ready to snap'. Fear played a large part in workers' narratives when discussing schizophrenia and the daily job of dealing with schizophrenics becoming part of the social relationships of the workplace. In this kind of formulation workers were drawing upon their working experience *and* on popular versions of schizophrenia as dangerousness and volatility leading to unpredictable behaviour.

Workers frequently deployed psychiatric terminology, especially diagnostic labels, to refer to the people they dealt with. Sarah, a social worker who worked in one of the drop-in centres, said she thought that schizophrenia took on different forms in

131

different people: 'delusions, ... hallucinating, hearing voices, paranoid behaviour' or 'more withdrawn, apathy ... they isolate themselves'. She is combining behaviour with diagnoses in much the same way DSM IV (American Psychiatric Association 1995) does. Francine, also a centre worker who is trained as a social worker, stumbles with psychiatric terminology, also combining it with behaviour and lifestyle:

> 'Psychiatric problems' and 'mental illness' [she says is an illness with psychotic symptoms, a loss of touch with 'reality']. ... A personality disorder is more of, your personality make-up. ... A very common personality disorder is borderline ... these people have a lot of trouble accepting limits ... and very often these are substance abusers.
>
> (Francine)

Centre workers like Robert, who has no particular professional training to equip him to work with people at all, frequently reiterate the view that schizophrenia is incurable and best managed with medication – a broadly medical view of the situation shared by many psychiatrists. His account of the hallucinations and voices that accompany schizophrenia links them with the dirt *he* evidently fears in his clients, repeating a version of schizophrenia we found among shelter clients. 'A lot of people just halluci-nate, they hear voices, umm, depending on severity, um, a lot of schizophrenia people are, are dirty, are dirty to the look and to the smell and they don't even realize it' (Robert). Others gave biomedical definitions such as 'chemical imbalance in the brain' and could list major symptoms: 'hallucinations', 'delusions', 'paranoia' and 'social withdrawal' (Warren). A minority – working in the tiny, well-resourced official community sector – believed that psychiatric knowledge was irrelevant and said they preferred to 'work with the person' in a broader and more individual way, which seems thoroughly commendable. Generally, workers' conceptions of schizophrenia are more likely to accept superficial versions of psychiatric knowledge 'worked through' the place in which they come into contact with madness. Homeless-shelter workers were unable to speak about schizophrenia outside of the complexity of social problems – like alcoholism and drug use – that their clients bring to them at work. In these accounts, schizophrenia is elided with dirt and fears of dangerousness and outbursts of uncontrolled behaviour arising from not keeping proper order, giving the place a particular character. Narratives of dangerousness and volatile behaviour are more prominent than in the accounts of schizophrenics, and there is evidence of a belief in biomedical thinking and symptom clusters that underlie presenting behaviour. Theirs is a version of psychiatric knowledge that foregrounds danger and the working envi-ronments in which madness is encountered. The hybrid versions of schizophrenia with which workers operate are the result of these factors: a smattering of psychiatry is worked through face-to-face contact conditions and popular understanding of danger-ousness grounded in experience located in a particular time and place. There is a sense in which these workers deal with whatever they have to deal with on a daily basis and that they use reworked rudimentary psychiatric understanding to do so. They have no sense of – or else they reject as nonsense – the complex theories of schizophrenia held by their clients and are consequently not able to respond to them. Cut loose from the asylum and the hospital, medical knowledge works its way into the social relationships of the new spaces used by the mentally distressed and the new semi-professional practices through which they are managed.

Conceptions of schizophrenia interact with *place* and other aspects of social context and circumstances of those who experience it, but there is no particular alliance between the nature of the place/client relationship and theories about what schizophrenia means, what causes it and so on. The crucial factor seems to be biographical circumstances that operate as the framework with which other explanations must coexist, as theories of schizophrenia and life details are massaged into place by each other as Rhona's attempt to incorporate notions of multiple personality so graphically illustrates. Conceptions of schizophrenia shape the field of future life possibilities with their limitations and problems governing what may be contemplated, attempted, achieved in the course of a life and the circumstances in which it can be lived. Enormous constraints are placed on the field of possibilities by schizophrenia from living situations, employment prospects, types of social relationships that can be envisaged and so on. This chapter has attempted to give a sense of the *self* and the *life* in so far as it is forged around conceptions of what may broadly be referred to as mental distress with which schizophrenics navigate the nooks and crannies of the city. Theories of schizophrenia affect who people think they are and the ways in which they might reasonably expect to conduct themselves in the spaces and contexts available to them. It is significant in charting their course and making decisions to decide whether someone is moved by conspiracy theories or biomedical theories of the nature and meaning of schizophrenia or some complex interaction of both. And it is significant in providing effective social spaces as contexts in which this kind of thinking can be accommodated and best served. Conspiracy theories especially are exacerbated by some of the contexts through which clients are administered in shelters and centres. Even if these *are* a symptom of the problem, conspiracy theories still operate as a plausible explanation for some events and experiences, especially those that cohere around black people and cannot be explained by other means. The content of madness is extremely important to those to whom this social position is assigned or who recognize it as applying to them and their situation. It is only when we crack open and examine the meaning of madness that we can begin the task of social accommodation and understanding that comes with living with it as a broader social and political problem that goes beyond the confines of psychiatric jurisdiction and knowledge.

6

DANGEROUSNESS AND
ENDANGERMENT

Philippe Feraro, who had a 'history of psychological problems', was shot dead by a Montréal police SWAT team in 1995 (*Hour* 6–12 July 1995). Armed with a pick, an axe and a knife – but not a firearm – he was alone inside his house at the time. Earlier, in 1993, a 25-year-old Trinidadian-born man allegedly forced his way into a neighbour's apartment in the rooming house where he lived. When the police were called, he threatened them with a blade but was otherwise unarmed. It was known that he had been released from Montréal's Pinel Institute for the criminally insane where he was treated for paranoid delusions. Police fired four shots near the base of his neck, something that, remarkably, given the position of his wounds, he survived (*Hour* 6–12 July 1995). Paolo Romanelli, a 'disturbed' 23-year-old who stabbed and injured a Montréal police officer in the shoulder was shot to death *after* he had retreated into his house (*Hour* 6–12 July 1995). In the neighbouring Province of Ontario (1988) Lester Donaldson, a 43-year-old 'psychiatric patient' who held six police officers at bay with a knife in his rooming house, was also shot dead by the city police. Edmund Wai Hong Yu, diagnosed as 'paranoid schizophrenic', and alone on a Toronto city bus and armed with a small shiny hammer was shot through the head by police in 1997. The evidence that he might be dangerous was that he was barred after getting into a fight with another man at a downtown homeless shelter, and that he had threatened a woman standing at the bus stop. He was described as 'likeable' rather than dangerous by one of the shelter workers (*Montréal Gazette* 22 February 1997). This was reported as the thirteenth fatal shooting by Toronto police since 1990, significantly one of only two fatal shootings in any recent year. The list of summary and brutal responses of the police in dealing with the mad can be continued for key cities on the other side of the border. The most recent addition to the list of mad victims of police marksmen is the shooting of a 29-year-old Jewish man, Gary Busch, in September 1999 who, armed with a hammer he was swinging around, was shot 12 times by New York City Police in Brooklyn. Described as 'sick and he did things that were strange' (the UK *Guardian* 11 September 1999) the response of the police has prompted a protest that includes the local orthodox Jewish community as part of a critique of police behaviour towards ethnic minorities. Dangerousness, as well as attaching itself to madness, is male and 'ethnic'.

In all of these cases the police shot to kill and not disable people believed to be too dangerous to be dealt with by other means – people who posed too great a risk to the police and to the public on whose behalf they act. Far from just revealing the most reactionary elements of the social climate, policing is the set of practices where practical action takes place and takes precedence over rhetoric and political posturing. Policing is the point – at which the police face the 'mad man' in the act of generating public terror – that social priorities are momentarily shuffled into place and the rights of the mad are sacrificed in defence of the public safety they are presumed to threaten. Police are in a position to act on and sustain myths of urban dangerousness in some acute moment of social truth not easily dismissed and with some lethal consequences. This is particularly so given the strategic position of law enforcement in a system that has reduced psychiatric incarceration and the deployment of constraint so that police are increasingly used to restore order among the mad in shelters, day centres and on the streets of the city, as we noted in Chapter 4. As psychiatry divests itself of the constraints and compulsions of the psychiatric wards and asylums, these tasks fall into other hands. A Toronto schizophrenic was recently jailed when he refused to comply with the court order requiring him to take his medication. The velvet glove of community care contains an all-purpose iron fist as forms of social danger become law and order issues. The police (and the criminal justice system) have, *de facto*, become a part of the social management of madness: and yet they readily admit that they are ill equipped and trained to deal with mental health issues or the bodies of the mad they confront at gunpoint. The (1999) legislation passed in Britain to allow the indefinite detention of people 'believed to be dangerous whether or not they have committed any dangerous act' underscores both the strategic position of policing and law enforcement in the social management of madness in Britain and other countries too, and the link between policing and public discomfort and fear around madness. Policing is an *integral*, if distinctive, aspect of social organization. There is a broader and more ambivalent social context to the demonization of madness that etches its place in the panoply of urban myths.

In addition to being shaped by police action, urban myths are also shaped by events, public reactions to events and the political and media contexts in which they are managed. The media is, perhaps, the most powerful global myth maker of our time. Greg Philo (1996: 96) shows in a different political context – Scotland – that media coverage was a highly significant source of information shaping public opinion on the dangerousness associated with madness generally, and with schizophrenia in particular. His interviews uncovered deep levels of fear surrounding schizophrenia in the popular imaginary. Clearly, the media produces the events that make this connection in a particular way so as to sustain madness as a key form of urban danger. This was particularly evident in the eruption of public/media anxiety sparked in Britain by the murder of Jonathan Zeito by Christopher Clunis, significantly a black schizophrenic, in December 1992. Clunis pushed Zeito under a London underground train and unleashed a flurry of media activity in which this awful event was replayed for more than a week on breakfast television serving as a daily reminder of the danger of unmedicated madness lurking on the street as a result of decades of community mental health policy. The pressure group bearing Zeito's name is still regularly referred to on issues concerning madness and public risk in Britain. Significantly, this event also contributed to the racialization (and gendering) of schizophrenia as a form of dangerousness. Young males, especially collectively and individually, have become a focus of fear of urban danger. And if we take into account the heavy-handed policing practices of urban police forces in Montréal, London and key US cities, it is evident that dangerousness is not just male, it is also *black*. Popular versions of racial and gendered dangerous subjectivities in our interviews were repeated as well as countered in individual's stories about themselves.[1] The Montréal media contained a smattering of stories raising anxiety about public safety as madness was transferred out of hospital custody. But it also, ambivalently, contains more sympathetic stories about the difficulties confronted by the families of schizophrenics. For example the *Montréal Gazette* (4 June 1998) carried a story 'Psychiatric Outpatients Suffering', which detailed the difficulties of the parents of a 34-year-old schizophrenic woman psychiatrists were reluctant to hospitalize, despite her having made several violent attacks on her parents. The local media is reasonably even handed in its treatment of madness: the mad appear both as a source of danger and family difficulty and concern. The ambivalence and liberality of the media when it comes to madness is clearly possible, but effectively countered by the actions of the local police force.

It matters whether urban myths of madness as dangerousness are professionally underwritten by those with authority to define madness. Psychiatric evidence that the deluded regularly act on their delusions would provide significant support for popular mythologies of urban danger. Although Parker *et al*. (1995) contend that psychiatry subscribes to its own versions of the demonology of madness, the American Psychiatric Association historically denied the association between mental disorder and violence. The Canadian Mental Health Association also denies links between madness and dangerousness and timed its pronouncement to coincide with a spate of subway assaults in Toronto for which schizophrenic suspects were arrested in 1998. The UK National Schizophrenia Fellowship pressure group, in addressing this theme, reported (*Guardian* 5 July 1993) that 40 people had died at the hands of diagnosed schizophrenics and other seriously mentally ill people in the last two years, but that 100 mentally ill people had committed suicide in the same time period. It argued that 17–18 per cent of schizophrenics attempt suicide. This supports the view that the mad pose a small element of danger, but are typically *endangered* rather than dangerous. This concurs with the spirit of decarceration – if the mad are dangerous, then they ought not to be let out of hospital. If they can be released, then they *must not* pose a public threat. But in Britain, as elsewhere, this comforting formulation about public safety has been disturbed by the Zeito murder and a small number of other high-profile murders by people with serious psychiatric diagnoses and personality disorders. Psychiatry may have developed a liberal grand narrative concerning serious forms of madness, but its (much-reduced) routine interaction with it and its willingness (at least in Britain) to concur with the incarceration of those *believed* to be dangerous and bow to the public demand for the prediction of dangerousness indicates the diversity of the stories about madness and its relationship to dangerousness of which psychiatry is capable. Under this kind of pressure to assuage public anxiety there is evidence of a shift in psychiatric grand narratives in the direction of the more popular view that the mad are, indeed, dangerous. James Beck, a Harvard-based psychiatrist, told the American Psychiatric Association that new research supported the view that there was a link between mental disorder and violent behaviour (*Montréal Gazette* 3 June 1998).

Policing, the media and psychiatry are only three of many sources of interconnected thought and social action concerning madness. The association between madness and dangerousness is, perhaps, best set in the broader context of urban mythology in which madness is one of many forms of social danger in the urban popular imaginary.[2] Fear of random attack, stranger danger, the association of certain parts of the urban landscape with unprovoked violence bears no necessary relationship with actual incidents or their frequency. They are about peoples' reading and use of public space. Arguments about levels of dangerousness in the private, domestic domain have not shifted the association between home as a place of safety and public (especially urban) space as open to multiple forms of dangerousness. The popular imaginary – not easily reshaped by statistical evidence – needs be taken seriously, not least because the reinsertion of the mad into the community demands their mutual coexistence with the rest of the population and the urban myths by which they live. City landscapes particularly are prone to the imagining of danger. Its maps of danger and safety are real enough in shaping its use. Fear of madness as dangerousness reconfigures urban space, homogenizing the spatial particularity of different parts of the urban landscape as the scenes of different kinds of mad lives described in Chapters 2, 3 and 4.

In the popular Canadian imaginary the urban landscapes of the United States are a source of *real* danger against which cities like Montréal, Toronto and Vancouver – although the centre of their own myths of urban danger – are, by comparison, rather safe. Vancouver in the early 1990s was in the grip of 'Asian gang fear' – its urban mythology reflecting public concern about levels and sources of immigration and its impact on the English–Canadian character of the city. Montréal's collective fear focuses on the province's political turmoil, the exodus of people and businesses and the impact of this on its prosperity and unemployment levels. Empty commercial space, especially in the city centre, prompted fear of decline, perhaps symbolically represented in the forms of human dereliction, which panhandled in front of it. Individual anxiety here, as elsewhere, focuses on personal safety in the urban routines of apparently random murder and attack on persons and property. The hold of madness on the public imaginary and its maps of dangerousness, is a part of this broader context of fear of random personal attack. Madness underwrites and gives meaning and content to the randomness and senselessness of urban violence: and this is its place in the overall political economy of local urban mythology. The mad have re-entered the demonology of modern urban life – lurking beneath the surface, indistinguishable from the rest of the population, an insidious threat that gives new form to the long-standing social anxiety that surrounds the *anomie* of urban existence, something that sociology has taken very seriously indeed.

The relationship between personal maps and use of urban landscape, urban myths of dangerousness and madness as a contemporary form of urban danger is clearly a complicated business involving myriad social/autobiographical processes that go well beyond the scope of this volume. All that can be undertaken here is to expose the myth of madness as dangerousness to some of the ethnographic evidence gathered in viewing the lives lived by the mad on and around the streets of the city; and to admit that unpacking urban myths in order to confront them with another version of reality is not particularly effective in the light of Philo's (1996: 84–6) finding that popular beliefs concerning madness and dangerousness are undisturbed when they are revealed to be founded on misinformation or mistakes in media reporting. Unmasking myth is, at one level, a pointless exercise. In being unsettled, myths do not necessarily loosen their hold on popular thinking. But on another level, to leave these myths unexamined is to collude in their hold over the popular imaginary – the source of their social power. The material garnered in this volume hints at some aspects of dangerousness – it would be dishonest to deny that madness carries a small burden of public risk – and raises important questions concerning public tolerance of risk and the social management of risk. Placed in the context of the broader picture, however, the evidence points in the opposite direction. The mad are not dangerous but 'endangered' and this theme is strongly present in the stories they tell and in the analysis of their social (spatial) management described in this volume.

Endangerment and vulnerability

Vulnerability and dangerousness are not mutually exclusive states of being: endangerment can produce its own forms of dangerousness. There are issues here of levels and kinds of dangerousness that are dealt with later in this chapter and questions to be asked concerning the 'dynamic' between dangerousness and vulnerability in individual biographies. For now, it is sufficient to note the ambivalence of vulnerability: that it can overbalance into forms of dangerousness. Jonathan, the street musician whom we met in Chapter 4 and earlier in the context of a discussion of some of the spatial practices of the mad in the city as a whole, expresses this ambivalence rather well. He suggests that to operate on the streets is to expose oneself to its dangers and psychological pressures *on top of* the kind of distress many of the mad carry around with them. To return to what he said earlier:

> That's why I wouldn't go panhandling. I mean, I deal well enough with rejection, but having 300 people a day telling you [screaming] 'Get a job you fuckin asshole' or just 'NO! NO! NO!' Two or three hundred 'Nos' in a day you start to twitch – you know, and then you have to deal with all the people who say like, 'Would you like to come over to my place?' That's it, it's seedy, seedy, crappy ... this city is around here sometimes. That's all it boils down to, everybody wants sex, money and drugs, you know. ... The city is full of them [the lonely]. You're going to get the people who go to McDonalds with machine guns, they're like, 'I'm lonely. I need a friend [mimics machine gun fire].' The city is full of them, I mean it seems to me that most street people are on a hair trigger right now, it's like they're borderline. ... [He makes an interesting use of a psychiatric term to discuss broader personal and social circumstances.] You give them a little push, you know, you say the wrong thing to a lot of street people and I think that you could just flip 'em right out, and have violence perpetrated against yourself.
>
> (Jonathan, Street Musician)

Jonathan describes the tensions of the street well, its population swelled by those with serious psychiatric problems. And he describes the vulnerability of those who live in close contact with the street and this – the combination of individual and social vulnerability among those whose lives hang in a delicate balance of psychological distress – was a dominant theme in our interviews.

The vulnerability of the mad arises from a number of sources set out in preceding chapters and can be briefly summarized here. Vulnerability is evident both from the individual narratives we recorded and from the analysis of the revolving and precarious spatial arrangements in which they were set. Chapter 5 discussed one of the most obvious sources of vulnerability – madness itself – the terror of hearing voices and seeing visions; the social consequences of existential crises; and living in a parallel reality to the rest of society. In addition to dealing with their own demons, the lack of personal space – on the street, in hostel dormitories, in drop-in centres and soup kitchens – means that the mad have also to live with the demons of one another, something that is obviously additionally unsettling. In Chapter 2, Rick gives harrowing testimony of his nights in a shelter dormitory listening to his neighbour wrestling with the internal terrors Rick was struggling to keep under control.

This implicates a second source of vulnerability organized by the spatial politics of close proximity and need that operates in shelters and soup kitchens. The mad are fearful of each other. They are fearful of others' erratic behaviour, standards of bodily hygiene (Chapters 3 and 4) and the possibility of others acting on the (sometimes alarming) advice of their demons. Survival depends on how they handle competition – there are power plays between them over the acquisition and defence of space as panhandling patches, seats in the soup kitchens and beds in the shelters. They fear the encroachment of others as well as their demons. As a potential resource in each other's circumstances – a source of spare change, cigarettes and favours – they fear the predatory attentions of one another. These vulnerabilities are spatially configured by their arrangement and competitive social relationships.

Other sources of vulnerability implicate the social (spatial) circumstances of the mad more directly. Those living on or around the street feel the precariousness of their survival, which takes constant effort and work on their part to maintain. Street life also precludes the ability to exclude others – to operate in a private space out of public view. Life is lived in a most public way – something that clearly contains its own forms of stress as well as competition in which almost nothing occurs outside of the gaze of

Plate 28   Clothes store at the drop-in centre

others. The street contains multiple dangers: violence and personal threat; invasion by others whose attentions are unwanted; arrest by the police; and so on. Those who circulate around hostels, rooming houses and the street express fears of personal decline and degeneration. They are made vulnerable by the precariousness of these shifting circumstances and the fear that they will get 'stuck'. Ironically they, and their circumstances, are both fixed and in free-fall. Those on the street who do not want to go into hostels are afraid they will end up there. Those in hostels who are not happy to be there are afraid they will never get out. The vulnerability of those in foster homes is the vulnerability of the child dependent upon the approval of the 'grown-ups' and the domestic regimes in which their needs and sense of aesthetic prevail. All of these spaces articulate different anxieties about being overturned or becoming frozen. Mobility (in space) is both an asset and a liability in these calculations. The reactions of the non-mad – who are in a position to call the police, have them carted off to the psychiatric wards and to deny them access to jobs and public places – are also a source of vulnerability and anxiety. The non-mad have a privileged relationship to public space.

The complex and interconnected texture of endangerment is somewhat further explored by looking at two lives – Eddy's and Lauryn's. Through these two quite different prisms we take a close-up look at particular forms of endangerment and see some of the ways in which it is given substance through gender and race. In the hostels and centres where we interviewed, being 'dangerous' or 'harmless' were important distinctions used by workers. When we were handed Eddy to interview, who was considered to be 'quite harmless', we were steered off another black man sitting in the corner who was described as 'dangerous'. Our informants often came with this sort of endorsement, especially in one particular hostel where we were always locked into a little room with them for the interview, and workers felt they had to assuage what they imagined and saw as *our* discomfort.

Eddy's vulnerability is palpable.[3] A black man born in Montréal, he presents an adolescent picture of himself although he is 40 years old. His account of himself is stuck in his youth at a time when he travelled in the United States with his friends and played in a band. He presents himself as 'lost' and 'abandoned' – themes that reveal and express his sense of vulnerability. His first abandonment – by his mother to foster parents – is a theme that is (worked up in psychiatric narrative and) repeated to account for other kinds of loss. He describes his condition as an 'acute case of psychiatry'! Something that involves being 'lost in my thoughts' and 'lost in society' – two connected versions of the loss, by which he makes sense of his life.

> Well I had, I was lost, I couldn't get a job, I was lost again, and I was on the street, you know, and I was more or less abandoned. I felt alone and lonely and scared, you know. Nowhere to go, being on the streets … and some of them [others on the street] are dirty … you get, you know, lost you know, and there's no such thing as mental illness. … It's like an accident, you know, you fall down and got to get back up, and sometimes you get lost in society. … Well they said there was schiz, schizophrenia, anxiety more or less schizophrenia, because I was really alone, you know, and you get anxious. If you've been alone things tend to close in on you, and I became very anxious. [His narrative continues reflecting on the bleaker side of humanity, wars and famines, showing a broader sense of the world and his particular connection to

it. Turning back to his own problems, he continues.] I felt it coming on for a while, being on the street, I felt it coming on myself. You know, staying in my room all by myself, all day long.

(Eddy)

Eddy had his first 'psychiatric fit' at 18 after leaving home because his foster parents became 'too strict'. His foster father was a porter, like other black men, working from Windsor railway station on the Canadian Pacific Railway in one of the few jobs available to black men. Eddy occupies (briefly), a number of jobs and homes, with others and then alone. His story is the product of over 20 years of hospital admissions and ECT treatments, and movement in and out of his own apartment and into shelters. The key to stability (and the opposite of loss), as he sees it, is having a job and a relationship to give his life the same structures as he thinks others have and rely on. The themes of 'loss', 'abandonment' and 'being lost' mesh perfectly with his feelings about living alone in what he sees as a big city. The size and anonymity of the city threaten him. He is threatened by others and hides away in the shelter where he has had a room of his own for the last two years. He is threatened by the general condition of the world in which it is set. He is threatened by his schizophrenia. And he is threatened by his lack of close relationships and a job. It is also evident, in this version of his life, that Eddy sees his life of insecurity on the streets as contributing to his psychological precariousness. The sources of Eddy's vulnerability are the ordinary things connecting him to the social world. And yet, in the public imaginary, as a black, male schizophrenic, he is the embodiment of dangerousness.

Lauryn's story – which is also gendered and raced but not in any straightforward or predictable way – illustrates other aspects of vulnerability. Aged 35, Lauryn moved to Montréal from Guyana with her older brother when she was 17. She works illegally doing housekeeping, the only kind of work she can get, while she waits to get her residence status regularized. She tells us she wants to pursue her education and become a teacher and get married. Her story reveals her financial vulnerability and the vulnerability of her emotional state: the two things being linked in her narrative.

> Schizophrenia is a, is some kind of mental illness that makes you do like, strange things, like hearing voices or seeing things and makes you think that this is the last day of the world … there is nothing else in this world that you can do. … I was in hospital because I couldn't sleep at night and I used to sit all alone in a lonely place thinking and my family think that I'm getting sick because people don't sit by themselves, but I don't want to talk, I don't want to do nothing, just sit there all day by themselves. Like looking in one position, so they took me to the hospital. … I told the doctor I'm okay, just its different stages of *me being in Montréal*, going through this hardship, couldn't find a job, can't have an education. … I'm a very active person in life. … I gave up everything, schooling, working, because I couldn't do anything, my mind was like blah [she subscribes to the stress/disease model of schizophrenia] because I couldn't concentrate on anything, but just my, like, you know, to live, to keep on living and not to be dead. … [Her recurring theme is the loneliness of life as a schizophrenic and this, along with her financial, and immigration-status, vulnerability, is a major part of her feeling

of 'exposure'. She speaks about some schizophrenics being a bit aggressive and adds]: I wouldn't go around hitting someone, it's hard for me to strike someone because I know myself, its not the right thing to do. ... [The significance of this emerges later when she admits that when someone looks crazy 'he could harm you'. She is persuaded to continue her theme of 'what crazy looks like' and describes another user of the drop-in to exemplify this description of madness.] He is wearing his pyjamas and you don't wear pyjamas on the street unless something is happening or unless there is an emergency ... doesn't look carefully, you know. *He could be hurt* [my emphasis, showing vulnerability combined with dangerousness] ... the way he sometimes, he says to me 'Oh I want some money. I need 5 cents to use the metro'. You can't use the metro with 5 cents. That means he is thinking about something else. ... I see him, like a person that is not really responsible for being a part, a friend ... he is dangerous – a danger to life, a danger to himself and a danger to the public. So I'm afraid, I'm afraid of him [and, she implies, of becoming him].

(Lauryn)

Lauryn's testimony is useful because it details her own sense of vulnerability *and* because she is able to articulate a version of 'madness as dangerousness', which may well resemble its meaning in the public imaginary, and which articulates the fear that is attached to looking and acting differently from other people. Although he may look untidy and be a nuisance, it is not clear precisely *how* the man she describes is dangerous. The symbolic representation of madness must be distinguished from dangerous behaviour – a theme that is taken up later in this chapter. Lauryn admits that she herself is fearful of being deported, and this is an important and fundamental part of her vulnerability. She lives in a private rooming house and uses drop-in centres for lunches and hanging around, spending the day with other people as an antidote to loneliness. She presents herself as emotionally vulnerable. She is socially isolated and fears personal disintegration. She is vulnerable in terms of her immigration situation and this consigns her to low-paid work (financial vulnerability) in domestic service where she is additionally vulnerable, as an illegal immigrant, to the demands of her employers. Psychological and social precariousness often collide in the lives of black immigrants. Like Eddy, Lauryn's vulnerability consists in the things connecting her, so tenuously, with the rest of the world as a black woman and illegal immigrant liable to summary deportation to the Caribbean. The point of these two sketches of Lauryn and Eddy is to say something about the social context and extent of vulnerability and its hold on mad black lives ironically conceptualized as dangerous.

Dangerousness

Mad people, as Lauryn noted, often look and behave in ways that are frightening. This raises public anxiety, but it does not make them dangerous. Informants' performances for us – and perhaps their more public performances, too – often played out versions of madness as erratic, unpredictable and bizarre behaviour. Any researcher who has spent time in an elevator at a homeless shelter with a man wearing a sandwich bag on his head who is standing too close will verify this! Appearance and behaviour combined with a renewed public visibility feeds popular perceptions of dangerousness, but this should not in itself be interpreted as dangerousness. What *looks* dangerous is not so necessarily. We need to go beyond the symbolic in order to get to grips with what dangerousness means in these contexts. We have also to discount as evidence of dangerousness the disturbances that sometimes erupt in shelters and drop-in centres generated by the competitive context of these spaces in which numbers of fairly fragile (and variously medicated/unmedicated) people wrestling with their own demons operate in spaces that are not designed to deal with their problems. This kind of institutionally induced conflict, although understandably threatening for the workers involved, is a product of the (*ad hoc*) system by which madness is socially managed and cannot be taken as *de facto* evidence of mad volatility. Acting out and conflicts are also just some of the ways in which the mad scare each other and those whose job it is to deal with them. Volatility and erratic behaviour are both a strategy for dealing with others and it is embedded in the spatial configuration and social relations of institutions managing madness. These outbursts look and feel dangerous. But are they? Is anybody *injured* in these circumstances? Are centres trashed or burned down? This, of course, raises questions about the meaning of dangerousness and it is this that we need to unpack a little.

In pursuing this discussion it is important to be a bit more precise about levels of dangerousness and the nature of dangerousness. There can be no doubt that the mad scare people, and they scare each other too, as Lauryn pointed out. There is no doubt also that they are liable in certain circumstances to erupt, fight and threaten the order of the environment in which they are managed. And there is no doubt that people feel threatened and harassed by being approached by them or having to walk past them on the street. In all of these ways the mad raise public anxiety. But if dangerousness means 'posing a threat to others, which is backed up by behaviour that causes physical harm or terrorizes', a reasonable interpretation of dangerousness, then most of the people we met were not dangerous. There were, in three cases only, incidents reporting harming and terrorizing other people in the stories we heard.[4] This is not an attempt to deny the dangerousness of madness, but to be more precise about it. Of course it can be argued (with some validity) that the truly dangerous are unlikely to agree to be interviewed or be available for interview. It can also be argued that informants are unlikely to reveal evidence of their dangerousness in an interview. This is actually unlikely, as a number of informants did tell stories of erratic and bizarre behaviour they probably thought we wanted to collect, and which sustained the public myths of madness as this particular version of dangerousness. But we maintain that these stories of erratic and bizarre behaviour are not the same as dangerousness as the capacity to harm or terrorize others. And, if three people were prepared to reveal their dangerousness, then there is no reason to suspect that others would be put off from doing so, especially as some of them clearly enjoyed trying to scare the interviewing team too. The three cases of dangerousness to show up in our interviews make it possible for us to reflect a bit further on what dangerousness actually means – specifically how and to whom were they a danger? And what was the social context producing each version of dangerousness? In what does the spatiality of dangerousness consist? These questions guide our unpacking of the meaning of dangerousness.

The first case is Guy. Guy presents himself as a 'Francophone' who was born and raised in Montréal. As his narrative progresses, he turns out to be Jewish, having changed his name to a classic French–Canadian name because 'I succeed with that name'. This tells us something about the local racial order's shuffling of ethnicities and establishing priorities that guide the calculation of belonging as well as the places where people choose to live and the jobs available to them. It also shows that some forms of ethnicity are highly malleable, as we saw with Samuel, the young man with the white skin and Jamaican leanings. In Guy's narrative Jews are dirty and rich, and, like his own family, connected with business. His family find him difficult to deal with although they make occasional visits to the homeless shelter where he lives. The dangerousness he describes is a one-off act of violence, not apparently repeated in the forty years that followed it, but it was the sort of unpredictable behaviour that terrorizes others and inflicts serious damage/death on the victim. It is his violent outburst that prompts the recognition that there is 'something wrong' and this in turn leads to his diagnosis of schizophrenia.

> When I was 16 [40 years ago] or something, I was playing ping pong and the guy wanted to take on the winner, he didn't want to take on the loser, to replace the loser, he wanted to replace the winner so ... got in a hassle, apparently he was a, an, apprentice policeman or something like that, he felt really piggy you know. I got mad and somehow I flung the ping pong bat at him and he, the ping pong bat cut him, cut his throat off, cut his head off apparently ... head fell off, fell over and his body was swimming around with the blood and everything, apparently. I don't know. [Why?] I've forgotten. It's very horrible that, the whole town watching or something. ... They put me in jail for that.
>
> (Guy)

Guy was kept in psychiatric detention for four years. He says that he doesn't see a doctor at all now, and then admits that he took himself to hospital a few months ago in search of asylum but was thrown out after three days. He also tells us that his spiritual life is guided by 'the dead' and 'the king of the underworld' and that he 'invests' in human beings and horses. Horseflesh, he says, is 'very sexy'. At this point the interviewer has heard enough. She terminates the interview and only agrees to continue on condition that Guy talks about his life in the shelter, and not this more central story that changed the course of his life. His account of 'the murder' is interesting. It is first reported with a note of disbelief 'apparently', as though relating what he has been told happened while he himself was 'absent', perhaps in a 'moment' of insanity. But later he shifts to reporting it in a more direct way that admits his responsibility in it and his involvement in the kinds of minor institutional scuffles that had occurred while he was in detention, placing himself more squarely in the frame as someone who (more routinely) uses violence as a strategy for dealing with others.

> I committed murder. It's awful. It was awful. I went crazy. [He doesn't relate other incidents of violence but has been in and out of secure psychiatric accommodation for many years. In fact, he says whatever happens around him *they*] put me in jail again. ... I have no mother any more. There's no home, no luggage, so I was going from hospital to hospital mostly, getting rooming houses. In the end I was tired. ... [Does he like living in a hostel?] It's very

good [compared to psychiatric hospital and prison], but I'm always arguing with somebody. ... I had some fights in jail. ... Practically every jail I was in, I was in a fight and in a, put in the hole [solitary] you know. ... You get very bored in jail you know, there is nothing to do. ... The boys [there] are misraised and misfits ... so there's always trouble. You get in a fight very easy. ... Turn around wrong. You're in a fight ... ping pong table, you know, it could be for TV. ... It could be anything at all. ... They weren't raised properly, weren't loved good, didn't have a good mother maybe, and they ended up in jail.

(Guy)

Guy's point is a good one. If violent people are locked up together, they deal with each other violently, imposing their own modes of operating on the social relationships of space, something anticipated in its architectural arrangement. His own dangerousness seems to be confined to this sort of context and to the one dramatic incident he describes. He is not routinely dangerous, except in jail and similar contexts, and he is not a public danger with the exception of one incident forty years ago. Is Guy still dangerous? There are no guarantees that he will not repeat the lethal and unprovoked attack of forty years ago, but so far he has not done so. The local psychiatric establishment, which leaves him free to wander the streets, seems prepared to take the risk and offer him no care or therapy at all in the community. His dangerousness is also tinged with vulnerability in his own account of it. His own fears and insecurities hinge on his unanchored and dispossessed condition as someone who is 'motherless', 'homeless' and 'luggageless'. He was also fearful of the electric shock therapy he was given in hospital. He does not see himself as dangerous although he does indirectly and eventually acknowledges that he once did a very dangerous thing.

Our second example of dangerousness is Pras,[5] who is dangerous in a different way from Guy. Now in his mid-thirties, Pras came to Montréal from Haiti with his (Haitian and European) biological parents before the age of 2, and by the age of 6 had been adopted by a (white) Francophone Québécois family. Clearly, this posed issues of ethnic identity for him as he wore chains in the second interview and used them to speak about his African identity through slavery, which the chains symbolized. He has a striking physical defect in the face that required extensive reconstructive surgery soon after he was born, and has left him with a hare lip and the speech difficulties that accompany this kind of deformity of the mouth. He is consequently very conscious of his appearance. At home in his rooming-house apartment he has a black tube light that he says makes his skin look a darker blue/black than it is. He is diagnosed schizophrenic. His story is very difficult to listen to both because of its disturbing content and because he breathes heavily and gets upset while he is speaking. He demands the same kind of reassurance from us as he has in the past clearly sought from the various psychiatrists to whom he has made his confession – that we will not report him to the police. He offers what is a chilling account of his dangerousness in a narrative context in which he positions himself as 'victim-turned-perpetrator', which we suspect as having been framed in various psychiatric encounters. His victimhood is secured in his account of his foster father's violence towards him and his mother, and his early sexual exploitation as a teenager by an older man who kept him locked up in a derelict apartment in Toronto from where he was worked as a male prostitute. It is this sequence of events that form the pattern in his 'compulsion-to-repeat' account of his adult life of dangerousness. His narrative takes up the highly significant period more than 10 years earlier when he was twenty and living with his foster family.

> I told him [violent foster father] off twice in the apartment, I did. First time was with a metal chain because he would hit me or hit my adoptive mother. The second time I hit him on the head with this cast iron, cast iron. The microphone, was, the base was cast iron, solid metal. I hit him with that, he was sleeping. ... I got him good. It's not me, it's not really but I have to do it, because he threw my mum on the floor, and had her by the neck. I went in the kitchen, got what you call it? A meat cleaver. [He is describing – as it later turns out – his third attack on his foster father.] A large one. I opened his head with it at the back. He fell down. I thought he was dead, he wasn't moving any more. ... I have, I have to do it. No, he wasn't moving, no! You think I'm gonna let him do it? No. I told my mum this is the last time I do it ... they didn't arrest me [not immediately but 'years' later]. ... I got acquitted; the charges were dropped completely. Yea, because of the circumstances. ... I learned from him in a way ... I did the only other thing with that girl, I hit her.
>
> (Pras)

If Pras felt that these attacks on his foster father were deserved, he does not feel the same way about what he – or a psychiatrist he has seen – sees as their repetition on his girlfriend a few years ago in Vancouver, because while he tells us about this he is breathing heavily and crying.

> I hit her. I hit her with something. You know. I don't know what happened. She, ah, she was not moving. ... God knows where she is now. If she's still alive. ... I'm not happy. No, I'm not happy about myself. No. No! I don't like myself. ... I don't feel good. I don't [in a conflation of inner state and outer appearance] look good either.
>
> (Pras)

His outburst is unresolved and he waits to see if the police will arrest him. It is in a later interview that we realize he is planning to do some equally unpleasant things to his current girlfriend, repeating the other dimension of his (sexual) victimization by the older man in Toronto. He swears us to secrecy, but the interviewer, rightly, voices her objections to his plan and makes it clear that this is not acceptable behaviour.

> I want to put her in a run-down building infested with cockroaches, and rats. ... I'll be good to her for a few weeks ... after that Toronto! I'll buy her gifts and then she has to pay for that. ... I'll put her in a night club ... work as a dancer, a dancing girl. ... I did it before ... I'll do it again, I know.
>
> (Pras)

Pras plans to sexually exploit and incarcerate his young girlfriend, luring her away from her family. He was very violent to a previous girlfriend and he killed his adoptive father. To whom is he dangerous? Is he dangerous to women with whom he develops close relationships and to violent men who threaten women to whom he is close? What is the nature of the threat he poses? His dangerousness has both sexual and violent aspects to it. It is also *active* and ongoing – hence our concern for the safety of his girlfriend and over the fact that we were compromised by being taken in to his confidence. He did not enjoy our disapproval and he is clearly ashamed of what he has done. He is neither boasting nor deliberately trying to raise our anxieties with his story. Like Guy, he is not being followed up by psychiatric agencies in the community although he is an active danger and although he has, at various times, sought their counsel, discretely bringing his dangerousness to their attention.

Our third version of dangerousness is drawn from Terrance's story. Terrance, who, like Pras is also in his thirties, lives in a rooming house and uses various centres on which he has a great deal of expertise. He speaks quickly and confidently. He is street and centre wise. Other drop-in centre users don't get away with much with him working as a volunteer: 'a position of trust and responsibility', of which he is discretely proud. He thinks of himself as 'Canadian', born and raised in Montréal. He says 'I'm (Anglophone) Québécois'. His mother is Mohawk, and his father Jamaican, but he has never met them as he grew up in 'the (child welfare) system' and these forms of ethnicity are not important in forming his sense of himself – his identity, as will become apparent, is written by other means, primarily through his sexuality. If he 'would identify with any cultural group', he says, it would be gays 'because they are an ostracized group' on the fringe of society, although they are in danger of becoming 'mainstream'. He says people who hate him because he's black don't know him, because there are many more pressing reasons to hate him. We pick up his story as he is telling us that he was told at the centre where he volunteers: 'Don't bring your boys up here'.

> One day, a couple of months ago, I brought my boy Mikey one day, brought him there, looked at him, we hung out for a bit and left. The next day I went back by myself and I said okay and I spoke to Des [the centre worker he was testing] ... it's like love the sinner hate the sin. And my point was, 'Are you going to refuse to feed this kid just because I'm sleeping with him?' And for me it was very important to make that point because this is one of the ways I gauge people. And Des, Des didn't blink. He took it right in his stride. He said, 'No I don't like what you're doing but I'm not gonna let him starve just because you're doing that'. ...
>
> The fact that I'm gay, that I'm bisexual, the fact that the majority of my lovers are in grade two [7 years old], they [the centre and the interviewer] are uncomfortable with that. ... You can accept me for what I am or you can fuck out of my face. [He goes on to say that people who deal with street people *have* to exercise tolerance, and his comment is also applied to those of us who interview them.] It's still a house of God [the drop-in is held in a church, and this is something which must be respected, but] he [Des] lets me bring my boys there. ... As long as I, have respect, you know I'm not going to start sucking ... them. But don't ask me to pretend he's not my lover either. ...

147

I've never been *diagnosed* as schizophrenic, but I've heard voices in my head all my life. ... The difference between me [and other mad people] is that I didn't listen to the voices ... it's bad enough what I'm doing already, you know, being a rapist and so on and so on ... [has been diagnosed as] manic depressive, obsessive compulsive. I've also been labelled as a homosexual pedophile. ... All of these descriptions are accurate to a certain point ... but none of them paint the complete picture. ... I put myself on a higher level [than others because he realized he had a problem and turned himself in to a psychiatrist for help]. ... And me, I chose this path and most people chose this [indicates the other way] path. So this is why I'm different. ... It's a chemical thing, you need to have a physical intervention. ... [He lists the drugs he refused because they weren't 'treating the issue', which is, as he himself describes it, that he beats people up and rapes them. He was given medication to reduce his sex drive, but it didn't work on him.] I had three boys every day [at the time he was taking the medication] every day ... and this is where the obsessive compulsive comes in. ... I was having sex on average six to ten hours a day. ...

I spent my first 7 or 8 years being a rape victim ... [in Montréal orphanages where he grew up] and this is of course what got into my head ... you spend your first 12 years being a victim and the next 15 years being a perpetrator. ... I still want to have my same basic tastes [in young boys] ... but I don't want to be a fucking psychotic rapist. ... [Like the other sexually predatory people he knows.] If I'd been brought up in a normal family ... [life might have been quite different]. I feel close to the people on the bottom ... in general, I identify most with the victims. I've been a kid. I've been a victim or a perpetrator.

(Terrance)

Terrance poses a more general and systematic *social danger* than Pras. A paedophile and serial rapist, he poses an almost indiscriminate danger to very young boys and also sometimes to women in the city. His description of himself as a 'predator hunting a herd of gazelles' is a chilling commentary on his map of the city in which he hunts. His version of the city as a hunting ground full of human quarry mirrors the conception of the city in public anxieties acted on by the police in their summary and violent treatment detailed at the beginning of this chapter. In his description of how he uses the city – a subject on which he is particularly eloquent – he is hunter and hunted; adult and child; victim and perpetrator. But, unlike Pras, the vulnerability aspect of Terrance's dangerousness is not deployed as explanation of what he does, or as a bid for sympathy from us. He is demanding of us something far more compromising – acceptance.

It may assuage public anxiety to know that Terrance is being treated for his sex drive, but it is somewhat less comforting to know that this is the result of a great deal of work on his part. He is – he tells us – the only person in his treatment programme who is not there because of a court order. He says the police are not interested in him because he is 'mental', and this means that they are unlikely to secure a conviction and are hence reluctant to waste police resources taking him through the criminal justice system. No liberal, he says that 'rape should be a capital offence', carrying a penalty of execution. Canada does not, of course, have the death penalty. That leaves the psychiatric system to deal with him, but it is interesting that he sees himself as in need of punishment rather than treatment and that death is the magnitude of threat needed to make him change his behaviour. Switching tack abruptly, he tells us how he reached the realization that he should be 'treated' when a female friend refused to leave him to look after her daughter. But having reached this realization he found it *very* difficult to get treatment. One day, in desperation, he tells us, he walked into a psychiatric clinic and demanded treatment, threatening to go out and rape another child if he was refused. Even this demand only got him an appointment the following day. It is his urge to rape in order to get sex that he wants treated, and not his preference for young boys, which he sees as a lifestyle preference. A good outcome for him would be a move to consensual sex, although this still raises serious questions of public interest concerning the age of his partners.

Terrance is not ashamed of or apologetic for what he does. He simply wants help in curbing the more violent and predatory aspects of his sexual appetite. We were acutely aware that in listening to his story he was demanding that we accept who he is and the lifestyle he has chosen, although he made this point indirectly, telling us about how he dealt with the drop-in centre. He put us in a very compromised position, something that he occasionally fudged by moving upwards, in the course of the interview, the age of the boys he has sex with from 7 to 15. Terrance knows how to lean on a liberal conscience. Where does acceptance of street people end and outrage at the rape of minors legitimately begin? Did the fact that he was an active public danger to underaged boys mean that we should break confidentiality and report him? But we knew this was a pointless concern as we were just one more party on a list of local community workers who knew what he did and he had tried reporting himself without success.

Finally, it is worth noting the context in which the stories relating dangerousness were collected. Having been impressed with the overwhelming vulnerability of our informants, we were convinced that none of them could be described as dangerous. In each of the three cases described in this chapter this information was forced upon us. In the case of Terrance, the interview proceeded along two parallel tracks. The interviewer stuck to his agenda, which was to gather information about the different centres and how they were used. Terrance provided this information, but in the context of stories about his sexual behaviour. The interviewer, who is gay, tried very hard *not* to engage with Terrance's frankly unnerving and distasteful account of his sexuality, but Terrance does not let him off the hook and relentlessly unravels his narrative. Terrance is also very convincing, and by the end of the interview it is difficult not to be drawn into his story, which is ultimately redeemed by his attempts to effect significant changes in himself and his behaviour. He and not the system is actively addressing his dangerousness. In Eddy's interview, the interviewer stops the interview and tries to redirect it back onto her agenda. She only agrees to continue when Eddy agrees to answer *her* questions. And in Pras's interview the interviewer actually objects to his plan to incarcerate and sexually exploit his girlfriend. It is not possible to collect this kind of material without feeling implicated in it and reacting to it.

This chapter raises a number of highly significant issues. City space is no more open to the particular forms of danger discussed in this chapter than domestic space.

In the public imagining of the city as dangerous it becomes a single, all-threatening place – something that is corroborated by Terrance's version of it. The possibility of containing dangerousness is part of the architectural arrangement that helps to generate it in the first place. All three of the men identified as dangerous live in the least supervised arrangement of private rooming houses, which allows them considerable autonomy and anonymity. However, they participate in centre activities as well as feeding regularly at soup kitchens – things that expose them to the public gaze. But apart from this, the spatial dimensions of dangerousness are unclear. There is the overwhelming, compounded, vulnerability of the mad that is *not* being addressed in consigning them to the crevices of the city and to situations where their vulnerability and insecurity is heightened. Solutions that reduce their sense of precariousness while not reducing their sense of active social management of their own lives need to be applied. If services were designed with this vulnerability as a central point, then the whole system would need to be, and should be, overhauled. Neglect is not acceptable. There are also broader social and political questions raised concerning public tolerance and the accommodation of madness on the streets of the city. Currently, the terms of coexistence between the mad and the not so mad in the city are governed by fear of dangerousness. Public tolerance of odd and erratic behaviour is an obvious first step in rewriting the terms of mutual public coexistence. So is the need to recognize that oddness does not mean that someone is dangerous. We have an obligation to think more clearly about dangerousness and to identify those who are likely to cause harm or terrorize others. Therapeutic public services have a duty to address these forms of dangerousness when they are identified and at the moment, from the limited evidence available, they are not doing so – something that heightens rather than assuages public anxiety. Risk and the prediction of risk are a tall order to place at the door of any group of professionals and this kind of concern needs to be placed in a broader social and political context of relations between the mad and the rest of society if community care is to have any kind of a future. If we are – as we must – to share the city, then on what terms might we do so?

CONCLUSION

Bedlam's collage of performance images, stories and interpretations of the grammar of city space are an invitation to imagine another world. A story of stories, it is conscious of its own backstage conditions of intellectual production and its methodological and intertextual flaws are left in place for you, the reader, to see. Its stories are the daily trudge of human existence and its crises. These are stories about the making of selves and social landscapes in the dialogues of mutual creation: in circumstances that constantly threaten to engulf the self and drag it into a black hole of despair. But in these stories the subjects are no mere hostage of circumstance and crises but active agents shaping selves through the activities of daily life and the scenes on which it is produced. You were invited to imagine the social world of the mad; the nature of their journeys and the scenes on which they are set; their ways of being; who they are; and of dealing with others' versions of what it means to be them.

You have heard from Daniel, the asylum historian, and witness/survivor of past and more barbaric regimes that invoke, for him, the imagery of a totalitarian politics and its acts of ethnic cleansing. You have seen the photographs of Anne who performed the story of her life and version of madness she could not tell in words. You have heard the stumbling silence of Alfred and his highly medicated and compliant fellow clients of foster care regimes. You have heard the confident street wisdom of Terrance charting his shift from (child) victim to (adult) predator/hunter stalking the streets of the city. You have heard the insights of Jonathan, the street musician, who watches the world on the street unfold. You have heard the unsettling whispered confessions of Pras, the man who wears chains to symbolize his ancestral relationship of slavery to the society in which he now lives. You know that Guy *could* smash your head in with a table tennis bat, but generally, he and the others are just as scared of you and each other as you are of them. You have heard the conspiracy theories of Rick – that veteran of the child welfare system who was thrown out of his foster home for trying to strangle his landlady/carer. Anthony, Evan, Paul and Michel have told you what it is like to live in a shelter and have described for you the pathways leading them there. You know about the relationship of mutual support between Jacques and Samuel and their plans to move into an apartment together recreating a version of Jamaica they can both live with. You have seen the inside of Joe and Dominique's rooming-house apartment and its ashtray-focused squalor. You have heard the tragic life Rhona replays as comedy in which her versions of madness are worked through the roles she plays as an extra in the Montréal film industry. You have heard the plaintive voice of Norma who lost every-thing she had stored in the church basement when the centre decided she was not coming back. You have heard the other women who had to give up their children or the chance of ever having children and the kinds of close personal relationships they crave but don't know how to have. You have heard stories of courage and survival, precariousness and vulnerability told by those who live on the edge of human survival plagued by the voices inside their heads with their terrible instructions. By the time you read this they will all have been back through the revolving door of the local psychiatric wards and have set off once again on their journeys around the city. If you live in or visit Montréal, you may have walked past them on your way down St Catherine's Street without knowing who they are.

These lives and their journeys contain many lessons – some of them abstract and analytical, some of them political, and some rather simple, concrete and practical. They raise fundamental questions about the boundaries of human existence and its moral and political frameworks. They also raise practical questions about appropriate forms of basic provision of shelter and nourishment and many other questions in between these two polarities of philosophy and food. Considering some of these questions and issues and dealing with some unfinished business offers a way of bringing the grim and hopeful story of *Bedlam* to a close. Scattered throughout the text and hovering menacingly just beneath its surface are a dispersed series of observations concerning some of the ways in which race and ethnicity are brought into play on *Bedlam*'s scenes. You may remember from the introduction that this text began as a story of race and was eclipsed by the more pressing story of madness. Raising some of these issues to the surface in a more direct and explicit discussion deals with a significant chunk of unfinished business *and* provides a route in to some of the more abstract issues raised by *Bedlam*. These concern the mapping of subjectivities and subject positions in place of larger social categories like race and ethnicity in an effort to provide a more finely tuned set of social distinctions. Race and ethnicity, as we shall see, in fact operate in ways that support this fragmentation and re-categorization of lives as forms of subjectivity and subject positions.

Race and ethnicity – like gender about which I know rather less – are neither central nor absent in the writing of mad subjectivities. The things that we refer to in using these analytical categories – for they are distinctions between lives used by social scientists in making sense of the world – are a part of the making of lives and its social scenes. They are entangled in the existential – in the ways in which lives are experienced as personal circumstances and the outcome of paths chosen – and in the administrative arrangements in which they are set. Craig's narrative of racialized (Jewish) suffering starkly showcases the oppressive nature of the asylum as a technique in the management of madness in its elision with the final erasure of genocide. The asylum's acts of compulsory incarceration, its social practices and social relations that permit and normalize its medical experiments are taken to their ultimate conclusion in the concentration camps of central Europe in the earlier part of the twentieth century. In Craig's story these are comparable regimes: two sets of administrative arrangements for dealing with certain categories of (unwanted) people. Without doubt, there are important lessons to be learned here about the operation of suffering and the mechanisms by which it is racialized in collective ancestral memory. But that's another discussion. For our purposes here, there are two significant points to be noted from this example. The first is that racial suffering inflects subsequent interpretations of events and modes of being administered to or dealt with, collected as individual or collective experience. The collectivizing of experience requires, of course, the appropriate narrative vehicles. Those dealing with people in the kinds of situations we describe in *Bedlam* need to be aware that people carry this sort of baggage with them. Race clearly operates at some general level in providing an explanation of suffering in the face of historical precedent. It is able to collect negative experiences of being dealt with and provide a coherent rationale for them. We will return to the racialization of administrative action later in considering the lessons we might learn from Rick's experience. The second concerns the 'meaning' of the asylum and its place in critiques of mental health care. There are some very strong hints in the stories heard in *Bedlam* as well as from other sources of critique that some kind of asylum – in the sense of refuge from the pressures of daily life – is what some people want and need. As others better qualified to do so have pointed out, in terms of social policy and provision the abolition of asylum was a mistake. Any attempt to reintroduce it, however, should be aware of its meaning in Craig's version of his biography. Although they served different political regimes, the asylum (and the prisons) and the death camps in central Europe, share common features in their organization and social relationships. And it is these things – and not their existence as a refuge – that are problematic. This remains a moot point as new forms of asylums do look as though they will be introduced. The trend, in Québec and elsewhere, is moving in the opposite direction with foster homes pegged to provide what asylum is available as a cottage industry. Similar criticisms can be made of prisons, which are clearly – for this and other reasons, too – unsuitable places to store the mad. Communication between patient and psychiatrists over the testing of new drugs also needs to be re-examined if there is – as we suggest – a widely held view (of which Craig's is the most extreme) that medical experiments are still conducted on the mad without their consent or understanding. These, of course, are general matters and not matters of race, but they are revealed in a particular way through the modality of race, which often serves to cast social mechanisms in a particular light. Craig's seemingly bizarre outburst raises all sorts of questions about the social relationships of contemporary community psychiatric care. Race and ethnicity operates as a prism through which broader issues of social experience and organization is usefully reviewed.

The operation of race in the mechanisms through which people are dealt with as welfare subjects or in other capacities is also shown in Rick's conspiracy theory of schizophrenia. Theories of schizophrenia, like race, also have broader social implications. Rick is not alone in his feeling of being administered by a plethora of apparatuses that appear to place him at the centre of their 'networks of control'. This experience of 'being administered' is not uniquely racial: we are all dealt with over different issues and as the bearers of other identities. But being administered *is* configured in a particular way in the local politics of race, which relays important explicit and subliminal social messages about the 'meaning' of those to whom they are applied. Not only is Rick's (and his father's) right to live in Canada scrutinized – as it is for all immigrants (although not all immigrants are treated the same, for example, those from Britain and France have little trouble having their job qualifications recognized) – but other apparatuses, too, are brought to bear on him as a black immigrant in a particular set of circumstances. These apparatuses – quite reasonably – feed his sense of conspiracy. His father, as a new immigrant from Jamaica, loses custody of his son in circumstances Rick is not clear about. Rick is then processed by the child welfare system rotating through a number of foster families; by an education system that puts him back a year with younger children *because* he has come from Jamaica; by the juvenile justice system and later the adult criminal justice system; *and* he is processed by the immigration authorities. In addition to all of this he becomes a client of the mental health system in circumstances he described in Chapter 5. This is a particular constellation of administrative apparatuses dealing with black men with immigrant biographies. It is a set of social processes and social relationships inflected by the racialized experiences of the professionals who operate them and by Rick's experiences of being administered. Professionals anticipate and deal with young Jamaican men in ways that take account of past experience and the social meanings attached to who they are and what their lives are like. This occurs in a context in which their own sense of entitlement – perhaps they are (white) English or French Canadians – is framed. In the dialogues of administrative action this in turn impacts on Rick's response to them and the outcome of their intervention. The local meaning attached to being a young male Jamaican immigrant and Rick's response to this is highly significant. But this operates in concert with other social processes unleashed by poverty, madness and, in Rick's case, legal infraction. Together these things configure the 'constellation of apparatuses' (and their professionals) dealing with Rick. Rick's 'version of blackness' is hence configured by and through the social processes that are brought to bear on him and his situation. I will later suggest that we may speak about Rick analytically in terms of the (racialized) processes brought to bear on his situation and *not* in terms of race as though race operated in some holistic way conferring social characteristics and situations that can be automatically and readily deduced from it. Race is always contextual and interactive. It is a part of the existential/administrative dialogues ordering lives and is hence embedded in the details of everyday life and the social mechanisms ordering it. It has no intrinsic meaning of its own but is given meaning in the contexts in which it operates in tandem with the other things going on around it. This lack of autonomy makes it a slippery customer to identify in practical and analytical terms. It is not difficult to imagine (although a more systematic analysis is beyond my competence) how this constellation of apparatuses and the local meaning of race would be adjusted by gender as questions concerning motherhood, sexuality and shelter were brought to the fore. Most importantly, when dealing with schizophrenia, racially generated feelings of conspiracy interact with it and compound it and it is this – and not the problem of cultural difference – that dogs the interaction between professionals and their ethnic minority clients. It is the local social consequences and meaning of racialized and ethnicized differences that professionals need to understand and not the cultures of their clients. What they need to know about their clients' cultures are their hybrid forms of culture and ethnicity in practice: what is talked and walked and lived locally and as part of a global dynamic on a daily basis.

Race and ethnicity operate in Rick's and the others' global trajectories. It is their globality that gives them a particular relationship to national, city and administrative space. Global migration *is* inflected with race and ethnicity but not in a straightforward way beyond the obvious point that people from poor countries try to move to richer ones, and that national wealth incorporates fault lines of racial and ethnic cleavage. In the stories we were told by the characters of *Bedlam*, global trajectories were a rather haphazard business. Those in the Caribbean with a sense of adventure or a couple of contacts to the north or the east set off for a new life armed with a travel brochure or a good deal from the local travel agent. They are edged out of home by the paucity of post-colonial opportunities. Colonialism, of course, had another, different, racial script. They operate with globally dispersed family networks whose relationships are reconfigured by the obscure (racialized) grammar of global migration. They wash up in an immigrant-receiving city like Montréal with poor employment prospects, few resources and depleted family networks. They do so at the end of the twentieth century after moves to keep Canada white have been abandoned in the 1960s as an explicit set of immigration procedures. Race – in this indirect sense – is about the movement of bodies in space as well as the social relationships configuring (global and other versions of) space. It is walked and travelled.

Locally, blackness has many meanings and this feeds the existential/administrative dialogues that generate *Bedlam*'s subjects. Some of these meanings are evident in the racialized geography of the local city space into which global migrants have been historically received. Little Burgundy was once the centre of black occupation when being a railway porter (or, for women, a domestic servant) was the main occupation of black immigrants, who invariably lived close to the railway station. Black occupation of the city is now more dispersed but still pronounced. Some of these local meanings are structured by the highest principles of human equality and political correctness. But others – and we sometimes catch sight of others in action rather than talk – are not. The tense and often violent relationship between local police and black Montréalers is an example of this. Thomas commented on the heavy-handed way in which the police had dealt with him . The treatment of the Ghanaian teacher William Kafe by his students at a school on the outskirts of Montréal tells another story about the meaning of blackness as centred on fears of invasion, servility and dirt. It was this, hovering just beneath the surface of racial civility, which allowed his students to chant 'Brule le negre' (burn the nigger) (Knowles 1996: 300). We heard no complaints of racism of this kind. Either school children were able to articulate what normally remains unsaid but thought, or, those who were mad *and* black had so many other complex problems that subtle and not so subtle forms of racial harassment faded into insignificance. Alternatively, there were no popular and ready-worked narratives of racial suffering – save those applied by Jews and natives – ready to convey this kind of information. But in this case we would expect borrowing from elsewhere – there are many narratives of this kind operating in the United States. Or instead, we would expect narratives of 'private suffering', such as those we collected from local black psychiatric nurses who deploy designer dress and education strategies to deal with the subtle and implied versions of themselves as black that they confront on a daily basis. The point is that racial 'microclimates' are ambiguous and uneven and very difficult to read. The stories we heard, however, reveal some aspects of the local racial order as well as some features of the position of the (racialized) mad within it.

This particular local racial order is (like others) complicated by contesting versions of whiteness so it is not just a matter of black and white – visibility and its obverse – operating as the axis of racialization. Guy indicated this in changing his name – it was German – to a very traditional French-Canadian name offering clues about the cauldron of white ethnicities in which he operates as a Jew. Chameleon-like he assimilates into the once subordinate but now politically dominant group in order to enhance his employment prospects because 'no one has Jews'. Other Jews took a different line and aligned themselves with the Anglophone community. This is a city in which all forms of ethnicity are also threaded through the prism of the two dominant language groups and the cross-cutting political allegiances upon which they lean. Forms of whiteness are significantly different from each other and 'French Canadianness', defined primarily in terms of the language of daily operation, often takes priority over the place of origin of ancestors. It is this flexibility and contextuality that allows it as an ethnic category to so readily absorb others, including Irish Catholics, into its ranks. Like other ethnicities, it is multifaceted and highly permeable – organized by lived forms of expedience and accommodation that take priority over ancestral place and the other aspects of the moveable feast of ethnicity. Ethnicity, like race, is part of the fabric of everyday life and this underscores its contextual, spatial and local character.

You see in *Bedlam* that race and ethnicity operate in other capacities too. They provide the substance of delusions that clearly rework plausible as well as imagined racialized social relationships and practices. The symbolism of race and racial politics worked by Black Nationalism and biblical imagery were especially potent in this regard. Race is more than 'written' upon identity as Winant (1994: 58) suggests. It is evidently, as I prefer to think of it, operational within the many social processes fabricating subjectivity and modes of being in, and connected with, the world at large. It is engraved upon our many acts of 'being' as existential/administrative inventions. Few race commentators observe more squarely biographical dimensions of race, which remain for them, matters subservient to social structure and process. The exceptions to this are those who write about identity in more personal terms, but in these cases biographies eclipse social process, again failing to make the (dialogical) connection between the two. Race (like ethnicity), as I have argued elsewhere, (Knowles 1999: 123) is a local, socially scripted formula deployed to sustain numerous forms of alterity. It textures the flows of human movement in space and the calculations concerning home and belonging and can sustain any range of social distinctions to which it can be plausibly applied. In this it operates as a resource in myriad political projects joining and separating one from another in the casting of claims and building of allegiances. It is symbolically represented in skin as well as in other icons that sometimes operate in the absence of skin – as Pras showed us – as well as to sustain the symbolism of skin. There are many things that could be said about race, but my intention here is merely to transact some of the unfinished business of the text and to find an entry point into a discussion of the utility of social categories.

Considering race augments, but does not alone provide, an adequate means of discussing the lives featured in *Bedlam*. The same is true of the other social categories that may be applied, such as poverty or madness. *Bedlam's* lives are peculiarly poised on the boundary of human existence. Their stories of loss and social erasure are poignantly captured in the visual image of dispossession in the pile of baggage deposited in the church basement. What could be more socially distancing and revealing of one's place in the scheme of things than shopping via a wooden pole from *outside* the shop? Or shuffling around the mall stairwell and side entrance wearing clothes that other people have discarded? Or surviving on food that health and hygiene regulations deem unsuitable for human consumption? Or having to spend the day in a space of consumption – an activity in which you will never participate and in whose domain you are barely tolerated? Or migrating around the city assembling the basic ingredients of human survival? Imagine being catered for via services delivered through the industrial and religious monuments of the nineteenth century – monuments of a social order that has long since ceased to exist. Or being out of time and out of place. Or having your daily life haunted by the demons in your head and their terrible instructions. Or being left to your own devices until the distress gets so terrible that you volunteer for hospital admission or are carted off by the police following some incident involving a public disturbance. Or knowing that you are an object of public fear and at the same time fearing others in the same position as yourself. Or competing with others for the basic elements of human survival. Or living in a context in which survival competes with the quest for community with others who are similarly placed. Or living on a rapidly shifting landscape in which the only things that occur *outside* of the gaze of others happen *inside* you. Imagine a world in which the only private spaces are thoughts and what happens on the inside of your body. Imagine being observed whilst sleeping, going to the toilet or eating your only meal of the day, or having nowhere to live save temporarily, or having nowhere to keep your things. Or, in another scenario, imagine being frozen in a state of permanent childhood in a domestic regime you do not control and in which your affairs are managed on your behalf and you are kept in a docile and drugged haze.

These are the lives produced by the regimes I have laid out for you and their conceptualization challenges the social categories – of gender, poverty, race, class and madness – we might want to use to discuss them. It is tempting to take analytic shelter in the complete fragmentation of individual lives and the descriptive powers of biography. But these lives share too many things in common for them to be so regarded. Three factors make us focus beyond the individual and force us to grapple with the limitations of 'social' categories. First, there are similarities in the trajectories and social circumstances surrounding these lives and their pathways into madness. Second, they are administered or managed by the same social mechanisms clothed in the illusory garments of 'community mental health care'. Third, they are the socially crafted products of a particular kind of regime and set of political priorities. The social processes outlined throughout the text produce these lives – processes that 'position' lives among others in the ways described. It is the grouping – or categorization – of these lives among other lives that we need to be able to describe and account for. Are they, for example, appropriately discussed as (peculiar) forms of citizenship? Citizenship is a useful if over-used concept in that it describes forms of participation, entitlement and the terms of social inclusion and exclusion. But the lives we have described in *Bedlam* demand some broader and more fundamental means of etching their place on the social landscape than is offered by an account of citizenship.

The lives we have described demand a way of discussing the casting of the self: a mapping of subjectivities as ways of being in the world. What *Bedlam* has described is a category of selves and the mechanisms – biographical and social – by which they were produced. In these selves dance the shadows of gender, ethnicity, race, madness and poverty that do not alone, or in combination, provide an adequate account of what we have seen on the streets of Montréal. These are categories of selves that are uniquely positioned as ways of being in the world. They are peculiar in the modes of existence available to them. They are created by a particular constellation of mechanisms that produce them and manage them. And they are uniquely connected to other selves and the world beyond the territories of the self in the nature of the social bonds themselves.

What I propose is the mapping of subjectivities through three sets of connected processes that have the effect of unravelling the usual social categories used to describe and position people in the social world. The first is a mapping of selves as distinctive ways of being in the world. This can be described in the fabrication and use of space, the routines and rituals of daily life and the conditions in which these things take place. What kinds of clothes and food are available and how are they secured? How *can* the day be spent? No one else uses city space in precisely the same way or on precisely the same terms as the characters in *Bedlam*. No other group has precisely the same relationship to conceptions of public danger or demons battling in their heads. And no other category of selves has quite the same relationship between local, national and global migratory patterns. The individual selves that propel them along slightly different pathways or the same pathways in different ways mediate all of these patterns.

The second set of processes is closely aligned with the first and consists of the mechanisms producing and managing a category of selves. *Bedlam* traces the webs of administrative processes producing and managing the lives under consideration. Some of these operate globally like the conditions that stipulate the means by which global economies are serviced and socially polarized. Or they operate on a national/local level, in the organization of welfare regimes and spectrum of potential client relationships they are prepared to sustain. We have noted in the retreat of psychiatry the apparatuses managing mad lives past and present and the slippage between them. And we noted the distributive mechanisms of the asylum's revolving door with those who man it interpreting kinds of madness and levels of self-determination. Add to this the valiant efforts of the voluntary sector, slumlords, long-distance psychiatry and re-deployed mothers and you have a network of social mechanisms producing and managing madness. None of these factors are individually significant but taken in combination they provide a set of circumstances positioning lives and forging subjectivities. The webs and maps of mechanisms we describe provide a means of understanding the lives in question and have the advantage of drawing some fine social distinctions between lives not drawn by other means.

Third and finally, more finely tuned social maps can be drawn by mapping the conduits connecting the self to other selves – not as communities but as cohabitants of a set of social circumstances. It is possible to draw together a group of selves by identifying the connections to the territories beyond the self. As with the processes producing selves, this is not a matter of individual connections or social bonds, but a constellation of connections producing a pattern that can be mapped. Conceptually, this is a rearrangement of a Durkheimian preoccupation with what fastens the individual to society. The people described in *Bedlam* are positioned by a particular configuration of social bonds. Conflict, fear and competition, for example, structure their relationships with each other. Their relationship to food and shelter – the basic ingredients of human survival – are always renegotiated and require specific forms of compliance. The same is true of their relationship to consumption, to health and hygiene regulations and clothes. Taken individually, these things seem trivial: but taken together they form a map of connections that are radically different from those that hold for other groups. The mapping of selves, the processes by which selves are produced and managed and the character of their connections with others provide a means of construing categories of people that highlight fine social distinctions obscured by bigger categories like gender, race, ethnicity, poverty and madness. This is not to suggest that these categories have no utility. On the contrary, they show up in the fragmentation of lives into selves and processes just outlined. The preceding analysis of race and ethnicity makes just this point. These things work precisely in the construction of selves and the (racialized) processes producing, managing and connecting them with others.

On the face of it concern with social categories are analytical issues. But in fact the analytical gyrations above have a broader than analytical significance. They provide subtle ways of thinking about people and ways of describing lives which display the texture of the social fabric showing up flaws which may otherwise remain hidden. Being mad can and does mean many things – hopefully you are by now convinced of this – and some of these meanings and their implications show up rather graphically in the (fragmented but systematic) analysis of this volume. Description and analysis are any way the tools of critique and political intervention. The analysis above draws attention to differences between mad subjectivities and the distance between the lives described and other subjectivities and ways of being in the world. There are vastly different ways of being human and social and *Bedlam*'s ways pose some awkward questions about the human condition and the ethical basis of existence. This is a political point arising from the analysis that offers a systematic basis for making such an observation. The point of any analysis is, of course, to open a set of circumstances to critical scrutiny. Drawing attention to the effects of a system inevitably opens a space for critical dialogue as a prelude to change. Broad and sweeping changes are needed at many levels in order to reshape the lives spoken for in *Bedlam*. The aim of any programme of change would have to involve a remodelling of mad selves by shifting the conditions in which their lives are made and managed so that the resulting selves more closely resembled the selves that occupy other social positions. The gap – between the mad and the not so mad – needs to be narrowed.

Broad and imaginative social changes necessarily begin humbly. There are many small interim improvements that would recast the lives of the mad. Untangling some of their more concrete needs is hardly rocket science. Private foster homes are not an appropriate environment for unusual people to live in. Different kinds of low-cost housing with different levels of care and support that do not disappear when someone fails to pay their rent or is readmitted to hospital are quite clearly needed. No one with serious (or for that matter mild) psychiatric difficulties should have to live in a homeless shelter or on the street. (Should *anyone* have to live in these conditions?) No one should have to gather together the ingredients of human survival on a daily basis – shelter, clothes, community and food could be provided in a more integrated way. If medication is to be administered – and this is something on which more consultation between users and the relevant professional bodies is needed – then it should be done in a more systematic and professional way by those who have some knowledge of what is involved. The helpful shelter soldier should not be handing out medication under the conditions in which he is forced to operate. The re-engagement of psychiatric authorities with the affairs of the chronically mad is not necessarily the best option. Living environments of care are far more central a requirement of the lives we have scrutinized. The mad, as we have seen, have a good sense of what kinds of psychiatric intervention they need and when – they have been referring themselves one way and another for years – and they should have easy user-friendly access to professional services with expertise in their particular constellation of personal and social problems. But the relevant authorities already know all of this and follow some of it for the elite cadre of the local mad population – those displaying the requisite family connections, correct levels of self-determination and the will to improve their lot. Evidently distinctions these authorities operate in determining who should get and who should be denied services is unjust. But obviously the services offered to the elite cannot be offered around more widely without a commitment to extend spending on this partic-ular group of clients. Holding the requirements of one group of needy against others is a particularly unpleasant business. But this particular group are big consumers of resources when their affairs erupt into the crises that punctuate their grim lives. Hospitalization, police time, prisons and courts are inappropriate and non-cost-effec-tive ways of dealing with the mad. Even if we narrowly take an accounting view of things, money would be better spent improving services and conditions, instead of dealing with crises.

Such changes not only require different methods of accounting, but broader shifts in political priorities so that the needs of the chronically mad are counted as legitimate and deserving of resources. It is difficult to visualize this kind of shift in the current political circumstances when even the traditional parties of the left are taking a tough line on entitlement by linking it to labour-force contribution. Such a narrow concep-tualization of social participation excludes many other kinds of worthwhile contribution. The political agendas of left and right need to be re-sensitized to the particular circumstances of the mad. *Bedlam*'s mad expose other aspects of politics not usually thought of in political terms because they are embedded in the built environ-ments in which we operate. They expose the grammar of the city and the importance placed on commercial space; they expose the lack of public space and consideration given to collective life. Municipal governments need to see land as more than real estate to be deployed in commercial activity for private profit and be more imagina-tive in providing the space for collective life that does not demand user fees. It is by these means that cities operate in the interests of some and not others. What Wolch and Dear describe as 'the geographies of neglect' are in fact geographies of political calculation that judge and do not value the contribution of all citizens.

Still broader social changes are also needed. Madness and dangerousness need to be uncoupled in the public imaginary. This involves thinking more clearly about the meaning of dangerousness and public consultation over the mechanisms by which active danger can be properly managed in ways that do not stigmatize the mad in general and that assuage public anxiety. The mad clearly occupy a strategic place in popular public concerns about safety and danger. The message that most mad people are not dangerous but vulnerable and endangered needs to be more effectively put across. This entails overhauling the existing relationship between the mad and the not so mad and rethinking the terms of our mutual coexistence, something that requires a major shift in the ways in which we think about madness.

How should we think about madness? Here we return to the beginning of this book and the reasons for writing it. *Bedlam* is an invitation to re-imagine the world of the mad in more positive, inclusive and less defensive terms. The voices you have heard told you what the descent into madness felt like as an experience. Social and personal disintegration was vividly recounted. You can have been left in doubt that the descent into madness is *the* crisis that brings into question the boundaries of human existence and the reality and reliability of sounds, sights and social relationships. It is the most shifting of personal landscapes and raises questions concerning the nature of identity and the fact of existence itself. It is about the rapid retreat of the certainties taken for granted and that formed the basis of being in the world. It is an experience that left people shaken about how and who to be in the world. Are we not in fact fascinated by the possibility of this kind of social and personal disintegration? Is it not an ever-present fact of social existence – a constant reminder – like homelessness – of what happens if we fall off the gravy train of survival, success and upward social mobility? The mad live at the centre of this terrible social parable. And it is this and their strategic position at the centre of fears about public safety and dangerousness that structures their relationship with the rest of us. We fear the mad and we fear *becoming* them. As well as contributing to the social place of madness, we also contribute to its meaning, which is socially scripted as well as being an individual experience. The mad worry, as you now know, about the terms in which you think about them. They are acutely aware that madness carries a burden of social and individual incapacity. These social scripts require our active or tacit consent and participation. They can be re-scripted, revisited, reconsidered and placed in a more sympathetic light. Ultimately relations between the mad and the not so mad pivot on social tolerance of divergent lifestyles, circumstances and public behaviour. On these matters we are collectively intensely intolerant, as the stories of *Bedlam* have shown.

APPENDIX
Brief biographical notes

This section contains biographical details for those informants who appear in several places in the text and to whom there is more than a brief reference. Those whose lives are more completely described in a single place, or who are only mentioned briefly in passing are omitted. The ages of the informants were recorded when the interview was conducted. See the Preface for more details on this.

Pras is 35. He came to Montréal from Haiti as a 17-month-old baby. His father is black Haitian and his mother is white. His skin is very pale and he wears chains and a padlock purchased from a hardware store to emphasize his black Caribbean heritage and his relationship to African slavery. At the age of 6, his family relationships break down and he is fostered to a French Canadian family. He moves through a succession of foster homes and as a teenager is exploited by an older man who runs him as a prostitute in Toronto. In one of his fostering arrangements, he murders his violent alcoholic Czech foster father because of the latter's violence towards his foster mother. He is subsequently violent with a girlfriend, but is unsure about whether he killed her. He is very conscious of his body, having been born with a harelip requiring early surgery. It impedes his speech and he is evidently self-conscious about speaking. He is diagnosed as being schizophrenic and has been in hospital many times. When we speak to him, he has been off his medication for seven weeks because he can't afford it. He lives alone in a small rooming-house apartment and takes his meals in local soup kitchens. He has lived in homeless hostels too.

Anne spent some time with the interviewing team but did not give an interview. Instead she performed her account of schizophrenia for the camera, directing all the shots of herself and her apartment. Her apartment is much nicer than the others we visited. She hinted that she had friends or relatives with money who would occasionally send her some. At one point she made Dabert photograph a $100 bill. She claims she is a psychiatrist and keeps filing cabinets of her own medical notes, perhaps mirroring her treatment by the system of psychiatric referral. Her telephone bill addresses her as 'Dr'. Her apartment contains some Mohawk symbols and her appearance also suggests native connections in her genealogy. Otherwise she has a slight 'oriental' appearance but is generally difficult to place in ethnic terms. She is in her fifties and has a diagnosis of schizophrenia, which she understands as involving multiple personalities.

Norma lives in a women's homeless shelter. She was interviewed there and became fairly upset in the course of the interview. When she subsequently failed to return to the shelter – as many residents do – the interviewing team were blamed for upsetting her. Norma is embroiled in a conflict with a former male partner who, along with his new partner, has custody of Norma's 11-year-old daughter. She originally came to Canada from Jamaica and her story consists of a series of abusive relationships with men. She is in her thirties and has worked as a prostitute.

Craig's interview, disconcertingly, took place in my office at the university. He lives in a local homeless shelter but did not want to be interviewed there. It was Craig who contacted us and insisted on being interviewed in order to give testimony of his experiences in local asylums between 1953 and 1967. He gives harrowing testimony of conditions in the asylums – which he feels he has a duty to remember on behalf of those who cannot. Mid-way through his interview he reveals the connection between this and another narrative – of Jewish suffering – focused on concentration camps in central Europe. He is a second-generation holocaust survivor. He is heavily built and very conscious that his body does not look as he wishes it to. He talks a great deal about food. He wears sunglasses and is in his late fifties/early sixties. He is acutely aware that he might look like a former 'mental patient' and needs constant reassurance on this point. He is the uncle of Daniel (20 years old), although not the uncle Daniel lives with. He is diagnosed as being schizophrenic and he thinks this is connected with his diabetes and cocaine binges. He is not particularly religious but observes the customary Jewish festivals. He has a large local family network with whom there is not much contact.

Jonathan is a street musician and panhandler with considerable expertise on how to live on and around the streets. He tells stories about others but says little about himself apart from detailing the ways in which he uses soup kitchens and food banks. He lives in a rooming house. He has lived in homeless shelters.

Alfred moved to Montréal as a child immigrant from Italy. He lived with his parents and sister until his parents died. He has had many periods in hospital, which he has difficulty in remembering. He lives in a foster home with Phyllis, where he has lived for the last 5 years. He is highly medicated, elderly, tired and cannot see why we want to interview him.

Evan was born in Montréal and describes himself as 'Irish Catholic'. He is 62 and slightly built with straight white hair. He is well spoken and well groomed and describes himself as coming from a middle-class Westmount family, having held a responsible position at one of Montréal's newspapers in the 1950s. He lives on the second 'psychiatric' floor of one of the local homeless hostels. He is very anxious about the other people who may want to harm him and so rarely ventures outside of the hostel. He is a reluctant homosexual – attracted to men while believing that this is 'wrong'. It is this and his living situation that renders him celibate. He has spent much of the last 23 years in and out of psychiatric hospital and remembers vividly the early round of local decarceration. The schizophrenia with which he is diagnosed is complicated by his alcoholism. And his large, local family network find him difficult to deal with.

Rick liked being interviewed – we interviewed him six times. His is 36 years old and arrived in Canada from Jamaica aged 11. He spent some of his childhood in foster homes and his father – with whom he lived on and off – was abusive toward him. His mother moved to England. He was thrown out of a foster home after a dispute with his carer in which he tried to strangle her. She was trying to curb his drug/alcohol use. He subsequently moved to a shelter where these were not uncommon problems, but where he feels he is missing out on a night-time social life. He is very concerned with money (his financial affairs are in public curatorship) and is very controlling in interviews, which meet some agenda of his own. He was diagnosed with schizophrenia and manic depression while still at school. His accounts of medical treatment comprise accounts of medical abuse, locked wards and conspiracy theories. He believes he was used to test medication. He has had a great deal to do with law enforcement agencies.

Gail, who is a little over 60 lives in the foster home she has lived in for the last 10 years with some other women who are also white, and among whom she operated like a spokesperson in relation to the project. The dynamics of collective living clearly bear her dominant imprint. Born in Scotland, Gail moved to Canada in the early 1950s. She describes her schizophrenia as a 'nervous breakdown'. She has experienced multiple hospitalizations over a 20-year period. She thinks that the stigma of mental illness lessens as you get older and attitudes have changed for the better. She is very dependent on living in the foster home and on her social worker. She says with a lot of drugs lying around it is 'tempting to mix and match'!

Terrance, who is in his thirties and lives in a rooming house was born in Montréal. He describes himself – when prompted, it is not so important to him – as a Jamaican Mohawk. Without prompting, he says he is 'Anglophone Québécois'. He uses food banks and soup kitchens and has experience of shelters, which he hates, preferring to live on the streets even in winter. He is highly self-directed, having got himself off drugs and alcohol and having gone to some lengths to seek treatment for his compulsive sexual activities with young boys. He describes himself as a paedophile rapist. Terrance presents himself as a victim turned predator, making the switch at the age of 11. At 7 he stabs his foster father – who raped him and another foster child – in the stomach – and ended up in local orphanages, where he was sexually abused by others. He was first hospitalized aged 11. He sees the city as a hunting ground for his sexual urges. He works as a volunteer in one of the drop-in centres where he challenges the management to allow him to bring 'his boys' if they are in need of food. He is the most extensive public danger of the three dangerous people to show up in our group of informants. He says he has depression and violent rages and has had delusions. He has had a great deal of contact with law enforcement agencies from an early age, when he was prone to destructive rampages. He is a forceful and persuasive character who wanted our approval and who delighted in making his gay interviewer squirm.

Derrik is a native who was born in Nova Scotia where he grew up on a reserve, and later moved to Toronto and Montréal. He arrived in Montréal recently through Arizona. He says he had little contact with native people. He was brought up by a white foster family until he was 14. He started university and then dropped out with 'catatonic schizophrenia' aged 23. He is a Christian, extremely bright and with great insight into his situation. He knows Montréal has one of the lowest costs of living in Canada, making it a suitable place to be poor. He tells us that people like Freud don't try and treat schizophrenics! He lives mostly in a rooming house but has spent time in homeless hostels. He eats in a soup kitchen but refused to be interviewed there, preferring Burger King instead where his friends provide an audience from an adjacent table while he polished off a large breakfast.

Dominique shares with Joe the tiny one-roomed grimy apartment featured in the photographs. He is 36 and came to Montréal from Winnipeg to find his mother, who had given him up for adoption as a child. He and his mother are of Greek descent and he lived with her for five years as a young adult. He was diagnosed schizophrenic around the trial, following an altercation with the person who fenced his stolen articles, in which he used his machete. He says that he takes his medication and now he feels 'back to normal' again. He smokes, with Joe, a lot of crack cocaine supplied by his landlord. He eats in soup kitchens and uses drop-in centres.

Thomas, who is in his mid-thirties, is of Jamaican descent. He is well dressed, highly articulate and artistic. He lives in his own apartment, staying in touch with his children and shows a great deal of insight into his situation. Unlike most of the other informants, his diagnosis is manic depression and he concurs with this. He realizes his blackness when a large number of police cars arrive to take him away from a local hotel, where he is speaking rather loudly. He earns a living in the arts.

Lauryn was interviewed three times. She is 35 years old and moved to Canada from Guyana, aged 17. All of her relatives are now in the UK and various parts of North America. Her mother died when she was 10 and her trip to Canada was to be the start of a new life, disentangling her from a relationship in Guyana. Because she has never regularized her immigration status, she works illegally in domestic work and child care. She lives in private rooming houses and uses soup kitchens and drop-in centres. Prior to this she lived with an aunt. She wants to have a family and continue her education so that she can get a different kind of job. The schizophrenic episode she was first diagnosed with began in her twenties. She has been hospitalized two or three times. Paul is her brother.

Michel is a 59-year-old French Canadian who has lived all of his life in Montréal. He now lives in a private room inside a shelter, which he likes very much. He described himself as a 'devout Catholic' who was studying to be a priest when he 'became sick' with schizophrenia. Somewhat ambiguously he also dates his sickness as coinciding with the end of an affair with an older married woman. He has spent 23 years in psychiatric hospital and has a large family who live locally. Although the interview team speak French, he insists on being interviewed in English, only using French when he has difficulty expressing himself. This shows that in terms of ethnicity there was no neutral place in which to stand and do this research. We were firmly associated with an English-speaking university.

Eddy (interviewed three times) is 40 years old. Born in Montréal, his parents migrated from Jamaica. Short and thin, he presents a very adolescent picture of himself. The best part of his life was when he was a young adult playing in a band that toured the United States. He presents himself as vulnerable and 'lost' as well as young: a cut-off musician whose career was terminated by his schizophrenia. 'Abandoned' by his mother as a child, he is subsequently brought up by a series of foster parents. He lives in a homeless shelter but has, in the past, lived in apartments and in a commune. He eats in soup kitchens where he also helps out. He has had several tours into hospital and is good at negotiating with psychiatrists over what is wrong with him.

Anthony is from Dominica and guards his Dominican passport. He came to Canada as a young adult on an excursion 'special' and stayed arriving in Québéc from Toronto, curious about its picturesque winter-scapes. He has yet to regularize his immigration status. He lives in the Mission homeless shelter. He is very concerned about standards of hygiene as well as the drug and alcohol habits of the other shelter users. He is adept at piecing together local resources such as soup kitchens and food banks.

Paul (who is Lauryn's brother) is 40. He came from Guyana as a teenager and speaks of its post-colonial collapse as a reason for migration. He lives in a shelter, having just given up his apartment to redirect his expenditure onto clothes for himself and his two children (aged 9 and 16) who live with his ex-wife. If he gives up his apartment for the month of August, he can buy school supplies for the start of the school year. His belongings are scattered around the apartments of his friends where he occasionally takes a break from the shelter and a shower. His schizophrenia is associated with the loss of his job and the breakdown of his six-year-old marriage. He has had a number of hospitalizations. He uses the soup kitchens and volunteers at one of the drop-in centres. He advanced the view that his sister's schizophrenia results from her failure to manage the stress in her life.

Jacques, who is 31, was born and raised in Montréal by his mother who, like his father left when he was young, migrated from Jamaica. Living in a shelter, he has developed a close friendship and mentoring role with Samuel. They are waiting to move into an apartment together in 'little Jamaica'. He describes himself as having 'mild schizophrenia', avoids 'crazies' and is very independent. He maintains a relationship with his mother and sisters who live locally but does not ask them for help. He has been in jail many times in circumstances he chooses not to elaborate. His friend Samuel is recently from Toronto. He is 18 and has one Dutch and one Jamaican parent. Although he looks white, he identifies with Jamaica as a place of belonging. He spends most of his time with Samuel.

Rhona is in her early fifties. She lives in an apartment and uses one of the drop-in centres. Her schizophrenia is precipitated in her mid-teens when her mother decides to move away from her grandmother. Her mother is Jewish and, she says her father was black. Her mother is very angry with her father and this surfaces around his blackness. She is physically abusive to Rhona. Rhona presents herself as a 'survivor'. She spent 4 years in a psychiatric hospital in the 1950s when this was still possible. She gets casual work as an 'extra' in some of the films made in Montréal.

Vincent, (40) whom we interviewed three times, was a child psychiatric patient because he was 'hyperactive'. Born in Canada and having lived most of his life in Montréal, with some periods in Toronto and Vancouver, he says his parents were from the West Indies. He seems not to know where exactly and says it (and they) are not important – it was 'the jungle'. He moves between rooming-house apartments and shelters. When we interviewed him, he was living at the Mission and using soup kitchens. Always smartly dressed he is very self-directed. He variously lived with his mother and father, his mother and then an aunt. He had an uncle who worked as a porter on the railway. By the age of 17, he was living on the streets and was already taking drugs. He is a conspiracy theorist who is convinced he was hospitalized for being rebellious. He has spent many years in and out of hospital since he was 7–9 years old.

NOTES

INTRODUCTION

1   Social citizenship, at least in the British context, is linked with Marshall's (1950) concept of social inclusion guaranteed by a baseline of provision through welfare (Morris 1996: 162). More generally and elsewhere it is about being a full member of a community – civic status – and a counterpoint to the underclass as an expression of social, moral and material exclusion. In the United States, William Julius Wilson used the term 'underclass' to refer to a racialized category of ghetto residents who lived in a milieu of joblessness, illegitimacy, welfare and crime: the truly disadvantaged who had become detached from mainstream society. It became a popular part of affluent America's working vocabulary in the early 1980s following a series of articles by Ken Auletta in the *New Yorker* deployed to discuss and justify the widening polarities of wealth and poverty (Jencks 1992: 120–42) attendant upon global restructuring. It is a contentious term and is not used in this volume to discuss the mentally distressed – not because many of its features of exclusion and separation do not apply – but because it lumps together some diverse social circumstances that need to be unpacked.

2   Parr and Philo (1995: 199) use the term 'mad' to reappropriate a word considered to be prejudicial or mocking to mark a distance from medico-psychiatric thinking, which uses mental illness as though it reveals the truth about mental distress and to make use of its potential in political campaigning. These are good reasons for using the term, to which I would like to add that it also reappropriates it as a part of popular thinking and deliberation by the mad, who use it to refer to themselves and to the antics of others. Mental distress is also a useful term that expresses some of the pain involved in living with madness. Madness and mental distress will therefore be used interchangeably throughout this volume.

3   The 'Quiet Revolution' refers to the liberation of Québéc in the 1960s from the oppression of the Duplesis regime of provincial government and its class of political elite, and the hold of the Catholic Church which made it the only feudal state 'north of the Rio Grande'. It marks the rapid modernization and secularization of Québéc society and coincides with the establishment of a modern welfare state, education system, a modern civil service and a nationalized system of electricity as well as some important forms of cultural and political reframing.

4   Bachrach's (1994: 4) discussion of the different service priorities of Canada and the US points to Canada's enhanced obligation to the needy, continuity of mental health care and principles of entitlement (Goering *et al.* 1994: 38). Unlike the US, Canada subscribes to universal entitlement to services as an essential basis for social participation (Bachrach 1994: 89) but doesn't implement it.

5   This estimate is supplied by some of the agencies campaigning around homelessness. There is no formal count by city planning services although one was planned and abandoned because of methodological difficulties involved in counting a mobile population.

6   There is a large literature about the complexity and veracity of psychiatric diagnoses, especially where issues of ethnicity and culture are concerned. See the work of Roland

Littlewood, Maurice Lipsedge, Suman Fernando, Laurence Kirmayer, and Ellen Corrin for some excellent examples. This volume is less concerned with issues of diagnoses and their appropriateness than with the ways in which diagnostic categories are used and understood by those to whom they are applied and those who come into daily contact with them through their work in informal community care situations.

7 Useful sources detailing the deinstitutionalization of US and Canadian psychiatric institutions includes David Rothman *The Discovery of the Asylum* (1990); Andrew Scull *Madhouses, Mad-Doctors and Madmen* (1981); Christopher Smith and John Giggs (eds) *Location and Stigma: Perspectives on Mental Health and Mental Health Care* (1988); Simon Goodwin *Comparative Mental Health Policy: From Institutional to Community Care* (1997); and Leona Bachrach 'Deinstitutionalization and Service Priorities in Canada and the United States', in Bachrach *et al.* (eds) *Mental Health Care in Canada* (1994).

8 Roland Littlewood and Maurice Lipsedge *Aliens and Alienists*, London: Unwin Hyman, (1989). Alienist was a nineteenth-century word used to refer to psychiatrists as the intermediaries between the social world and the mentally ill, 'aliens', who were seen as irrational, mysterious and abnormal outsiders-in-our-midst.

1 VOICE, IMAGE AND TEXT

1 Different interviewers would call forth different versions of the same informant, sometimes colluding with them in steering away from difficult areas or in being prepared to ask difficult and uncomfortable questions. Without having anything systematic to report, gender was clearly important in interview dynamics with flirtation, attempts to impress and threats crossing gender lines and with stand-offs occasionally marking the relationships between male interviewers and male informants.

2 I have argued elsewhere that political commitments as well as researchers' autobiography is significant in shaping research activity, choices of location and so on.

3 This is sustained by some of the classic accounts of sociological writing. George Herbert Mead points out in *On Social Psychology* (Chicago: University of Chicago Press, 1964) that the self is manufactured out of social experience and always socially structured. Goffman's ([1961] 1986) *Asylums* offers a conception of the self moulded by the spatial regimes of the asylum (although he does not express his work in spatial terms, it is highly concerned with space), which violate the territories and structures of the self. This is as much a sociological account of the self as of the asylum.

4 Key texts concerning the nature of space are Lefebvre *The Production of Space* (1996), Doreen Massey *Place, Space and Gender* (1994), and Pile and Thrift's edited collection *Mapping the Subject* (1995). These texts contribute to the conceptualization of space as political, as etched by time, as occupied by social relationships and the processes and strategies of everyday life. Particularly useful – and neglected in this volume – is Massey's (1994) comment that the spatial and the temporal need to be treated together. Space in these various formulations is active in the constitution of objects and human subjectivities and in forging and sustaining the symbolic.

5 Ricoeur (1991: 31) repeats Socrates' comment that an examined life is a life recounted. People constantly tell their stories to themselves and others and in this way constitute themselves as meaningful social beings in time and space. Life, says Ricoeur, is the field of constructive activity 'borrowed from narrative understanding, by which we attempt to discover and not simply impose from the outside the narrative identity which constitutes us' (Ricoeur 1991: 32). It is through narratives that we play out the existential possibilities of ways of being.

6 Margolis's (1999: 65) discussion of how Bourdieu negotiates the boundaries between the existentialism of Sartre and the structuralism of Lévi-Strauss without falling completely into either captures rather well the intended theoretical tension underlying *Bedlam*. Bourdieu, he says, has a way of insisting that human agents are neither automatically following social rules nor exercising existential freedom and that their actions are not to be understood in terms of their obedience to rules but in terms of exploiting the realistic strategies available.

7 The terms 'system' and 'service' are, of course, used very loosely to refer to what exists by way of *ad hoc* facilities. They are not strictly speaking services in the usual sense of the word, nor are they a part of any system set up to deal with specific groups of clients.

8 See Diltey (Erben 1993: 15) and Merton (Stanley 1993) on modern hermeneutic biography and its use in social analysis.

9 For a discussion of memory and the individual working of collective memories, see Pierre Nora (1989); Luisa Passerini (1992), who points out that memory is how we give meaning to our lives; and Alessandro Portelli (1991), who shows how meaning is what matters and how detail is rearranged to suit interpretations of events. Ricoeur's (1991: 31) observation that memory is the present of the past is also a useful insight. Memory involves the recasting of the past through the present and its concerns and social relationships.

10 See the output of the Centre for Biography in Social Policy (1998) *Social Strategies in Risk Society* (*SOSTRIS*), Working Paper 2, published at the University of East London, for a cogent discussion of the social locatedness of biographical interviewing.

11 Freeman's (1993) *Rewriting the Self* conceptualizes the self as a narrative enterprise written from the available social material and memories of childhood in which acts of selective re-collection of bits of the past are assembled in the construction and reconstruction of whom we are. He also usefully discusses the narrative genres in which the stories of the self are told.

12 The Nation of Islam is primarily organized from the United States, but makes sorties over the Canadian border holding rallies and recruiting in black urban areas. Its pitch is the rewriting of history inserting high black civilization and nobility and mobilizing a popular anti-white rhetoric. It is an aggressive form of Black Nationalism curiously becoming established in Canada, although it lacks the kind of history of black revolt and protest that is well established in the United States.

13 Barham (1984: 6) points out that schizophrenics – if this indeed is what they are, as schizophrenia is one of the most highly contested, politically manipulated and least under-stood diagnostic categories in psychiatry – are productive social agents who make sense of their own lives.

14 Massey's (1994) distinction between place and space provides guidance. Space is used in this volume to refer to the general analytic category, from which place with its *identity* and *meaning* – the particular characteristics with which space is invested – are derived.

15 Permission to photograph individuals was obtained with signed consent forms in every case. People in general were very trusting about the ways in which we might use these photographs.

16 Gregory Bateson and Margaret Mead (1942) in *Balinese Character* used photographs extensively.

17 Slum clearance may have brought benefits to the poor, but it was also to the advantage of builders and developers and was in this respect, because of its impact on established communities, controversial. Photographing this process locates images within the realist documentary tradition that is connected to its use as a documentary method in anthro-pology. The social realism of images, of course, is most seriously challenged by more modern technologies for the generation and reconstruction of images using computers.

18 Images of Bedlam by Hogarth and others (Gilman 1982: 52–7) provided popular images of confinement and madness during this period.

19 The concept of confinement in the seventeenth century was represented visually in the ship of fools and in the caged madman, which shows the insane closed in a self-contained world (Gilman 1982: 47–9). Gilman (1982: 123, 194) also discusses the aesthetic nature of madness – its visualization – images of wild men which go back to the Middle Ages in Blake's work 'museums of living pathology' and Charcot's drawings of psychiatric patients in the late nineteenth century.

20 Madness is also conceptualized in a racial discourse: Morel provided images with his point that the insane were a degenerate variant of the 'natural race' (cited in Gilman 1982: 171). And degenerate appearances were represented visually.

21 See George Stocking (1969).

22 Hugh Welch Diamond's 1856 paper delivered to the Royal Photographic Society 'On the Application of Photography to the Physiognomic and Mental Phenomena of Insanity', which resulted from his work in the Surrey Asylum (Tagg 1988: 77) was part of an era in which 'picturing' became a tool in the delineation and treatment of insanity as well as a mechanism for record keeping and the circulation of professional knowledge.

23 He read the transcripts and met informants, sitting in on interviews and listening to tapes of past interviews.

2 MADNESS AND THE GRAMMAR OF URBAN SPACE

1 The first asylums in the United States were opened in 1721 (Scull 1981: 145).

2 For an account of the broader social conditions in which the nineteenth-century asylums in Montréal were set, see Bettina Bradbury (1993).

3 Don Gillmor (1987) in *I Swear by Apollo. Dr Ewan Cameron and the CIA Brainwashing Experiments*, using records which became available in the United States in the 1980s shows that the Allen Memorial Hospital was used by the CIA in the early 1950s to field test LSD in experiments to control human behaviour. This was known as de-patterning in which people could be programmed to act against their will – the ultimate cold war weapon. When this connection was discovered there were protests about Canadian independence in relation to American scientific/political agendas and it was thereafter stipulated those sources of research funding be publicly declared. What is of rather more interest is the clinical setting at the Allen and in other psychiatric hospitals in which extensive clinical experiments with ECT and insulin shock treatments without consent from patients or relatives was given a free hand.

4 In our findings, family scenes feature as flash points and support for episodes of distress and feelings of relationship failure much more than they feature as a supportive network to be drawn-on in a crisis. On the other side of the family equation, mad relatives impose an enormous strain on daily life and family emotional/financial resources. The asylums that are being closed could be seen as monuments to the family's inability, historically, to sustain difficult and chronically distressed relatives. In this context the plans of policy makers to support families in caring for their mad relatives are hopelessly unrealistic.

5 Mental health disorders in general have a higher prevalence rate – twice as frequent – among the economically disadvantaged as the population as a whole (Health Services Promotion Branch of Health and Welfare Canada, 1990: 113).

6 Mercier and White (1994: 42) claim that the Castonguay–Nepveu Reforms of 1971 restructured, medicalized and professionalized the mental health care system integrating it into a newly created public network of health and social service centres that acted as a precursor to policies adopted in 1989 to further cut costs and fill the gaps in 'service delivery'. No doubt this was the intention of these reforms and an intention that is realized in one small part of the system. More accessible parts of the community system are the local community service centres – CLSCs – which are walk-in clinics. There is also the *virage ambulatoire*, designed to return people home from hospital as soon as possible. These are the community structures put in place of all aspects of hospital care, not just psychiatry. Although the CLSCs work quite well, the community health care system as a whole (not just those parts intended to deliver mental health services) are poorly developed. The general picture in Québéc and elsewhere in Canada is that health services are focused on hospital.

7 The retreat of state provision creates a gap in which private agencies provide particular aspects of health and social welfare services at a profit.

8 There was a fierce debate in Québéc about whether landlords could demand that welfare clients' rents be paid directly to them. The landlords lost and so any arrangement of this kind that exists would have to be with the tenants' 'permission'.

9 Most of our informants drawn from the rooming-house sector reported poor connections with family networks.

10 Being 'on a programme' refers to the arrangement with centres whereby users become volunteers undertaking particular jobs in the centre in exchange for higher welfare payments. It is only possible to do this for a year at a time as such positions are in high demand.

11 Research by Tessler and Dennis (1992) cited in Goodwin (1997: 128) based in Los Angeles found that a sample of homeless people was 38 times more likely to be diagnosed as being schizophrenic, 38 times more likely to have had a manic episode in the last two months and five times as likely to have a depressive episode pointing to the significance of mental distress among homeless people. Similar rates are found for Canada according to Goodwin (1997).

12 Literally translated, this means 'without tree'.

13 There are local complaints by some families of the mentally distressed who consider psychiatrists to be overly timid in the use of legal instruments in respect of the mentally distressed (*Montréal Gazette* 4 June 1998). This provides an interesting counterpoint to some heavy-handed treatment of the mad by the police indicated in passing in this chapter but treated in more detail in Chapter 6 in the context of a discussion of dangerousness.

14 The 1990s produced a series of complaints from the black community in Montréal about the heavy-handed manner in which the police treated them. There were a number of police shootings of black crime suspects in which the police were acquitted as well as general harassment by the police of black citizens and deteriorating community relations. See Clifton Ruggles and Olivia Rovinescu *Outsider Blues* (Halifax: Fernwood Publishing, 1996).

15 Racial order refers to the social organization of access and exclusion, symbolism, social processes and social relationships creating and confirming race as an aspect of social recognition (Winant 1994: 267–70). Race and ethnicity are not, of course, the same thing but they frequently operate in tandem as locally contextualized social and political categories.

3 INTERIOR SPACE, AESTHETICS AND SUBJECTIVITIES

1 Massey (1991) uses the concept of power geometry to discuss the ways in which individuals and social groups are differentially placed in relation to social processes such as globalization.

2 Anne reappears in Chapter 5 as the subject of various photographs (mentioned in Chapter 1) she directed and which are used to develop a discussion of the meaning of madness as schizophrenia.

3 He insists on being interviewed in English although his interviewers are Francophones and only switches to French when he cannot find a word he needs in English.

4 This is another example of the uses of law enforcement agencies to add to those outlined in Chapter 2.

5 We noted in a number of these drop-in centres and soup kitchens that women and ethnic minority men operated from the edges of the room. In one particular soup kitchen where the interviewers – some of whom were black – spent a great deal of time, we noticed that the number of visible minority users increased. In Britain there are community centres specifically for those with psychiatric difficulties and within this sector there are those for black people to use. They do, however, operate particular versions of blackness staked out in the symbolism of food, pictures of black leaders on the walls and activities. Hence, they operate specific versions of blackness that have their own forms of exclusion. With the exception of centres intended for native Canadians, there are no separate, ethnically defined, centres in Montréal as mental health provision is not seen in these terms.

6 In this particular soup kitchen interviewers helped out on a regular basis as volunteers.

4 LIVING IN TRANSIT

1 'The social' is too general a term for this volume, which locates 'social processes', 'social mechanisms' and 'social relationships' in the texture of space instead. It is used in this

chapter in order to begin to speak about the social bonds connecting people to things beyond the individual to public or collective life of culture of some sort.

2 Those living in foster care situation live much more stable and less mobile lives although there are levels of mobility associated with this kind of situation. Foster home clients sometimes move between homes or leave to live in other kinds of arrangements.

3 Pras appears in Chapter 1 in a discussion of the performance aspects of interviews. He wears chains to speak of black enslavement.

4 This adds to the discussion in Chapter 2 about the grammar of the city in its overall arrangement. The intention of this chapter is to give a sense of how the various parts of the city are connected by the lives that walk between them.

5 'SCHIZOPHRENIC' LIVES

1 It is evident from the fragments of the Diagnostic Statistical Manual (DSM) IV (American Psychiatric Association 1995) cited, that key concepts are open to wide interpretation and that certain social norms are assumed to operate and form the backdrop against which the social abnormalities composing madness can be charted. Although DSM it is intended as a world-wide guide to the classification and identification of mental pathologies, its vague formulation of normality are clearly open to political manipulation sustaining the accusation that it is used on those who flout social norms and the political regimes sustaining them as in the uses of psychiatry in the former Soviet Union.

2 The current and previous versions of the DSM have been extensively criticized for bias towards western values, behaviour conceptions of the persona and social norms.

3 This, of course, does not mean that there are no in-built racial and ethnic biases in the use of certain diagnostic categories, but simply that they have not been investigated. Although nothing can be drawn from it, a large proportion of our schizophrenic informant group belonged to a visible minority.

4 *Cry the Invisible* edited by Michael Susko (1991) is a collection of writings and stories by the homeless mentally ill in the United States and which details their invisibility and wandering and is offered as a part of a broader quest for voice and advocacy. This is a very effective collection of stories but does not place this group of people in their broader social, professional and political context. *Shrink Resistant: the Struggle Against Psychiatry in Canada* edited by Bonnie Burstow and Don Weitz (1988) is a similar collection of stories by mainly hospitalized psychiatric patients drawn from across Canada with some striking examples of complaints of ECT treatments. While this is also a very intriguing and rich collection of stories, it, too, suffers from a lack of political/social contextualization as well as its focus on hospitalization, which has largely, been phased out. Its key explanatory devices are social control and experimentation.

5 Rhona lives in a private rooming house apartment.

6 Rick lives in one of the religious-run shelters.

7 Craig lives in a shelter.

8 Wyclif lived in a private apartment/rooming house with his wife and 17-month-old baby when we first met him. When his relationship broke up, he was moving around sleeping at friends' places.

9 Lacan says that hallucinations are sourced in the subject's history in the symbolic order so that the symbolic, the imaginary and the real are important registers in understanding psychoses (Jacques-Alain Miller, *The Psychoses. The Seminars of Jaques Lacan Book III 1955–6* (London: Routledge, 1993): 8–13).

10 Myrna lives in a private rooming apartment with her boyfriend.

11 Joan, who is extremely neatly dressed and self-directed, has one of the places in the formal community sector in a group home.

12 Bernard, who is French Canadian, lives in a foster home.

13 Norma lives in a women's shelter.

14 Tina lives in a foster home.

15 Derrik lives in a rooming house and has spent time in homeless shelters. He eats in one of the soup kitchens, which is how we got access to him.

6 DANGEROUSNESS AND ENDANGERMENT

1 In our group of informants we didn't find any women who described themselves in terms of dangerousness, but we did find many men who saw themselves – like the women – as endangered and vulnerable.
2 The urban popular imaginary features in the work of a number of cultural theorists. It is about producing a commentary on popular thought and discussing the meanings of urban environments. Phil Cohen (1996: 171) uses it particularly effectively to discuss the narratives and images of different parts of the city and its racial maps of exclusion and belonging.
3 Parts of Eddy's story feature in Chapter 5 in the context of theories of the meaning of schizophrenia.
4 In identifying three cases of dangerousness, we have discounted the story of machete-waving Dominique related in Chapter 3 as although at first it seemed as if he had attacked his employer with a machete, subsequent versions of his story suggested that it was, in fact, Dominique who was cut in these encounters and not his employer.
5 We first met Pras and his chained performance in Chapter 1 and refer to bits of his story in subsequent chapters.

BIBLIOGRAPHY

American Psychiatric Association (1995) *Diagnostic Statistical Manual of Mental Disorders*, Washington, DC: American Psychiatric Association.

Bachrach, L. (1994) 'Deinstitutionalization and service priorities in Canada and the United States', in L. Bachrach, P. Goering and D. Wasylenki (eds) *Mental Health Care in Canada, New Directions for Mental Health Services* 61: 3–9.

Barham, P. (1984) *Schizophrenia and Human Value*, Oxford: Basil Blackwell.

—— (1992) *Closing the Asylum*, London: Penguin Books.

Bateson, G. and Mead, M. (1942) *Balinese Character*, New York: The New York Academy of Sciences.

Bourdieu, P. (1990) *Photography: A Middle-brow Art*, London: Polity Press.

Bradbury, B. (1993) 'Pigs, cows and boarders: non-wage forms of survival among Montreal families 1861–1891', in B. Fox (ed.) *Family Patterns and Gender Relations*, Toronto: Oxford University Press.

Burstow, B. and Weitz, D. (1988) *Shrink Resistant: the Struggle Against Psychiatry in Canada*, Vancouver: New Star Books.

Busfield, J. (1986) *Managing Madness*, London: Unwin Hyman.

Caygill, H. (1997) 'The future of Berlin's Potsdammer Platz', *The Limits of Globalization*, London: Routledge.

Centre for Biography in Social Policy (1998) *SOSTRIS Working Papers 2 and 3, Case Study Materials*, London: Jessica Kingsley.

Church, K. (1995) *Forbidden Narratives: Critical Autobiography as Social Science*, New York: Gordon and Breach.

Cohen, P. (1996) 'All white on the night? Narratives of nativism on the Isle of Dogs', in T. Butler and M. Rustin (eds) *Rising in the East*, London: Lawrence and Wishart.

Collier, J. and Collier, M. (1986) *Visual Anthropology: Photography as a Research Method*, Albuquerque: University of New Mexico Press.

Crossley, N. (1994) *The Politics of Subjectivity*, Aldershot: Avebury.

de Certeau, M. (1988) *The Practice of Everyday Life*, Berkley: University of California Press.

Denzin, N.K. (1989) *Interpretative Interactionism*, London: Sage.

Desjarlais, R. (1997) *Shelter Blues: Sanity and Selfhood Among the Homeless*, Philadelphia: University of Pennsylvania Press.

Donald, J. (1995) 'The city, the cinema: modern spaces', in C. Jenks (ed.) *Visual Culture*, London: Routledge.

Erben, M. (1993) 'The problem of other lives: social perspectives on written biography', *Sociology* 27 (1): 15–26.

Estroff, S. (1981) *Making it Crazy*, Berkeley: University of California Press.

Faris, R.E.L. and Dunham, H.W. (1965) *Mental Disorders in Urban Areas: An Ecological Study of Schizophrenia and Other Psychoses*, Chicago: The University of Chicago Press (originally published in 1939).

Farquhar, J. (1997) '"Friendly visitors" can cut mental health costs', press release from Montréal General Hospital, 30 January 1997.

Fernando, S. (1991) *Mental Health, Race and Culture*, London: Macmillan.

Freeman, M. (1993) *Rewriting the Self: History, Memory, Narrative*, London: Routledge.

Freeman, S.J.J. (1994) 'An overview of Canada's mental health system', in L. Bachrach, P. Goering and D. Wasylenki (eds) *Mental Health Care in Canada. New Directions for Mental Health Services* 61: 11–20.

Frisch, M. and Rogovin, M. (1993) *Portraits in Steel*, Ithaca: Cornell University Press.

Fyfe, G. and Law, J. (1988) 'Introduction: on the invisibility of the visual', in G. Fyfe and J. Law (eds) *Picturing Power: Visual Depictions and Social Relations*, London: Routledge.

Gillmor, D. (1987) *I Swear by Apollo: Dr Ewan Cemeron and the CIA Brainwashing Experiments*, Montréal: Eden Press.

Gilman, S. (1982) *Seeing the Insane*, New York: John Wiley & Sons.

Goering, P., Wasylenki, D. and Macnaughton, E. (eds) (1994) 'Planning mental health services', in L. Bachrach, P. Goering and D. Wasylenki (eds). *Mental Health Care in Canada: Directions for Mental Health Services*, 61: 31–40.

Goffman, E. (1986) *Asylums: Essays on the Social Situation of Mental Patients and Other Inmates*, London: Penguin (first published 1961).

Goodwin, S. (1997) *Comparative Mental Health Policy: From Institutional to Community Care*, London: Sage.

Gouvernement du Québec, Ministère de la Sante et des Services Sociaux (1990) *Mental Health Policy*, Québéc City: Gouvernement du Québéc.

Harper, D. (1986) 'Meaning and work: a study in photo elicitation', *Current Sociology* 34 (3): 24–45.

Health Services and Promotion Branch of Health and Welfare Canada (1990) *Mental Health Services in Canada*, Ontario: Federal Government.

Henny, L.M. (1986) 'A short history of visual sociology', *Current Sociology* 34 (3): 1–4.

Hevey, D. (1992) *The Creatures Time Forgot: Photography and Disability Imagery*, London: Routledge.

Jencks, C. (1992) *Rethinking Social Policy: Race, Poverty and the Underclass*, Cambridge, Mass: Harvard University Press.

—— (ed.) (1995) 'The centrality of the eye in western culture: an introduction', *Visual Culture*, London: Routledge.

Keating, P. (1993) *La Science du Mal: L'Institution de la Psychiatrie au Québéc*, Montréal: Boreal.

Keith, M. and Pile, S. (1993) 'Introduction, parts 1 and 2', in M. Keith and S. Pile (eds) *Place and the Politics of Identity*, London: Routledge.

Knowles, C. (1996) 'Racism and psychiatry', *Transcultural Psychiatric Research Review* XXXIII (3): 297–318.

—— (1997) 'Race and place in 'schizophrenic' narratives', *Rising East* 1 (1): 78–96.

—— (1999) 'Race, identity and lives', *Sociological Review* 47 (1): 110–35.

Lavoie-Roux, T. (1990) 'Forward', to *Mental Health Policy*, Québéc City: Gouvernement du Québéc.

Law, J. and Whittaker, J. (1988) 'On the art of representation: Notes on the politics of visualization', in G. Fyfe and J. Law (eds) *Picturing Power: Visual Depiction and Social Relations*, London: Routledge.

Lefebvre, H. (1994) *Everyday Life in the Modern World*, New Brunswick: Transaction Publishers.

—— (1996) *The Production of Space*, Oxford: Blackwell.

Littlewood, R. (1998) *The Butterfly and the Serpent: Essays in Psychiatry, Race and Religion*, London: Free Association.

Littlewood, R. and Lipsedge, M. (1989) *Aliens and Alienists*, London: Unwin Hyman.

Margolis, J. (1999) 'Pierre Bourdieu: habitus and the logic of practice', in R. Shusterman (ed.) *Bourdieu: A Critical Reader*, Oxford: Blackwell.

Massey, D. (1991) 'A global sense of place', *Marxism Today* 24–9 (June).

—— (1993) 'Politics and space/time', in M. Keith and S. Pile (eds) *Place and the Politics of Identity*, London: Routledge.

—— (1994) *Place, Space and Gender*, Minneapolis: University of Minnesota Press.

Mead, G.H. (1964) *On Social Psychology*, Chicago: University of Chicago Press.

Mercier, C. and White, D. (1994) 'Mental health policy in Québéc: Challenges for an integrated system', in L. Bachrach, P. Goering and D. Wasylenki (eds) *Mental Health Care in Canada: New Directions for Mental Health Services* 61: 41–51.

Mingione, E. (1996) (ed.) *Urban Poverty and the Underclass: A Reader*, Oxford: Blackwell.

Ministère de la Sante et des Service Sociale (1997) (Therese Lavoie-Roux) 'Forward', to *Mental Health Policy*, Québéc City: Gouvernement du Québéc.

Morris, L. (1996) 'Dangerous classes: neglected aspects of the underclass debate', in E. Mingione (ed.) *Urban Poverty and the Underclass: A Reader*, Oxford: Blackwell.

Nora, P. (1989) 'Between history and memory: les lieux de memoire', *Representations* 26: 7–25.

Parker, I., Georgaca, E., Harper, D., McLaughlin, T. and Stowell-Smith, M. (1995) *Deconstructing Psychopathology*, London: Sage.

Parr, H. and Philo, C. (1995) 'Mapping "mad" identities', in S. Pile and N. Thrift (eds) *Mapping the Subject*, London: Routledge.

Passerini, L. (1992) 'Introduction', in L. Passerini (ed.) *Memory and Totalitarianism*, Oxford: Oxford University Press.

Philo, C. (1989) ' "Enough to drive one mad": the organization of space in the 19th-century lunatic asylums', in J. Wolch and M. Dear (eds) *The Power of Geography: How Territory Shapes Social Life*, Boston: Unwin Hyman.

Philo, G. (ed.) (1996) *Media and Mental Distress*, London: Longman.

Pile, S. and Thrift, N. (1995) *Mapping the Subject*, London: Routledge.

Portelli, A. (1991) *The Death of Luigi Trastulli and Other Stories: Form and Meaning in Oral History*, Albany: State University of New York Press.

Rapport, N. (1997) 'Movement and identity: narrations of home in a world in motion', paper presented at Concordia University, Montréal.

Rose, N. (1989) *Governing the Soul*, London: Routledge.

Rothman, D. (1990) *The Rediscovery of the Asylum*, Boston: Little, Brown and Company.

Ricoeur, P. (1991) 'Life in quest of narrative', in D. Wood (ed.) *On Paul Ricoeur*, London: Routledge.

Rouverol, A. (1999) *'I was Content and not Content'. The Story of Linda Lord and the Closing of Penobscot Poultry*, Carbondale: Southern Illinois University Press.

Ruggles, C. and Rovinescu, O. (1996) *Outsider Blues*, Halifax: Nova Scotia.

Sassen, S. (1991) *The Global City: New York, London, Tokyo*, Princeton: Princeton University Press.

—— (1994) 'The urban complex in a world economy', *International Social Science Journal* 139: 43–62.

Scull, A. (1977) *Decarceration Community Treatment and the Deviant: A Radical View*, New Jersey: Prentice Hall.

—— (1981) *Madhouses, Mad-Doctors and Madmen*, London: Athlone Press.

Segal, S.P. and Baumohl, J. (1988) 'No place like home: reflections on sheltering a diverse population', in C.J. Smith and J. Giggs (eds) *Location and Stigma: Contemporary Perspectives on Mental Health and Mental Health Care*, Boston: Unwin Hyman.

Skultans, V. (1998) *The Testimony of Lives*, London: Routledge.

Smith, C. and Giggs, J. (eds) 1988 *Location and Stigma: Perspectives on Mental Health Care*, Boston: Unwin Hyman.

Sontag, S. (1990) *On Photography*, New York: Anchor Books, Doubleday.

Spaniol, L. and Koehler, M. (eds) (1994) *The Experience of Recovery*, Boston: Center for Psychiatric Rehabilitation, Sargent College of Allied Health Professionals, Boston University.

Stanley, L. (1993) 'On auto/biography in sociology', *Sociology* 27 (1): 41–52.

Stocking, G. W. (1969) *Race, Culture and Evolution*, New York: Free Press.

Susko, M. (ed.) (1991) *Cry the Invisible*, Baltimore: Conservatory Press.

Tagg, J. (1988) *The Burden of Representation: Essays on Photographies and Histories*, Amherst: The University of Massachusetts Press.

Taylor, C. (1999) 'To follow a rule', in R. Shusterman (ed.) *Bourdieu: A Critical Reader*, Oxford: Blackwell.

Taylor, M.S. and Dear, M. (1982) *Not on Our Street: Community Attitudes to Mental Health Care*, London: Pion.

Winant, H. (1994) *Racial Conditions*, Minneapolis: University of Minnesota Press.

Wolch, J. and Dear, M. (1987) *Landscapes of Despair*, Oxford: Polity Press.

—— (1993) *Malign Neglect: Homelessness in an America City*, San Fancisco: Jossey-Bass Publishers.

Wolch, J.R., Nelson, C.A. and Rubalcaba, A. (eds) (1988) 'To back wards? Prospects for reinstitutionalization of the mentally disabled', in C.J. Smith and J. Giggs (eds) *Location and Stigma: Contemporary Perspectives on Mental Health and Mental Health Care*, Boston: Unwin Hyman.

INDEX

Note: Page numbers followed by 'n' refer to notes